FROM A
TO B

Also by DAVID AXE

NONFICTION

Army 101: Inside ROTC in a Time of War

War Bots: How U.S. Military Robots Are Transforming War in Iraq, Afghanistan, and the Future

GRAPHIC NOVELS

War Fix

War Is Boring: Bored Stiff, Scared to Death in the World's Worst War Zones

FROM A TO B

How Logistics Fuels American Power and Prosperity

DAVID AXE

Potomac Books
Washington, D.C.

Library of Congress Cataloging-in-Publication Data
Axe, David.
　From A to B: how logistics fuels American power & prosperity / David Axe. —
1st ed.
　　p. cm.
　Includes bibliographical references and index.
　ISBN 978-1-59797-525-4 (hardcover)
　ISBN 978-1-61234-130-9 (electronic edition)
　1. Logistics. 2. Transportation, Military—United States. 3. Military supplies—
Transportation—United States. 4. United States—Armed Forces—Transportation.
5. Infrastructure (Economics)—United States. I. Title.
　U168.A94 2012
　355.4'110973—dc23
　　　　　　　　　　　　　　　2011019984

Printed in the United States of America on acid-free paper that meets the American National Standards Institute Z39-48 Standard.

Potomac Books
22841 Quicksilver Drive
Dulles, Virginia 20166

First Edition

10 9 8 7 6 5 4 3 2 1

Contents

Preface   vii

PART ONE   1   "They're the Lifeline"   3
                    2   Secret Sauce   19
                    3   Backseat Driver   33

PART TWO   4   Frankenstein's Automonster   47
                    5   Mixed Breed   63
                    6   Parsing Parcels   79

PART THREE   7   The Greatest Lakes   91
                    8   Medical Care, Anywhere   107
                    9   The $3 Billion Maritime
                        Operating Company, with Guns   121

PART FOUR   10   Big Blimpin'   139
                   11   Air Donkeys   149
                   12   UPS—in Space   171

PART FIVE   13   A Bowling Ball through a Soda Straw   191

                    Notes   213
                    Selected Bibliography   231
                    Index   233
                    About the Author   245

Preface

It was one of the most momentous innovations in all of human history. Sometime in the Middle Paleolithic era, between 300,000 and 30,000 years ago, bands of early modern humans in Africa began meeting to swap possessions. Food, tools, raw materials—the traded items might have included anything one group had in abundance that another group did not but needed. Trade developed before people had vehicles or even domesticated animals and before they began building permanent settlements.

With those innovations, beginning around 12,000 years ago, trade boomed. Traditional footpaths between villages expanded to accommodate animals. Hand-drawn, wheel-less carts called "travois" allowed people to haul heavier loads over longer distances, faster. Hitching carts to animals further boosted their efficiency. So did wheels, appearing around 5,000 years ago. Watercraft and caravans followed as humans spread across Africa, then outward across the planet, building resource-intensive permanent settlements to guarantee their territorial gains.

Logistics—the art and practice of moving stuff between two points—enabled humanity's rise. Today all human societies are, to some degree, dependent on transportation and logistics for their survival. The global economy, with its concentrations of specialization—oil and raw materials in the Middle East, Africa, and Asia; assembly in India and China; research, management, and high-tech manufacturing in Europe and the United States—is utterly dependent on efficient transportation to bring together all the elements of production and distribute the products worldwide.

All nations need logistics. But few nations need logistics as acutely as does the United States. America is a big country separated from many of its most important trading partners by great distances. Despite being geographically isolated from other world powers, the U.S. aspires to police the world system by deploying its sophisticated military to all corners of the planet. American power and prosperity require the efficient movement of huge quantities of goods and large numbers people over long range.

I grew up in Detroit, Michigan, in the 1990s during a boom for the domestic automobile industry. My father was one of millions of Michiganders earning a good living designing and building cars. Today American automakers have fallen on hard times. But even in the depths of a global recession, Detroit still develops and manufactures a large proportion of the world's transportation technology.

The act of making cars, trucks, and other logistical systems itself requires the support of an impressive logistical system: labor, raw materials, and finished goods course through the American Midwest's transportation networks like blood through veins and arteries. A half-decade immersed in transportation stamped on me a deep appreciation for, and fascination with, logistics. This book is a reflection of my Detroit youth.

It's also the product of the five years I spent covering U.S. military operations all over the world. In daily life in America, it's possible to ignore the constant churning of our logistical networks, so carefully concealed are most of their grittiest functions. At war, logistics is impossible to ignore. If the ground convoys, cargo planes, and helicopters can't reach your outpost, you might go hungry, thirsty, and defenseless. If your ship can't fit in some remote port, you're stuck at sea. When natural or manmade disasters strike and the U.S. military races to help, logistics can make all the difference between the victims living another day or quietly perishing amid the desperation and rubble.

From A to B does not pretend to be comprehensive. Time and space constraints, and the vagaries of my access as a journalist, determined what I could include and what I must regrettably leave out. That's why there's a full chapter on fringe research into robotic space transports but little mention of the thousands of locomotives that haul much of our raw material on one of the world's most extensive rail networks. I humbly offer this book as a series of snapshots from inside America's logistical culture, intended only to spark greater interest in, and stronger support for, our logistical professionals and their hard and important work.

From A to B is based largely on my own firsthand reporting. All quotations not attributed to another source are from conversations I had with sources or directly overheard. All mistakes are my own.

PART ONE

"They're the Lifeline"

J. J. Johnson shakes his head. Through the rain-spattered windshield of his truck, down the road in the dark, the forty-four-year-old Floridian watches two mud-caked "big rigs"—tractor-trailers— from the U.S. Army's 1052nd Transportation Company jockey for position on the wet gravel.

It's January 24, 2005, at Logistics Support Area Anaconda, a sprawling, sixty-five-hundred-acre base north of Baghdad. The 1052nd is organizing a supply convoy to another U.S. base in Tikrit, fifty miles away. It's around the hundredth such convoy since the unit's deployment in February 2004. All told, the 1052nd's 120 soldiers have put several hundred thousand miles on their trucks in a year of hard driving.

The 1052nd is just one of scores of transportation companies in the U.S. Army, together representing the backbone of the largest trucking fleet in the world: more than 200,000 vehicles of dozens of varieties, from the hundred-ton Heavy Equipment Transporter to the 2.5-ton "deuce-and-a-half," operated by 25,000 full-time truck drivers, plus hundreds of thousands of soldiers who count driving as a side job.

To keep supplies flowing in Iraq, the army has deployed more than 20,000 trucks, a tenth of its fleet, and contracted with civilian firms to provide thousands more drivers and rigs. Johnson, an employee of Kellogg Brown & Root (KBR), a Halliburton subsidiary, is one of these civilians.

The 1052nd is at the leading edge of one of the largest and most sophisticated logistical campaigns on Earth, at a time when logistics has become the key to American power and prosperity. But the big picture, however awe-inspiring, is hard to see when, from the truckers' perspectives, even the most impressive logistical campaign just looks like mud, metal, rubber, and diesel fumes.

In the twenty-first century, logistics—the practice of moving people and stuff over long distances—has been refined to an exact science, with a creative component as intuitive as any fine art. But to many of the practitioners, logistics is dirty, dangerous work. The 1052nd's truckers know this better than anyone.

Actually, the 1052nd and its civilian cohorts have been lucky. For a year now, transportation companies in Iraq have been getting plastered. Most companies have lost two or three guys during their year-long tours. But halfway through the 1052nd's deployment, just one trooper has been killed. Forty-two-year-old Sgt. Jerome Lemon was decapitated on October 27, 2004, by a suicide bomber riding a motorcycle.

Lemon's death hit the unit hard. One 1052nd soldier painted a memorial to the sergeant on a portion of the concrete wall surrounding the unit's living area. Still, the 1052nd isn't unaware of how lucky it's been. Sgt. Robert McClary, tonight's convoy commander, says his company has "karma." But from where Johnson is sitting, watching the convoy try to get itself sorted, it looks like that karma's all been spent.

Like two distracted pedestrians desperate to avoid colliding on a sidewalk, the tan-painted big rigs back up, half-turn, hesitate, and defer, their drivers trying to work out who should go first and when. Their little dance throws off the entire convoy. A dozen trucks and trailers, plus several Humvees sporting machine guns and grenade launchers, scatter to make room for the jousting rigs—then try to find their way back in line.

In the middle of this are several white-painted KBR trucks, including Johnson's. The white trucks are stationary, seemingly stoic, waiting out the confusion. Their drivers, who have many more miles under their belts than the army truckers, have seen this sort of thing before.

It's a bad start to a bad night, at the bleakest hour of the two-year-old war in Iraq.

For a year, there has been "a concerted effort on the part of the enemy to try to interfere with our lines of communication, our main supply routes," Brig. Gen. Mark Kimmitt said.[1] Insurgents have been targeting lightly protected supply units like the 1052nd during their daily supply runs between bases. Roadside bombs, rockets, and suicide bombers have killed hundreds of

Truck mechanics from the 1052nd Transportation Company, deployed to Logistics Support Area Anaconda, near Balad, Iraq, in January 2005. DAVID AXE

army drivers, mechanics, and other logisticians, and wounded thousands more.

Surviving this "convoy war" means driving fast, sticking close to the truck in front of you, and staying alert through twelve-hour long-hauls in the dead of night. And all that means lots of careful planning, good leadership—and teamwork, teamwork, teamwork.

Tonight at Anaconda, teamwork is thin on the ground. Soldiers and contractors assigned to the 1052nd's convoy observe the confusion with dismay. "They're going to get somebody killed," a Humvee driver on loan from the New Hampshire National Guard tells his gunner.

Johnson has been thinking the same thing. "I hope it ain't me," he mutters. Outside, the rain slackens. That, at least, is something. For the time being, Anaconda will be a little less unpleasant place to wait.

For America's logisticians, working around the clock to sustain American power and prosperity in an increasingly dangerous and competitive world, a brief letup in the rain is the only break they will get.

■ ■ ■ ■

In World War II, the typical American soldier carried thirty-five pounds of gear worth just a couple hundred dollars in today's currency.

By the beginning of the Iraq War in 2003 the American fighting man's kit included weapons, armor, and radios valued at tens of thousands of dollars and weighing nearly seventy pounds altogether. To defeat twenty-first-century enemies, a soldier needs more gadgetry than ever before, not to mention more ammunition, more gasoline for his vehicle, more food and medicine to stay fit, and more creature comforts to keep him happy despite the long separation from his family.[2]

All that stuff has to travel thousands of miles to reach him. It's for that reason that the Iraq supply effort at its peak amounted to one of the biggest sustained long-distance logistical operations in history. And as the Iraq War wound down in 2009 and 2010, the War in Afghanistan, which had begun in 2001, escalated. The overall logistical burden for the United States never lightened.

How big did it get? In the four months of buildup that preceded the March 2003 invasion of Iraq, U.S. Transportation Command—aka TRANSCOM, the Pentagon's in-house shipping agency—delivered just over 1 million tons of cargo and 258,000 passengers, using 3,900 round-trips by airplanes and 150 by ships. Counting pilots, ship's crews, cargo handlers, bookkeepers, warehouse workers, and other logisticians, the prewar supply push employed 150,000 soldiers, sailors, marines, airmen, and civilian contractors.[3]

By contrast, United Parcel Service (UPS), the world's largest express shipping company with roughly 425,000 employees, in a typical four-month period delivers around 5 million tons of cargo in *all the world*.

In terms of sheer scale, the only challengers to the Iraq buildup were the U.S. military's logistical efforts supporting two other historic invasions: Operation Desert Storm in January 1991—2.4 million tons of cargo and around 600,000 people over six months[4]—and the June 1944 Allied attack on German-held France, with 17 million tons of supplies and more than a million troops moved in the two years prior to D-Day.[5]

But taking into account post-invasion supplies, the logistical effort of the Iraq War was bigger by far.

After the invasion, TRANSCOM settled into a long-term effort to supply the military's fight against Iraqi insurgents while maintaining the flow of materials into Afghanistan, as well. This actually meant an *increase* in the pace of operations. In all of 2008, TRANSCOM dispatched 17,600 plane trips and 1,800 sea voyages to the Middle East, a 50 percent increase in the rate of air shipments and a whopping 400 percent jump for sea shipments.[6]

Put another way, logistics for the Iraq War alone represented one of the world's biggest express delivery companies, operating at full capacity on a permanent basis and serving just one country. Anaconda, the 1052nd's base in north-central Iraq, was the major hub for this military "super-UPS."

■ ■ ■ ■

In the months following the invasion of Iraq, the camp that would become Anaconda sprouted like a mushroom patch around a derelict Iraqi air force station.

With its long runway and access to all the major national highways, the base had two of the three things American military planners always look for in a supply hub. The only thing missing was a deepwater harbor. But, in fact, Iraq like Afghanistan is very nearly landlocked, with just a tiny, rusting, and cluttered port in the south near Basra. So most of the beans, bullets, gasoline, and other stuff that fuels the war effort comes from American factories and warehouses by sea to Kuwait instead of Iraq, in a nonstop train of cargo vessels overseen by Military Sealift Command (MSC), TRANSCOM's sea component.

In 2007, Sealift Command boss Rear Adm. Robert Reilly puts into perspective the scale of the sealift. "Since the global war on terrorism began in 2001, Military Sealift Command has delivered enough vehicles, supplies, spare parts, and ammunition to fill a supply train that would stretch from Washington, D.C., to Las Vegas—and enough fuel to fill a man-made lake a mile across and almost 70 feet deep."

In Kuwait, U.S. Navy and civilian logisticians break down the mountains of sea freight into two categories: the stuff that has to move fast, regardless of cost, and all the rest. Priority cargo is shoved into aircraft bound for Anaconda or one of the outlying logistical bases. The routine supplies, including all the fuel, makes its way four hundred miles north on truck convoys.

At Anaconda and a few smaller logistical bases, the supplies are further broken down into lighter loads, piled onto smaller convoys with tougher escorts, and spirited by night to the combat units.

It's an almost inconceivably vast and complex system, one that, in 2005, employs more than half of the roughly 150,000 American troops in Iraq, plus another 50,000 civilian contractors and countless subcontractors, in addition to TRANSCOM's 150,000 personnel. "They're the lifeline," boasts army captain Catherine Wilkinson, an Anaconda spokesperson.

The last hundred miles of the supply chain are the most dangerous—and it's this last stretch that falls to such units as the 1052nd. There are roughly a dozen transportation companies at Anaconda in January 2005. Every day they each run a couple convoys. Every day, at least one of them comes under attack. The attacks range from pissed-off teenagers hurling stones to inaccurate snipers to coordinated ambushes with insurgents firing rockets and detonating powerful roadside bombs.

The attack that claimed Jerome Lemon in October 2004 was an innovative one. Most roadside bombs are buried or concealed in debris and triggered by remote control. To kill Lemon, an insurgent strapped the bomb to his own chest, hopped on a bike, and motored right up alongside Lemon's rig. It was the kind of thing nobody had anticipated and against which it's hard to erect defenses. You can't very well scour Iraq's roads of all motorists.

Iraq's roads are bad, decayed from decades of neglect. The weather is alternately scorching hot, with towering dust storms, and miserably wet, with cold, driving rains and ankle-deep mud that only further erodes the awful roads. And rain or shine, there might be bad guys around every bend.

By April 2004, Iraqi insurgents had figured out that attacking heavily armed American infantry battalions was pretty much pointless suicide. So they probed the U.S. war machine for design flaws and discovered what the Pentagon had long known: that the America's huge, sophisticated supply network is both its greatest strength—and its biggest weakness.

Poorly armed American logistical troops, with their lumbering, lightly armored trucks and predictable routes along major roads, are easy targets. The insurgents know it, and so do the logisticians themselves.

The 1052nd's bumbling this night in January 2005 is due mostly to professional inexperience. But the accumulated stress from an entire year of serious risk-taking plays no small part. The supply units "done did the biggest part" in the war and "got no props for it," says Jeremiah Cumbee, a twenty-three-year-old specialist. "We are all expendable," reads one sad scribble in the 1052nd's latrine.

Their equipment is old: the rigs themselves date from the early eighties. Their combat training is minimal: just a few weeks running drills in Kuwait before heading north. Their mission isn't to hunt and kill—it's to haul and hand out everything from yogurt to diesel fuel to prepackaged rocket launchers.

Because during peacetime the army prefers to spend more money on the combat troops, the truckers are mostly reservists and guardsmen—that is, part-timers. Back home they are farmers, factory workers, officer clerks, students, and, yes, truck drivers. Here, in Iraq, they are civilians under a thin veneer of army tan, doing a job that, on the face of it, is mostly civilian in nature.

Problem is, they're trying to do that job in the middle of a war zone.

The presence of so many civilian contractors among the army logisticians, from KBR especially, does more to highlight their similarities than their differences. If anything, the contractors are *more* soldierly. Most of them, Johnson included, joined up after retiring from the military. Johnson, a former army sergeant, has more combat experience than pretty much anybody in the 1052nd, and it shows.

Just the other day, on another supply run with the 1052nd, insurgents opened fire on Johnson's unarmed truck. Tracers skipped off the road, rounds pinged off his rig. "We got gun trucks in the front, gun trucks in the back, and every army rig's got somebody riding shotgun with an M-16," Johnson recalls. "We got, like, fifty weapons on this convoy, but not a single person shoots back. Not a single one!" Thanks to dumb luck or insurgents' notoriously bad aim, or both, Johnson and the 1052nd escaped.

Like McClary says: "Karma."

Tonight the 1052nd is hauling supplies, including an entire trailer of mail, to the First Infantry Division in Tikrit. But first they have to get lined up, briefed by the convoy commander, then dispatched by Anaconda's movements coordinators—like air traffic controllers for trucks. With ground escorts in the form of Humvee "gun trucks," Apache helicopters flitting overhead, and a dozen different units guarding the terrain between here and Tikrit, tonight's supply run is a complicated affair.

To the infantry, logisticians' jobs look easy: they don't fight battles, and they rarely kill anyone. But it's a deceptive ease.

In fact, logistics is probably the most complex aspect of military planning, especially for the United States, which, as the world's only superpower, prepares to intervene anywhere on the globe at short notice. That means getting people and stuff from point A to point B, quickly, efficiently, and safely.

"Amateurs study tactics; professionals study logistics," Gen. Omar Bradley once said, according to legend. In this new age of American power, that's never been more true.

And never has a military precept applied so perfectly to the civilian world. For world-beating logistics isn't just the backbone of America's global military power—it also sustains the world's biggest economy.

Indeed, there's an important and poorly understood overlap between our military and civilian logistical systems, as Johnson and his fellow contractors in Iraq demonstrate. The military and corporate sectors both use the same processes, many of the same hardware, and collaborate to develop new ideas and technologies.

In the U.S., military and civilian logistics egg each other on, each driving innovation in the other in an endless and accelerating cycle that promises to extend America's logistical dominance. By the same token, flaws and weaknesses in one sector can creep into the other. The 1052nd's vulnerable, quarter-century-old big rigs, for example, are indicative of old-age issues appearing across our logistical systems.

■ ■ ■ ■

Most of what we Americans consume has to cross borders and oceans to reach us, in a sort of mirror image of the Iraq logistical push. To deliver our imports, every year shippers use millions of trips by ships, airplanes, trucks, and trains to deposit some 20 million shipping containers on U.S. soil, accounting for billions of tons of imported goods.[7]

Much of what we manufacture also gets transported abroad, using all the same methods that TRANSCOM uses, only with a much wider range of destinations. Exports account for a steadily increasing proportion of American manufacturing.

Ironically, among the most valuable U.S. export commodities are the very transportation equipment that we and other countries use to carry the world's goods. In recent years, America has sold more than $40 billion worth of airplanes and $100 billion in cars and trucks annually to foreign customers. Transportation isn't just the figurative *container* for our prosperity—it's also the *content* of that container.[8]

In total, we import around $2 trillion in foreign goods every year, from oil to clothes to auto parts. Meanwhile we export a trillion bucks worth of finished cars, airplanes, chemicals, grain, and other stuff. Goods traded over distance account for nearly a quarter of America's gross domestic product (GDP) in 2003, up from just over a tenth a decade prior.[9]

The next-biggest world trader, Germany, exports just two-thirds as much stuff as the U.S. and imports less than half of what we do. Trader number three, Japan, exports around half as much as us and imports a third.

Some of our imports and exports go by rail, road, and river to and from Canada and Mexico; the rest bobs across the oceans in the holds of cargo ships or streaks through the clouds inside freighter planes. Logistics is key even for goods that are made and sold in the United States. It's roughly as far from California to New York as it is from New York to London. American roads, rails, inland waterways, and air terminals shifted more than 16 billion tons of goods in 2001, and that sum has only increased since then.

To handle all this stuff, we've got the world's biggest and arguably most advanced logistical network, with 4 million miles of highway, more than five thousand airports with paved runways, more than one hundred fifty ports, one hundred forty thousand miles of railroads, and waterways totaling twenty-five thousand miles.[10] The transportation business alone employs one out of thirteen American workers and accounts for 9 percent of our GDP.[11]

Logistics is "the connective tissue that makes the global economy work," according to University of Pennsylvania professor George Day[12]—and "an essential component of America's global competitiveness," in the words of Thomas Donohue, CEO of the U.S. Chamber of Commerce.[13]

But in the early years of the new century, American logistics is under attack, literally and figuratively—not just in Iraq and Afghanistan, but at home and abroad as old infrastructure decays and investment in new roads, rails, runways, ports, and ships falls short. The last big construction boom for American infrastructure was in the 1950s and 1960s, at a time when the economy was just a fifth its present size. A subsequent boom in the 1980s was comparatively much smaller. The transportation infrastructure component of the 2009 "stimulus package" was smaller still: less than $50 billion, spread across several years and hundreds of projects.[14]

A road bridge collapse in Minnesota in 2007 that killed thirteen people drew attention to the condition of American transportation infrastructure. The I-35W Mississippi River Bridge in Minneapolis was forty years old when it collapsed but still the youngest river-crossing built on a new site in the whole city. The National Transportation Safety Board chalked up the span's failure to components called "gusset plates" that were built too thin. Their failure was exacerbated by three hundred tons of construction material that workers had piled onto the bridge in order to conduct some repair work.

But the broader issue was about more than gusset plates. In 1990 the federal government had labeled the I-35 bridge and tens of thousands other U.S. spans, as "structurally deficient." In 2005 there were seventy thousand bridges in that category.[15] Engineers warned that without repairs, Seattle's double-decker Alaskan Way viaduct freeway, traveled by one hundred thousand cars and trucks a day, might collapse in an earthquake.

Our infrastructure worries are bigger than just bridges. Due to underfunding, American seaports are too small and too inefficient, and three-quarters of them will suffer "significant capacity problems," according to John Vickerman, an analyst with trade group Transystems.[16] The list of problems goes on.

"The value of foreign trade to the U.S. economy will nearly triple from the equivalent of 13 percent of GDP in 1990 to 35 percent by 2020," the American Association of State Highway and Transportation Officials claimed. "Instead of reducing barriers to this trading boom, America is increasing them by trying to squeeze a greater amount of product through its increasingly congested logistical pipeline."[17]

Truer words were never spoken with regard to the Great Lakes, a vital shipping channel that connects American coal and steel to American power plants and factories. Great Lakes ports and channels had a maintenance backlog of more $1 billion in 2007.

What's more, the vehicles that flow through this infrastructure also need improvement. Cars and trucks gobble too much gasoline and diesel. Ships and trains dominate the "big and slow" shipping market, while airplanes handle smaller stuff that needs to move fast. But there's nothing between the two extremes to move moderate cargoes faster than ships and cheaper than planes. Hybrid cars and airships are potential solutions, but both face big obstacles.

America's transportation woes have got a lot of very important people very worried. President Barack Obama successfully campaigned on a promise to boost investment in logistics. "The need for 21st-century transportation networks has never been greater," Obama wrote in his campaign platform.

"However, too many of our nation's railways, highways, bridges, airports and neighborhood streets are slowly decaying due to lack of investment and strategic long-term planning. . . . America's long-term competitiveness depends on the stability of our critical infrastructure."[18]

Obama promised to "make strengthening our transportation systems, including our roads and bridges, a top priority." Not just because we need the infrastructure to facilitate trade, but because building the infrastructure itself is a major component of our economy. Obama also promised a million new jobs building infrastructure. Again, logistics isn't just the figurative container for our prosperity. It's also the stuff inside that container.

To be sure, even Obama's boost to logistics might not be enough. The administration's $800 billion stimulus package, crafted to boost the American economy at a time of credit freezes, huge manufacturing cuts, and shrinking employment, included just $48 billion for transportation infrastructure.

The nation's governors said that even before the stimulus bill passed in February 2008, they already had $64 billion in unfunded infrastructure projects ready to break ground. The American Society of Civil Engineers estimated the five-year backlog in infrastructure investment at $1.6 trillion.[19] Obama's plan amounted to a "drop in the bucket," according to Robert Yaro, a New York-based civic planner.[20]

Obama countered by saying the stimulus bill was only meant to "lay the groundwork" for a long-term plan to rebuild the country's logistical systems. "The key for us is making sure that we jump-start that economy in a way that doesn't just deal with the short term, doesn't just create jobs immediately, but also puts us on a glide path for long-term, sustainable economic growth," he said.[21]

America's unrivaled ability to move things from point A to point B promises another century of power and prosperity. But it won't happen without more investment, plus a lot of hard work and creativity from university researchers, corporate bosses, and the 10 million everyday Americans who drive our trucks, man our cargo ships, pack our shipping containers, and stock our warehouses.

And it won't happen without continued sacrifice from the hundreds of thousands of military logisticians who, even more than the fighting troops, embody America's willingness and ability to shape world events, no matter how far away.

■ ■ ■ ■

Back at Anaconda on that wet January morning, Sergeant McClary, the convoy commander, finally gets all his trucks in the right order. Doors swing open. Soldiers hop out of rigs. "Prayer time," J. J. Johnson notes.

Crunching over wet gravel, weaving around deep puddles, Johnson follows the crowd to a lumber gazebo rising like an island from a sea of fresh mud. The 1052nd and its attached contractors and New Hampshire guardsmen huddle for warmth while McClary uses a penlight to read some reminders about the route off a soggy sheet of paper. Then he clears his throat and asks somebody named Quentin Graham if he'll "do the honors."

Graham, a young specialist, strips his cap from his shaved head and bows to heaven. "Let's pray," he intones in a voice that cuts through the gurgle of diesel engines. Johnson tugs off his wool watch cap, closes his eyes, and tucks his chin into his chest. Soldiers and civilians do the same.

Over their heads, beyond Anaconda's earthen walls, green tracers arc into the sky. One of the earlier convoys is under attack.

"Our enemies lie in wait," Graham prays. "Protect us, oh Father God. Amen."

Fifty voices sound in unison: "Amen."

"Praying. It's what the 1052nd does best," muses Johnson as he climbs back into his truck. He reaches his right arm behind him and adjusts the bulletproof Kevlar curtain that surrounds his driver's seat. It's the only armor on his rig or any of the other seven hundred KBR trucks in Iraq. He focuses on the road and on the red headlights of the trailer ahead of him as the 1052nd convoy starts up. Once it has stretched out and reached a top speed of around 40 miles per hour, the convoy will be more than a mile long.

The line of trucks, trailers, and Humvees maneuvers toward the gate—and onto the dark, dangerous highways of occupied Iraq. Not ten miles from Anaconda, McClary's voice growls from the convoy's radios, ordering everyone to pull over and stay alert. Someone says he had spotted a bomb up ahead.

"What the—" Johnson begins. If it really is a bomb, there's no choice but to stop. But jumpy, overworked soldiers are always seeing things that aren't there. And slowing down or stopping because somebody hasn't been sleeping well just puts everyone's lives in danger for nothing. You never pull over in Iraq unless you absolutely have to. Speed is life; stopping is death. Strung out over a mile of exposed road, the 1052nd will be sitting ducks.

Like family vacationers taking an impromptu highway bathroom break, the convoy edges onto the side of the road, stretching like an accordion as each driver tries to maintain his distance from the truck in front of him. Johnson shifts into neutral, props his elbow on the door, leans his head in his palm, watches rain splatter on the side window just inches from his face, and sighs.

On the radio, McClary confers with his drivers then beams a request back to Anaconda for assistance. The 1052nd isn't equipped to identify and disable roadside bombs. For that, it needs a specialized engineering team.

On the plus side, the convoy is just a few minutes' drive from base. On the down side, insurgent bombers have been busy tonight, and the engineer team has a laundry list hours long. The 1052nd will have to wait its turn.

So wait they do, Johnson growing more frustrated, and nervous, by the minute. So frustrated and nervous that, when the engineers' headlights appear as yellow flecks in the distance, he exhales a breath he doesn't realize he's been holding.

The engineers trundle past in a motley assortment of hardware specially adapted to the bomb-disposal mission. Behind up-armored Humvee gun-trucks comes a high, spindly vehicle that looks like an extra-tall backhoe but with what looks like a downward-facing satellite disk in place of the hoe. That's a Meerkat, a South African-designed truck equipped with an X-ray scanner for detecting metal bombs and built "frangible" so that it harmlessly breaks apart in the event of a blast, protecting the driver in his cocoon-like armored cabin.

After the Meerkat, there's something huge, blocky, and tall, the automotive equivalent of a territorial bull. The six-wheeled Buffalo, also designed by South Africans, is built high-riding and thick-skinned to resist even the most powerful blast and comes fitted with a robotic, telescoping arm for probing and shattering improvised bombs.

The road and Johnson's rig shake as the Buffalo muscles past. All eyes on the convoy are glued to the vehicle's massive flank, for tonight this strange vehicle is their salvation. After the Meerkat makes a quick and inconclusive pass with its X-ray scanner, the Buffalo noses up to where the soldier says he saw a bomb and probes roadside trash with its robotic arm.

As Johnson suspected, there was no bomb—just a harmless pile of debris. Does the false alarm reflect poorly on the 1052nd? Maybe, although army drivers *are* trained not to take chances with suspected bombs. One thing's for sure: whether the bomb is real or not does nothing to tarnish the engineers', and their lumbering Buffalo trucks', reputations as lifesavers.

Little does the 1052nd know, the Buffalo will soon help save the Pentagon's entire logistical system from destruction by ever-more effective insurgent attacks. Heavily armored vehicles derived from the Buffalo's blast-resistant design will soon arrive in Iraq by the thousands aboard cargo planes and ships, helping "harden" the transportation companies and turning the tide of the convoy war.

These so-called Mine-Resistant Ambush-Protected trucks—"MRAPs," for short—represent the best of America's logistical culture, combining common sense, borrowed ideas, and high technology in a million-dollar package too expensive for smaller nations but affordable to a country that builds its transportation infrastructure on a continental scale.

■ ■ ■ ■

Between 2006 and 2010, the Pentagon spent $15 billion to buy some fifteen thousand of the MRAP armored trucks from a slew of companies, each with its own slightly different design. One of the biggest MRAP manufacturers is Illinois-based Navistar International, the world's fourth-biggest truck-maker and a major global exporter. Navistar describes itself as one of the few companies that can build MRAPs fast enough to meet the Pentagon's needs.

But the first MRAP-maker was, in many ways, Navistar's polar opposite—and a prime example of the workshop culture that fuels America's logistical innovation. Before they were even called MRAPs, the blastproof armored vehicles were hand-constructed by Force Protection, a tiny company operating out of a defunct General Electrics engine factory in rural Ladson, South Carolina.

On a sweltering South Carolina afternoon in summer 2006, Force Protection vice president Mike Aldrich—a wiry, energetic man—leads a tour of the company's sole production line. Actually, it isn't a true line, but a series of stalls where each truck is pieced together by workers wearing blue jeans, T-shirts, hard hats, and protective goggles. The armored trucks couldn't have more proletarian roots.

Each starts as a fully built commercial truck: a Mack, in the case of Force Protection's "Buffalo" model. The truck is stripped down to its chassis and everything else is discarded. Around the chassis the workers weld a single-piece "monocoque" hull with a characteristic sloped shape. To the naked hull they add mirrors, lights, doors, and bulletproof windows. Out the door the nearly complete behemoths roll, to a holding area where inspectors pore over them with clipboards and checklists.

Next, the big trucks make the short trip down I-26 to a navy facility in Charleston that adds all the radios, digital maps, and other military gizmos. From Charleston, the vehicles board a navy transport ship or an air force C-17 or C-5 airlifter bound for Iraq or, later, Afghanistan.

The impression at Ladson this summer is one of a small firm working hard but with lots of room to grow and opportunity for improvement. According to Aldrich, the current stalls occupy just a fraction of the available space on the existing campus. A true assembly line, versus stall production, would improve efficiency, but at a production rate of just a truck per day efficiency isn't really an issue. There are plans in place to expand, improve, and accelerate production, but they are timed to match gradually increasing demand.

What's missing at Ladson this summer is any sense of urgency. And for good reason. The tiny firm—with just four hundred workers—is finally turning a tidy profit after nine years of losing money and is only now eyeing an IPO. In mid-2006, blastproof trucks represent a niche military market. Only specialized units such as engineers and bomb squads even use them.

It won't be until year's end that the Pentagon will give the tough vehicles their four-letter acronym and make plans to hugely boost production. When demand swells from just a few dozen MRAPs per year to literally thousands, Force Protection will find its artisan-and-workshop setup too slow, too small, and hard to scale upward.

"Our goal right now is to field the MRAP as we know it today as rapidly possible," Marine Corps brigadier general Mike Brogan, the MRAP program manager, says a year after Aldrich's factory tour. So the majority of MRAP orders go to big defense firms that already possess large assembly-line-style factories—General Dynamics and BAE Systems, for instance—or to major civilian truck manufacturers such as Navistar that can adapt their production lines to military models. By 2008, Navistar is building almost all the

MRAPs, churning them out from its Mississippi factory at a rate of fifteen per day.

Only America, with its huge, diverse, and flexible industrial base for transportation products, can take a mom-and-pop idea like Force Protection's and transition it to mass production in just months.

Incidentally, the MRAPs demonstrate other strengths of the American logistical system. Each vehicle weighs at least fifteen tons, some as many as twenty-five. Normally, anything that heavy gets shipped overseas in the hold of a cargo vessel. At that weight, air freight just isn't cost-effective.

But the MRAPs are so badly needed that the Pentagon organizes an airlift campaign involving scores of military heavy-lift aircraft, plus chartered Antonovs and 747s, to deliver the first several thousand MRAPs directly from the U.S. to the troops overseas, at a total cost of $750 million. The MRAP airlift represents a "logistical surge" within the logistical surge that is the entire Iraq and Afghanistan supply effort. And only the U.S. has the transportation resources to pull it off.

But for all their in-the-nick-of-time genius, the MRAPs are only a stopgap solution to a long-term problem. To ensure that military supply lines are never again endangered the way they've been in Iraq, in 2007 the Pentagon looked to cutting-edge technology a generation beyond anything in a mere armored truck.

And in doing so, the Pentagon demonstrated the symbiotic relationship between America's military and civilian logistical systems. For our power abroad, and prosperity at home, both spring from the same expert ability to move people and things, quickly and efficiently, over long distance, through even the harshest conditions.

2

Secret Sauce

The "convoy war" of 2004 and 2005 really rattled Washington. With improvised bombs costing just a few hundred dollars plus the fanatical willpower of suicide-minded jihadists, Iraqi insurgents came close to collapsing America's vast, delicate supply lines—and with them, the entire war effort.

The worst months—April and November 2004, both with around 140 American deaths—inspired the first organized congressional opposition since the invasion. Sixty-nine representatives, many of them citing the mounting death toll, joined the "Out of Iraq" caucus to talk about ending the conflict. Not much came of it, but it was the thought that counted.

Desperate army logisticians tried everything to turn the tide in Iraq. At bases scattered across the desert, mechanics welded scraps of steel onto trucks' doors to protect the drivers from blasts. One armor shop at Camp Buehring in Kuwait nicknamed itself "Mad Max" after the jerry-rigged war vehicles in the classic Mel Gibson action flick.

Sometimes this "hillbilly armor" did more harm than good. Slap on the wrong kind of metal or botch the weld, and you might just create more lethal fragments in the event of a blast. Plus the extra weight—up to a ton and a half, depending on the vehicle model—ground down trucks' suspensions, wore out their engines, and chopped years off their useful lives. The army said it would cost $35 billion to buy replacements.

"A truck ain't a tank," McClary declared one cold afternoon at Anaconda. He twitched his wiry moustache and rolled his bulky shoulders under his tan and green uniform. At moments like this, the thirty-six-year-old sergeant sounded more like John Wayne than the factory manager he was in civilian life. McClary said he preferred to ditch the hillbilly armor and trust in God. "*Insh'allah*," he drawled, borrowing an Arabic term meaning, "If God wills it."

But as a philosophy, *insh'allah* had few adherents in the Pentagon. So planners tried hauling more supplies by air—a solution that was possible only because of the U.S. military's unrivaled logistics resources: more than five thousand helicopters and around a thousand supply planes in all. The army reassigned some of its twin-rotor CH-47 troop transport choppers and the air force ponied up a couple dozen of the 38-ton C-130 airlifters and their 140-ton C-17 cousins.

But shipping cargo by air costs at least three times as much as driving it. "I'm totally disinterested in the cost," said Gen. John Jumper, the air force's top officer. "It will be paid for. We'll do what it takes."[1]

But Jumper's successor sang a different tune when the $200 million C-17s started wearing out in Iraq. "We are burning up C-17s at an unexpected rate," Gen. Michael Moseley said in 2006.[2] In 2007, for the third year in a row, he asked Congress for an extra $4 billion, outside the regular defense budget, to buy more of the gigantic airplanes from Boeing. Congress was not pleased. Nineteen senators cowrote a letter telling Moseley to quit asking for extra airlifter cash.

The quick fixes just weren't sustainable. Casualties on convoys tumbled in 2006, thanks to the armor-and-airplanes combo, but the Pentagon still needed a long-term solution if it wanted to keep fighting wars at the time and place of the government's choosing. So budgeteers poured billions of dollars into ensuring that supply lines would never again be as at-risk as they'd been for two years in Iraq.

The result was an explosion of "techs," or technical solutions—some futuristic, some brutally simple, others embarrassingly naive—for spotting, disabling, and absorbing the blasts from suicide bombers and improvised explosive devices (IEDs).

On the gee-whiz end of the spectrum, with $80 million New Jersey-based DRS devised a sensor that could detect bombs—even buried ones—by way of sophisticated "change detection." Simply put, the sensor compared one snapshot to a later one to see if anyone had added anything or disturbed the ground. But it did it on various wavelengths, both infrared and visible, and with clever software algorithms for reading the changes in terrain. To top it off, Northrop Grumman in Los Angeles built a robot helicopter to carry the new gizmo.

Meanwhile, in Tucson, an ambitious new company called Ionatron sank $200 million into developing bomb-defeating "applied energetics"—aka, ray guns. The concept was straightforward: hang one of the firm's patented Joint IED Neutralizers on a truck in the front of a convoy. The laser-aimed gun would shoot a bolt of lightning to fry a bomb's metal components before it could explode.

Unfortunately for Ionatron's shareholders, the engineering was way more complicated than the concept, and the ray gun failed Pentagon tests. "Not yet mature," one general said rather graciously. The company's stock nosedived. Investors sued management. The company changed its name, trying to shake off its bad rep.[3]

MRAPs were a far better solution, and the companies building them thrived where Ionatron faltered. But John Young, the program manager for the blast-resistant trucks, urged caution. "The current MRAP designs we are buying are not a panacea." He was right. When MRAPs shrugged off the existing bombs, insurgents made their bombs bigger. Soon, MRAPs were getting blown up, too.

There was just one way to guarantee that no American soldiers died in attacks on supply convoys. It wasn't more choppers, airplanes, and armor, nor any technology for spotting bombs before they exploded. No, the only way to ensure nobody got hurt on supply runs was to totally remove the people from the convoys.

In a word, robots.

■ ■ ■ ■

Robotics "is a serious mission for the military," says Tony Tether, the jocular, sixty-something director of the Pentagon's D.C.-based fringe research arm, the Defense Advanced Research Projects Agency, or DARPA. "If we can reduce the number of people who are driving convoys in a place like Iraq or Afghanistan, we would definitely reduce the infrastructure to take care of those people."

Tether isn't the first Pentagon bigwig to gab about swapping out people for robots. But he for one puts up some money to back the rhetoric. In the spirit of the $10 million "X Prize," which inspired the first commercial space flight in 2004, Tether offers a $3.5 million pot split between the first three robot designs to finish a fifty-five-mile obstacle course simulating a supply run in Iraq.

DARPA dubbed the event—held November 3, 2007, at an abandoned Air Force base in Victorville, California—"Urban Challenge." It's actually the agency's third robot race since 2004 but the first driven by a real military need and attracting proven technology.

When DARPA announced Urban Challenge in 2006, students, engineers, and scientists all over the world, many of them veterans of the previous races, scrambled to put together the perfect team and the smartest, toughest 'bot. There were few rules about who could compete and with what, but in time a standard script emerged.

First you need a "platform": Chevy's Tahoe SUV and the basic Land Rover are two of the most popular. To that you add sensors for "eyes" (light-detection and ranging laser scanners, tiny radars, and optical cameras) and the custom-written software algorithms that function as "thoughts" for the robot's microprocessor "brain."

Teams match big corporate sponsors such as General Motors and Ford, which donate the platforms, with scrappy university robot squads and European engineers specializing in lasers, radars, and 3-D imaging. Major defense firms such as Lockheed Martin quietly slip cash and parts to some teams in exchange for discreet logos on their robots' sides. Tech scribe Tim Oren compares the Urban Challenge robot squads to NASCAR teams: "All business with lots of sponsorship money at stake now."[4]

"I'm excited about this project, more excited about it than almost anything we've done," Larry Burns, GM's top researcher, says after the company joined Carnegie Mellon University's team.[5] "We couldn't be more excited," echoes Dave Tuttle, leader of the University of Texas team sponsored by a local used-car dealer.[6] "Funny," comments one reader on the popular *TG Daily* technology blog, "humans are excited by their own replacement research."

Indeed they are. Eighty-nine teams register by the deadline, fifty-three make the first cut, thirty-six reach the semifinals, and, amid a lot of griping from those disqualified, just eleven pack up their 'bots for the final showdown in Victorville.

On the cold, gray morning of the race, hundreds of shivering spectators pack the stands, and thousands more all over the world keep tabs via blogs and live newscasts as the robots warm up in their pits. Teams in jumpsuits scramble to make last-minute tweaks. They wipe off sensors, checked gas gauges and tire pressure, and tinker with a few lines of code. At last they trot off, and the robots are alone.

If it's possible for trucks to seem tense, these sure do.

■ ■ ■ ■

Urban Challenge turns out to be a bigger deal than anyone had anticipated. The competition's requirements—build a 'bot that could safely navigate the Victorville course in under six hours while obeying California traffic laws—are simple enough that seemingly every team has a different interpretation of the whole *point* of the exercise.

Tether talks about developing robotic convoys for the military. This is the application that Wisconsin manufacturer Oshkosh imagines when it decides to enter its fifteen-ton Marine Corps supply truck in the race. But every other team picks a lightweight civilian vehicle, and talk about all the amazing potential commercial spin-offs from all this robot design work.

Sven Strohband from Volkswagen, which has donated a Passat to Stanford University's team, says that robotic vehicles, constantly beaming messages to each other, would be able to line up in each other's slipstreams on the highway, timing subtle movements to stay in line. This ballet might boost fuel efficiency by as much as 20 percent, reduce traffic jams, and help avoid the kinds of accidents human drivers get into when they're tired, distracted, or plain stupid.

"Cars are unsafe. We kill something like 42,000 people per year, and most of those deaths are due to human error," Sebastian Thrun, Stanford's team leader, chimes in. "Cars are inefficient. They require a lot of time and attention to drive. . . . I think that autonomous cars will really change society."[7]

"Horse-driven carriages were replaced by human-driven autos in the 20th century," says Raj Rajkumar, the professor who led the research and development behind GM's and Carnegie Mellon's "Boss" robot, a black-and-blue Tahoe. "We will see autonomously driven vehicles in the first half of the 21st century, changing transportation again forever."[8]

The Marine Corps unwittingly illustrates the evolution Rajkumar has in mind when it sends an honor guard to open Urban Challenge. With thousands watching, the four marines on blond-haired horses march in formation, bearing the U.S. colors, past the robot pits, and toward Tether's perch on a tall metal stand.

Things are going great until one of the horses spooks and breaks rank. The other horses panic, too, and the whole formation collapses into a confusing scrum of flying tails, bucking heads, and pissed-off riders. Spectators cringe sympathetically as the marines retreat—something marines don't often do.

If the horses are an omen, only Norman Whitaker, the wiry DARPA race manager, takes note. "Anyone who tells you they know what is going to happen is lying," he mutters. He says he's especially worried what might happen when two robots meet up for the first time somewhere on the course.

Tether, for his part, cheerily glosses over the horses' antics and Whitaker's concerns. "Don't hit anybody!" he sings, and waves a green flag to start the race. One by one, the Urban Challenge contestants roll up to the starting line, their cabins disturbingly vacant, sensors spinning, yellow lights flashing on their roofs as warnings that no human drivers are aboard.

Slowly, with just a smattering of self-conscious applause (after all, who's listening?) and intermittent warning beeps disturbing the awed silence, the robots enter the course and start feeling their ways around the base's winding residential streets, four-way intersections, soft merges, and looping roundabouts. Sooner or later they'll cross each other's paths and the paths of human-driven DARPA cars sprinkled along the course to simulate traffic.

None of the 'bots are expected to exceed fifteen miles per hour, but DARPA isn't taking any chances. The agency's drivers all wear helmets and heavy-duty seatbelts. Some are fairly accomplished amateur racers in their spare time. Are they worried about the robots going nuts on the course? "No, not really," one says. "From what we've seen, they've been better than most people, actually."

■ ■ ■ ■

Still, as Whitaker predicted, those meetings between groups of robots, as well as between 'bots and human drivers, will be Urban Challenge's toughest tests—and an all-too-real symbol of the future of American road transport. Some day, robots will take their places in supply convoys and on our highways, first as assistants then as solo drivers, gradually boosting safety and efficiency, and squeezing out more productivity—especially from the trucking industry, whose biggest limitation is the physical endurance of its 2 million drivers.

The *New York Times* estimated that sleepy truckers were factors in as much as 30 percent of all highway deaths, but every effort by the federal government to impose stricter sleep rules met with howls of protest from the industry.[9] A proposed law limiting drivers to a twelve-hour shift daily would force companies to hire 100,000 new drivers just to keep up with demand, one trade group said.

But pressure to perform pushed drivers to their limits. "You're so tired you feel as shaky as when you have the flu," one veteran trucker confessed. "You overreact, like a drunken driver, jerking the rig to the right, then back, trying to keep it between the lines."[10]

Robotic autopilots could take over more than nine-tenths of a typical trucking route, extending drivers' endurance without endangering anybody. This according to one experiment, way back in 1995, that can be reckoned the great-granddaddy of Urban Challenge.

Todd Jochem, a grinning, bespectacled doctoral student from Carnegie Mellon, and his diminutive partner Dean Pomerleau took turns manning the gas and brakes while a custom-built, shoebox-size robot, plugged into the cigarette lighter, steered their 1990 Pontiac Trans Sport, dubbed "Navlab 5," nearly 2,800 miles from Pittsburgh to San Diego. Jochem and Pomerleau had to take the wheel for just the rainiest, most treacherous fifty-three miles—less than two percent of the trip.

"Boring, mostly," is how Pomerleau described the experiment to reporters. "Astonishing," is the word the men's end-of-trip press release used. "The goal," they wrote, "is to use technology, similar to that used in Navlab 5, to create a safer and more efficient national highway system."[11]

They didn't dwell on the fact that the Pentagon had paid for much of the development, perhaps anticipating that one day robotic drivers might also come to the rescue of besieged army truckers.

■ ■ ■ ■

But before robots can get their driver's licenses and hit our roads and our combat zones en masse, they have to prove they can get along with human drivers, and with each other, on a scale bigger than Jochem and Pomerleau's experiment. Urban Challenge is the first test. And despite being held on flat terrain in perfectly clear weather—rain and fog being about the only things no team was prepared to tackle—not every 'bot passes.

Oshkosh's TerraMax is the first to crack up. The giant yellow truck, its cameras peering in all directions, completes a couple circuits of the course, beep-beeping its way safely past several other robots and DARPA cars before easing into an empty lot for a parking test. The goal is to pull into a parking place, idle for a moment, then proceed on its way. But TerraMax doesn't even make it to the space. What's gone wrong, nobody knows for sure, but the 'bot suddenly sidles up on an abandoned building adjacent to the lot and nudges it with a black fender.

Oshkosh's TerraMax robotic truck languishes after crashing at the Urban Challenge robot race in Victorville, California, in November 2007. DAVID AXE

Just like that, TerraMax is disqualified. But it's not alone. Four other robots get canned for minor scrapes and join the yellow behemoth in impound. When reporters start sniffing around the impound lot, Urban Challenge lackeys rope it off with police tape.

The Massachusetts Institute of Technology's maroon Land Rover almost joins the benched robots. A couple hours into the race, the MIT 'bot gets aggressive, accelerating to pass a DARPA car, then moving to slingshot around Cornell's sluggish Tahoe. But MIT misjudges the lane change and taps Cornell's left front bumper. The two robots pause, algorithms crunching all these new sensations, while behind them Stanford's Passat idles, scanning ahead with its lasers, waiting to see what might happen next.

A couple minutes later, MIT and Cornell peel apart in hesitant jerks, both a little battered but still in the race. Reporters narrating live video feeds comment that the interaction almost has human qualities to it.

But what they are seeing are actually the programmer's personalities. "If one of these cars changes lanes or makes a turn smoothly, it's because some dedicated zealot stayed up late one night tuning the crazy thing until it looked just so," one Cornell team member will write later. "That's what makes it just as much a labor of love as anything else—the perfect example of art imitating life."

And like in the real-life arts of logistics, especially trucking, the winner of Urban Challenge's simulated supply run is the contestant that kept the steadiest pace and avoided major tangles, all thanks to the most rigorous planning.

After four hours and ten minutes, Carnegie Mellon's Tahoe trundles across the finish line, past Tether, ever the showman, who is waving a giant checkered flag. The 'bot has averaged fourteen miles per hour, just 0.3 miles per hour better than second-place Stanford. Virginia Tech nabs third with thirteen miles per hour—and three more teams, including MIT, limp across the finish line around the six-hour mark.

"So what are you guys going to do next?" a relieved Whitaker asks an MIT team member as he exits the pits. "We don't know," he says. "You tell us."

But Whitaker and Tether are mum. They just disappear into their offices with reams of data, without even mentioning when the next, and fourth, robot challenge might take place. Their silence is perhaps as intentional as the vague objectives they laid out eighteen months prior when first announcing Urban Challenge. The lack of any specific direction has meant every team pursuing a slightly different application with slightly different results. Now, postrace, the teams all come up with different but equally valid ideas for the next race.

One team leader proposes a long-distance road race through night and bad weather, finally forcing the sensor experts and programmers to contend with the rain, snow, dust, and darkness that human drivers deal with every day. The team from Virginia Tech proposes focusing mostly on "swarm" behavior—that is, somehow getting robots to work together in large groups, like in convoys. Thrun, the Stanford leader, wants to see 'bots handle sharper corners and faster top speeds—and to go head-to-head with human racers.

Thrun gets his wish—sort of. In April 2008, Stanford's Urban Challenge racer, Junior, meets up with the Urban Challenge 'bots from Carnegie Mellon and the University of Pennsylvania for a rematch during a lull in the Long Beach Grand Prix. The three robots do just a single lap of the two-mile downtown course, versus the fifty miles they had to travel for Urban Challenge. But they do it faster: thirty miles per hour, on average, compared to just fourteen miles per hour for the Urban Challenge winner. And they race in front of a crowd of up to 300,000 people, instead of the mere hundreds that attended Urban Challenge.[12]

Long Beach doesn't advance the technology very much, but it introduces hundreds of thousands of people to the robotic vehicles that, some day, might drive them to work, deliver their packages, and haul the goods that stock the shelves at the local Walmart.

Getting the public comfortable with robots is especially important for that period of overlap that will inevitably follow the introduction of the first autonomous cars and trucks, a period when robot drivers and human drivers will share the road. For as one robot developer discovers when it builds the first robotic military supply truck on the basis of its Urban Challenge racer, people don't always trust robots enough to drive alongside them.

■ ■ ■ ■

Perceptek didn't make it past the Urban Challenge semi-finals, but that doesn't stop the Colorado firm from installing a stripped-down version of its Urban Challenge technology into two military supply trucks and sending the 'bots down to a Virginia army base for tests. The army's Detroit-based Tank and Automotive Research and Development Command, or TARDEC, sends people to watch and learn. They call the test program "Convoy Active Safety Technology," or CAST.

The goal, according to army engineer Ed Schoenherr, is to come up with a convoy autopilot that costs just $20,000 per copy and can be sent to Iraq soon. Some Urban Challenge teams, by contrast, spent more than $100,000 on sensors alone—and only Oshkosh's TerraMax was really military-grade. With a robotic autopilot doing most of the driving, soldiers can stay rested, stay alert, and keep an eye out for attacks. This is a bit shy of the fully autonomous supply convoys Tether imagines, but it's a huge step in the right direction and might save lives.

On November 1, 2007, on a hilly roadway surrounded by forest at the army's mostly abandoned Fort A. P. Hill, Chris Hall, a stocky, bearded

Perceptek engineer, climbs into one of the five-ton CAST vehicles, while his coworker Peter Jarvis gets into the other. Hall turns the key. The nondescript robotic truck rumbles to life.

To start, they both drive manually. Jarvis takes the lead; Hall pulls in close behind. As the trucks crest a hill, Hall mashes a cartoonish red button installed on his dash—and takes his hands off the wheel and his feet off the gas and brake. He leans back, alert but relaxed. The wheel turns itself. The pedals work all on their own, pressing and rising like some prop at an automotive edition of Disney World's Haunted Mansion.

Hall's truck stays right behind Jarvis's, up and down the hill and around several turns. Where the lead truck goes, the other follows—but not stupidly. For in addition to keeping a camera on the leader, the "follower" truck also watches the road, twitching to stay in its lane. And if other cameras sense something dashing across its path—an animal, a wayward car, a person—the truck screeches to a halt. All the while, the two trucks swap data on their speed and positions as a backup, so they can do their little dance even if the cameras go blind.

Jarvis is still driving because the army requires it, for safety reasons. But behind that one human-driven truck, you can line up as many 'bots as you want. "They follow like baby ducks," Maj. Gen. Charles Cartwright said. And the Perceptek crew insists that replacing the human leader with another 'bot is not a technical challenge—it's all about getting the army to trust robots.

Here, on the cusp of achieving what they say they want—replacing living, breathing, bleeding drivers with utterly reliable and fearless robots—the army brass discover that they, and many younger soldiers, just don't trust a machine to do a man's job, at least not entirely.

"We're having to fight the Hollywood effect," army engineer Bernard Theisen says, referring to a long list of sci-fi movies pitting scrappy human survivors against genocidal robots. *Terminator. The Matrix. Transformers.* Asisat Animashaun, an army researcher, says trust needs time to catch up to technology. "We're building trust through exposure." Soldiers starts warming up to Perceptek's 'bots after just a couple rides, she says, and after that their ability to spot attacks jumps by 25 percent.

After the Virginia tests, Perceptek and the army bring in Lockheed Martin for a consult, then go back to the labs and tweak the CAST hardware and algorithms. The developers take this improved 'bot out to a Nevada test range in October 2008 and invite two Nevada National Guard transportation companies to try it out.

The results are encouraging. The improved robot autopilot is 93 percent more reliable and can drive more than one hundred miles at fifty miles per hour without a glitch. Soldiers show 25-percent boosts to their target-spotting ability right out of the gate.

Based on the Nevada results, the army says it might take CAST to war as early as 2013. Had the 'bot been available eight years earlier, it could have helped the 1052nd sort out its convoys quicker and more safely, and might have freed up the unit's drivers to scan and shoot instead of just drive.

Would that have prevented incidents like the 1052nd's roadside-bomb false alarm or the earlier ambush where Johnson, the KBR driver, said the 1052nd drivers never shot back? Would it have prevented the motorcycle suicide bomber from sneaking up on Sergeant Lemon? Would it have rendered the $15 billion MRAP program redundant?

It's hard to say. But looking to the future, the army is banking on robot trucks to make future logistical operations safer, more efficient, and more resistant to enemy attack. And the auto industry is hoping to capitalize on those advancements in to improve our domestic transport systems.

With DARPA's robot races driving the research, and small companies such as Perceptek translating the racers into useful equipment and slowly converting believers, in a few years military supply convoys might have robotic autopilots, helping drivers stay alert for enemy attacks—or even allowing a single human driver to lead several unmanned trucks.

A decade or so after that, convoys might be entirely autonomous, effectively eliminating the possibility of massive casualties such as those that threatened to derail the Iraq war effort in 2004 and 2005. Meanwhile, the same techs that are saving American lives in war zones might help reduce congestion, gas consumption, and highway accidents back home—and could revolutionize the trucking industry.

With Urban Challenge, DARPA unwittingly hit a sweet spot in America's logistical needs, one where a serious military requirement intersected with the unexpected wants of the automotive industry, shippers, energy firms, city planners, and safety advocates—and maybe even drivers themselves. Urban Challenge gave engineers the shove they needed to combine existing technologies into something that might add up to more than the sum of its parts.

"Everybody owns a car in the United States," Tether said during one of his many energetic interviews before Urban Challenge. "You can buy these computers commercially, the sensors are even available commercially and even the actuators to make the car do what you want are somewhat available commercially because of the handicapped market. The only thing missing now," he said, "is somebody's imagination—the secret sauce."[13]

He was talking about robotic racers, but he may as well have been referring to America's entire logistical culture. The raw material's already in place: the roads and ports, the engineers and laborers, the academic theory and practical skills. All that's needed to transform the ways we move stuff from one point to another—in other words, to better take advantage of our greatest strength as a nation—is a little creativity.

Lucky for us, our logistical culture has creativity in abundance. Nowhere is that more evident than in the workshops and laboratories of America's biggest industry. In 2009 and 2010, the Detroit automakers were in trouble. Tumbling sales of outmoded designs and a global credit freeze forced General Motors, Ford, and Chrysler to slash payrolls, shutter factories, and retire decades-old brands.

But for all their struggles, the automakers weren't about to surrender and fold. Crisis lends urgency to reform movements that had been gaining momentum for years. For better or worse, cars and trucks are the most important component of our land-based logistics—and cars and trucks are hurting *bad*. It could be more than a decade before military robotics reach the civilian car industry, perhaps resulting in an automotive revolution. In the meantime, Detroit automakers count on making today's cars twice as efficient, itself no mean feat for technology already so highly refined.

That's the challenge for automakers at a time when logistics are under stress: how to inject new life into a stale idea.

3

Backseat Driver

"The [San Francisco] Bay area transit system can operate without a driver," points out Rodney Brooks, a robot designer at MIT and one of the cofounders of iRobot, a company that builds bomb-disposal 'bots for the military. "It ended up having a driver because people were more comfortable."

Trust. It's a problem with robots throughout the military and civilians spheres, Brooks says. Just because a machine *can* do a thing, doesn't mean we *want* it to.

The trust issue began to have implications for the military in the early 2000s. It was then that a tile-shaped inspection robot developed by the University of Utah and refined by the army's TARDEC began early user tests. The Omni-Directional Inspection System, or ODIS—a small, flat, wheeled robot carrying tiny video cameras and meant for peering at the undersides of cars to spot bombs—was fully autonomous in its first incarnation. Surprisingly, this turned out to be a problem for some operators.

"Autonomous" means different things to different people, and there's no clear consensus on what exactly qualifies as "full autonomy," for at some point all robots at least *communicate* with human handlers. The point is that ODIS could go about most of its tasks without any human interaction. It could approach an idling vehicle, check under and around it, and detect anything suspicious such as a bomb. But during early tests, users complained, saying they wanted something they could control more, according to TARDEC's Terry Tierney.

So army engineers took the basic ODIS and made it dumber, tethering it to a handheld remote control much like a kid's toy. Today the dumbed-down

ODIS is in military use in Iraq and Afghanistan and with law enforcement agencies in the U.S. But it's relatively manpower-intensive, more than it needs to be, because of the discomfort of those early test operators.

These days, many engineers voluntarily limit the degree of autonomy they build into new 'bot designs, even if the technology enables a far higher degree of independence. Bomb-disposal troops, for instance, prefer relatively dumb robots that they control at every step from inside the protective shells of their armored vehicles. "The algorithms exist" to expand bomb-'bot capability, says Bill Smuda, another TARDEC engineer, but designers have to balance capability, cost, and soldiers' preferences—and bomb squads prefer using the drones essentially as direct surrogates for, or extensions of, human beings, rather than as complementary systems that leverage robots' unique, and autonomous, abilities.

One way to build greater trust between soldiers and robots is to design 'bots that communicate the same way human beings do with body language. That's where Brooks, a balding man with arched eyebrows that give him a mischievous air, comes in. At his lab at MIT, he is working on design elements—some functional, some purely cosmetic—that might help facilitate better human-robot relationships and perhaps persuade people to allow robots greater autonomy. Brooks's ideas will only work with certain kinds of ground robots, but at least it's a start.

"Suppose I want to show you how to perform some manufacturing task," the Australian-born Brooks says. "I come up to you, I put stuff in the center of your gaze, and then maybe use little hand motions to indicate that this is what I want you to pay attention to. Then I glance at your eyeballs to make sure you're looking at what I want you to. All the time I'm talking, I'm looking constantly back and forth at your eyes and hands, and you're looking back and forth at my eyes."

Brooks call these "intuitive social cues" and says robots should be able to mimic them. "Eventually people will need an intuitive understanding of what robots' intent is—and having that signaled intent be consistent with their actions."

It's all about gestures and gazes, Brooks says. Engineers could add structures simulating eyes and brows to a more autonomous bomb-disposal robot, and connect those to certain behaviors. In other words, before the 'bot reaches out its telescopic claw-arm to grab something, it makes a subtle "facial" gesture to announce its intent to reach.

The "eyes" themselves don't *necessarily* need to do anything else but communicate intent, Brooks says, but that's not to say that they can't be functional. The robot's navigational cameras could double as its emotive eyes. "Gaze," Brooks says, "is a pretty good functional coupling."

Regardless, the eyes don't need to appear very human. The gesture is more important than the eyes' actual appearance, Brooks says. Indeed, emotive structures that appear *too* human tend to have the opposite effect than intended: they inspire an instinctual revulsion in people. This effect is called the "uncanny valley"—a term coined by Japanese robot designer Masahiro Mori in the 1970s.

In light of this, designing emotive structures requires a delicate balance, as Maryland-based Vecna discovered with its prototype Battlefield Extract Assist Robot, funded by the U.S. Army. BEAR's function, carrying injured troops off the battlefield, dictates a fairly human-like form, with hands, arms, legs, and a simple face—all features that lend themselves to the "uncanny valley" effect. So the designers gave the face a deliberately exaggerated cartoon-like appearance, with big round eyes and stubby ears like a giant teddy bear.

The bottom line is that you've got to take people's feelings into account when you design machines meant to work in close proximity with people. That realization has driven the development of a new discipline, one that didn't really exist until just a few years ago.

Eight thousand years after Egyptians first hitched plows to their oxen, there are very few truly novel ideas in the field of transportation and logistics. Most transportation technologies are, by the same token, pretty mature—even robots have been around more than sixty years. But there's a lot of room for improvement where people and technology meet. Engineers call this point of contact, "human factors." It's "the scientific discipline concerned with the understanding of interactions among humans and other elements of a system," according to the Human Factors and Ergonomics Society.[1]

"Human factors has come to increased prominence over recent years," designer Patrick Jordan noted in an article. But there was lots of room for improvement, then and now. "Users must be 'humanized,'" Jordan wrote. "Users must be understood as rational *and* emotional beings rather than being regarded as just physical and cognitive components of a system."[2]

That's one of the biggest obstacles facing DARPA's robot racers and the Army's CAST robotic convoy autopilots. And it's a huge problem for the engineers tasked with saving American logistics from itself, at a time of rising costs, decaying infrastructure, and general economic gloom. We've got the technology, much of it robotic, to improve the way we move stuff around. But to exploit this technology, we have to find ways to get feeling people and thinking machines to work together. Since we can't easily or quickly change the design of the human mind, that means making robots more like people. Just not *too* like people.

■ ■ ■ ■

In June 2009, in a nondescript field in a nondescript corner on the MIT campus, a mostly normal-looking forklift does what millions of forklifts do every day all over the world: it rolls up to a pallet, lowers and inserts its forks, and lifts the pallet.

There's just one different thing about the forklift. Like with the Urban Challenge racers and Perceptek's robotic cargo truck, there's nobody sitting at the forklift's controls. Obeying a human command, the machine manipulates the pallet entirely on its own. It's a seemingly simple gesture with huge implications for the robot forklift's creators and for the whole American logistical system, for it represents the culmination of an important experiment in getting a robot to think like a man.

The robo-forklift is the product of a twenty-five-person team laboring two years in MIT's workshops and classrooms, with funding from the U.S. Army. Led by Seth Teller, an expert in what he calls "situationally aware computing," the team derives its forklift's brain from the inner workings of MIT's Urban Challenge racer, in the same way Perceptek based its robotic convoy technology on its own non-qualifying racer.

A forklift might, at first glance, seem less impressive than a self-driving war-zone convoy, but in reality Teller's forklift represents several major advancements compared even to Perceptek's impressive robot autopilot.

"The focus of my lab is to develop the ability for machines to have a representation of their environment, in order to move and work purposefully in the world—the same way people that build up a mental model of the world, where things are connected in space," explains Teller, an energetic, youthful-looking man with a permanent five-o'clock shadow.

By contrast, Perceptek's CAST 'bots have only a very basic understanding of the world around them. Like baby ducks lined up behind their momma, a convoy of CAST trucks plays a simple game of follow-the-leader, each truck sensing and following the truck in front of it. Only the lead truck is required to react to a weaving road, hills, puddles, oil spills, and deer darting across its path—and in Perceptek's initial concept for CAST, that mother truck would have a full-time human driver paying close attention to his surroundings.

A Perceptek employee demonstrates the "follower" function in his Convoy Active Safety Technology–equipped supply truck during tests in Virginia in 2007. DAVID AXE

Teller's bot, on the other hand, is designed to sense a warehouse in much the same way a human worker would. The robo-forklift that lifts that first pallet in the summer of 2009 is a standard commercial model, weighing three tons, with a three-thousand-pound lifting ability. Only its computerized brain is custom-made. Even the controller the human operator uses to "talk" to the forklift is an off-the-shelf model. The standard interface is via a simple application on a Nokia smartphone—although the 'bot is also programmed to respond to voice commands. For eyes, the 'bot has the same kinds of lidar and optical sensors that MIT and other schools fitted to their Urban Challenge racers.

Where the forklift differs from other robots is in its ability to safely work in a complex environment alongside human beings without any extra infrastructure devoted solely to it, Teller says. There have even been robotic forklifts before Teller's, but these traveled along special lanes inside a warehouse or workspace. These previous robo-forklifts did not truly mix with human beings, for they weren't responsive enough to avoid harming them. Accidents were pretty much inevitable.

Teller's 'bot is smart enough to sense and avoid people, while deftly manipulating pallets in what Teller calls a "semi-structured environment"—say, a rush-job army supply depot close to a battle zone or a bustling corporate warehouse during the holidays. All it needs to get started is a "guided tour" of the facility so that it can internally map out the area, noting landmarks and obstacles with its sensors. This tour basically entails a person driving the forklift around for a few minutes and letting it see its surroundings.

The MIT forklift's flexibility and reliability make it useful for real-world jobs and even combat applications—although Teller estimates it might take up to two years to make the design production-ready. In the meantime, he adds, technologies refined for the forklift might find their way into other unmanned logistical systems. The result, in a few years, could be frontline supply lines that seamlessly mix an ever-shrinking number of people with an ever-growing number of machines, thus exposing fewer human beings to attack—and all without sacrificing the capacity and responsiveness of today's manned logistical systems.

All thanks to that simple but profound notion that Brooks championed. You've got to take people's feelings into account when you build machines to work alongside them.

"We think lot of our techniques are broadly applicable to other robots," Teller says. The speech interface, for one. "Another piece is the narrated guided tour," he adds. "There's a major disconnect now between the languages people speak and those robots speak. Now people take pains to express an environment in terms a robot can understand—usually GPS coordinates. But people don't think in GPS terms; they think in terms of landmarks. So we want to make robots that come all the way to people and do the bidding of people on human terms. Our robot does that."

■ ■ ■ ■

Jim Sayer's problem is pretty much the reverse of Teller's. Where Teller is working to get robots to obey people in the context of ever-more-intimate man-machine teams, Sayer's trying to get people to obey their 'bots. The potential reward is safer and more efficient transportation, if only people can be convinced to better trust thinking technology—and provided Sayer can make the tech truly earn that trust.

Sayer, a short, studious-looking man, works at the University of Michigan's Transportation Research Institute, UMTRI for short. The institute is just a quick walk from the university's other transportation-focused body, the so-called Automotive Research Center. Where ARC is focused on "heavy" projects such as propulsion, often with military applications, UMTRI works on brainier stuff.

Stuff like Sayer's current project, the Integrated Vehicle-Based Safety System, a suite of sensors and algorithms that function as a very basic robotic driver—sort of a civilian analogue to CAST. IVBSS has supporters across industry, government, and the military. Honda, Navistar, defense contractor Battelle, and the Michigan Department of Transportation have all ponied up cash for the program.

On a snowy morning in early January 2010, Sayer runs up several flights of stairs to his office overlooking U of M's workmanlike, almost nondescript campus. He's late for an appointment to describe his safety system and its triumphs and tribulations since launching in 2005. Sayer arrives red-faced and barely pauses before launching into an enthusiastic monologue as gigantic snowflakes sweep across the windowpane behind him.

What IVBSS is, Sayer says, is a "stand-alone system addressing all crash threats." The system's "eyes" and "ears"—a combination of GPS, radar, lidar, and cameras—keep tabs on four things: the possibility of a forward collision, lateral drift across road lanes, merging, and speed going around a curve. When the vehicle exceeds pre-programmed safety limits,—going too fast around a corner or crossing the yellow line on a two-way road, IVBSS warns the driver with an alarm. A car or truck equipped with the system is, in theory, much safer than one without. Lane-drift alone accounts for a fifth of all highway fatalities, Sayer says. IVBSS is basically a slightly dumber form of the computer brain inside Teller's forklift that allows that 'bot to wheel around a warehouse without squishing people.

Assembling the technologies for the safety system isn't terribly difficult—it's all stuff in use, separately, in different applications. In 2007, Sayer's team fitted IVBSS to sixteen Honda Accords and issued them to volunteer drivers.

For two years these drivers used their "smart" Accords like they would any personal vehicle. The UMTRI team monitored the performance and periodically surveyed the drivers. What they found would not have surprised someone like Brooks or Teller. "The biggest potential stumbling block," Sayer says, "is user acceptance." How do you get drivers to trust machines to do some of the driving for them?

The problem got even worse when UMTRI installed the safety system in ten Navistar commercial trucks and delivered them to Conway Freight, a trucking company based just down the road from the U of M campus. Truckers more than most people need safety systems, in light of the sheer number of hours they spend on the road. But Conway's drivers actually liked IVBSS less than the regular commuters did.

Part of the problem was the nature of what engineers would call trucking "duty cycle"—the fairly narrow range of circumstances in which big rigs are used. They do a lot of high-speed cruising on highways. That kind of duty makes the safety system's job harder. For the collision warning, IVBSS's sensors must gaze farther down the road for a commercial truck than for a personal vehicle, owing to the higher speeds and the truck's greater mass and thus braking distance. UMTRI amended its design to better suit truckers, but it was too late to change everybody's mind. Still, Sayer points out, "it only has to save your butt once and you forget the nuisances."

Based on the user tests that ended in December 2009, UMTRI is modifying the safety system so it can adapt to different duty cycles and even to the habits of particular drivers. The modified IVBSS should do this adapting all on its own. The system doesn't have to be "hard-coded," Sayer says. "It could learn about the attributes of the individual driver."

UMTRI did some early work on this adaptive safety system with the Accords. Sayer and his team kept track of what alarms the test drivers ignored. If a particular type of alarm—turning speed, for instance—were consistently ignored by one driver, it's probably because that driver has a driving style that pushes the boundary of what others might consider safe but that might not actually be hazardous, in the strictest sense.

Future incarnations of IVBSS might take that same adaptive principle and apply it to a broader range of driver behaviors. Over time, the safety system would come to understand its owner's "driver personality" and figure out how best to compromise between this personality and a reasonable conception of safety.

That kind of software intuition is the bridge linking today's rudimentary "warning"-based safety systems to the robotic autopilots of the near future that are just beginning to emerge in the Urban Challenge races, CAST and Teller's forklift. People will eventually accept intrusive safety systems like IVBSS, Sayer contends, especially once automakers start offering them in standard car packages. The benefits are inarguable. Again, people's comfort level is the biggest obstacle. "You've just got to have a slow introduction until you build that trust," Sayer says.

And once drivers open their doors to robotic assistance, there's no stopping a rapid technological progression toward ever-greater automation. It won't be long before most cars have the same brains as the Urban Challenge racers but also accommodate human drivers. Driving will be a collaborative process between feeling people and thinking machines.

The federal government is banking on it. The U.S. Department of Transportation's Intellidrive, a $100-million-a-year research initiative launched in the 1990s, is sketching out the basic parameters of robot-assisted driving. Intellidrive is "focused on advancing connectivity among vehicles and roadway infrastructure in order to significantly improve the safety and mobility of the U.S. transportation system," according to the program's website.[3]

Early on, Intellidrive envisioned installing magnetic strips on all U.S. roadways, plus sensors on all American cars and trucks for reading the strips. A vehicle would automatically follow the strips, staying perfectly within its lane until the driver deliberately overrides it. The kind of infrastructure hardwiring was one of the fundamental tenets of Intellidrive: future versions might have included highways that supported a seamless wireless data network for communicating with vehicles, warning them about traffic jams and other hazards.

Then someone calculated the potential cost of essentially digging up and rebuilding every mile of roadway in America. "Hundreds of trillions of dollars," Sayer says it would cost. That realization forced a profound shift in thinking within the Intellidrive office. The change happened to coincide with the broader movement throughout the U.S. economy toward mobile, open-architecture networks. Think cell phones, as opposed to hardwired landlines. The future, Sayer says, is in "vehicle-to-vehicle" communications.

First we let simple robots basically perch on our shoulders as we drive, warning us when we drift out of our lane or turn too fast. Growing more comfortable, we might eventually allow our robot copilot to actually control the car in emergencies and while we're just cruising on the highway. The next step would be to give our robot drivers permission to talk to each other, so that cars aren't just dumb, isolated machines. If vehicles are allowed to communicate, then every car and truck on the road is a sensing, acting node in a dynamic network that optimizes its own performance while doing its best to protect all of its nodes.

Less congestion should be one result. If cars can warn each other about traffic jams and coordinate to send everyone along appropriate alternative routes, everyone would spend less time stuck in traffic.

Safety should also improve, the way Sayer imagines it. "You've got twenty cars driving down I-696 that communicate, out of one hundred on the road," he says. "You've got an icy spot at the intersection with Dequindre." When one car hits that ice, it tells every other car that's "listening," and these cars warn their drivers. "You'll get the message," Sayer says.

But he worries: "Will you trust it?" If we allow the cars to share in the driving, they could conceivably slow on their own when they reach the icy spot. But granting them that leeway is itself a leap of faith for us.

Since we've abandoned the idea of multitrillion-dollar, hardwired "smart" roads, the technical obstacles are actually quite small. The systems for gathering the data that would flow across a future driving network are already in place. Most cars and trucks have onboard computers that record performance and maintenance data. Many commercial vehicles, and even some personal cars with OnStar and similar systems, plug these computers into transmitters that beam key data points to some collection center for analysis.

That's called "telematics." Building a vehicle-to-vehicle network would simply involve taking the existing data and telematics and broadcasting widely instead of narrowly. Every new car or truck that rolls off the factory floor would have a transmitter and a receiver, plus displays for the human occupant and computer algorithms for the robotic autopilot, enabling it to make decisions based on what the network tells it.

It would be as though the Urban Challenge racers both cooperated with human drivers and cooperated with each other. Rather than competitors, they would be teammates. "That's where the future is," Sayer says. Getting to there from here is not so much about developing new technology as it is convincing people to let existing technology play a bigger role in their driving.

Again, it boils down to trust.

With IVBSS, Sayer is trying to determine prevailing attitudes and, hopefully, begin to change them. "What we're really interested in is how drivers respond," he says. He's not discouraged by all the negative feedback he's gotten so far—he's challenged by it. "There's a lot to be done," he says.

PART **TWO**

4
Frankenstein's Automonster

Trust is one reason we haven't surrendered our cars to greater robotic control. Another is that we plain *love* driving all by ourselves, the old-fashioned way.

Among the world's leading powers, the United States is the most heavily dependent on roads. In 1999 there were around 3.9 million miles of public roads in America—that's sixty feet of road per person.[1] That included 46,000 miles of freeway. China, by contrast, had just 2.2 million miles of public roads in 2007—eight feet per person—and 26,000 miles of freeway.[2]

Americans drive more than most people. Before 2005, the U.S. had more cars, and more cars per person, than any other country, according to the Organisation for Economic Co-operation and Development. Then, for some reason that no one has adequately explained, Portugal inched slightly ahead of the U.S. in per-capita car ownership, with just shy of 800 cars per 1,000 people.[3]

Still, when car ownership, average driving hours per person per year, and other factors are combined, Americans come out on top as the world's biggest drivers. There's a good reason for this: suburbia. The massive expansion of American suburbs after World War II spread more people over a larger swath of the countryside, farther and farther from their jobs. "Because more people own cars in rural areas than urban areas in the U.S., suburban sprawl is often considered the reason Americans rely so heavily on cars," *Forbes* reported in a 2008 article.[4]

But the article overlooked an important and curious fact. It was the car that encouraged the sprawl that, in turn, made the car so necessary—and at the same time sustained a century of economic and cultural development that mostly hinged on the production and use of automobiles. Gavin Wright, a professor at Stanford University, described this odd circularity in a 2007 article.

According to Wright, America enjoyed what he called an economic "surge" in the 1950s, to become the wealthiest and most influential country in the world. "One major component of this performance reflected a continuation of 19th century strengths in natural resources and mass-production industries," Wright wrote. "The most dramatic example was the automobile industry, a blend of mass-production methods, cheap materials and fuels. Although large, gas-guzzling Americans cars were clearly designed for the domestic market, the combination of scale economies and technology was powerful enough to dominate world motor vehicle trade in the 1920s."[5]

That domination had huge implications for American society. Employment was the root of it. In 1950, more than 200,000 people worked in car plants in Detroit alone, while nationwide several million worked in the auto industry.[6] These jobs were unusually productive for the whole economy. Every auto job sustained at least three jobs outside the immediate industry, from the laborers who mined the raw materials and the shippers who hauled them to the shopkeepers who sold the factory workers shoes and jeans and the short-order cooks who fed them on their lunch breaks. The car companies were the strong core of the weighty industrial center around which the whole U.S. economy revolved.

Cars made us rich. The richer we got, the more we could afford the very cars whose manufacture had made us wealthy in the first place. The Great Depression was a hiccup, of course, and so was World War II. In 1945, the final year of the war, factories were still producing war goods and Americans just weren't shopping. Detroit sold 70,000 cars that year. But five years later, with millions of former soldiers back at work and the economy retooled for consumer production, market conditions intersected with the auto industry's decades of accumulated expertise, in a perfect union of supply and demand. In 1950, American carmakers sold six million vehicles.[7]

"It was a great love story of man and machine," columnist P. J. O'Rourke wrote about American car culture in the 1950s. "The road to the future was paved with bliss."[8]

The destination, the future itself, was somewhat less blissful. The car explosion unleashed forces that changed our society in good ways and bad.

Wright described the "broad trajectory of adaptation to the automobile, including demographic trends such as suburbanization and regional migration." With so much changing, so fast, no one really knew where it would all end. If our adaptation to a massive influx of personal transportation technology represented "a road . . . to the future," as O'Rourke described it, it was a road with a blind curve.[9]

For one, "we got married and moved to the suburbs," O'Rourke continued. Because, with cars and the highways that government built to speed cars along, we *could*.[10] 1950 was the first year that more Americans lived in the suburbs than in the cities. In 1940 fewer than 20 percent of housing units were in the suburbs. Fifty years later, nearly half were.

Naturally, industry followed us into the 'burbs. This included the car plants that had fueled the prosperity that enabled the initial car purchases that had sent us speeding out of the crowded cities in the first place. "Between 1945 and 1957, the Big Three auto companies built 25 new plants in metropolitan Detroit, all of them outside the city," historian Thomas Sugrue wrote.[11]

That migration of people and industry had tragic, unforeseen effects. With far fewer auto factories and their workers, cities such as Detroit slowly collapsed. In the Motor City in the 1960s, "what had been some of the densest sections of the city were now a veritable wasteland, pockmarked by empty storefronts, rubble-strewn vacant lots and boarded up houses," Sugrue wrote. The suburbs, by contrast, became a closed loop of steadily increasing wealth and slowly decreasing factory employment, all founded on the explosion of car purchases after World War II.[12]

Urban residents who had missed out on the postwar car-buying binge found they could no longer afford to participate in the car-based economy. Without your own car, "getting from the central city to an outlying plant was time-consuming and costly," according to Sugrue. "In a vicious circle, those who lived in places abandoned by the auto and related industries and who were frozen out of suburban housing markets had to rely on the most expensive form of private transportation, because of public transit cuts, to get to jobs."[13]

Most of those who had cars kept their jobs. Many of those who didn't have cars lost their jobs. But even this dichotomy didn't last. Suburban Americans' skyrocketing standard of living made it more and more expensive to build cars anywhere in America. To stay ahead of foreign-based competition, Detroit began exporting production to countries where labor was cheaper.

By 1990 there were half as many factory workers in U.S. car companies as in 1950. It was an increasingly white-collar industry: suburban Americans designed, engineered, and managed car lines; Mexicans and Canadians and later Chinese assembled the actual vehicles. In America more and more auto wealth was concentrated in fewer and fewer hands in places farther and farther from the cities as the changes sparked by the car played out to their logical and tragic extremes.

Between 1950 and 2009, the annual number of miles the average American drove quadrupled. "Being away from central cities meant Americans had to spend more of their time driving," O'Rourke wrote. "Over the years 'away' got farther away. Eventually this meant that Americans had to spend all of their time driving." Ironically, driving became more and more important even as the industry that gave birth to driving slowly, and tragically, collapsed. The collapse began in those places that could least afford to lose the industry, because they had already lost so much.[14]

From his home in Flint, Michigan, a former factory town and a place that in 2009 embodied the extremes of the "car century," filmmaker Michael Moore summed up the brutal experience of those left behind when the cars carried American industry out to the suburbs and later outside U.S. borders. The auto industry—specifically General Motors—"ruined my hometown and brought misery, divorce, alcoholism, homelessness, physical and mental debilitation, and drug addiction to the people I grew up with," Moore wrote.[15]

Not to mention that the car in part fueled a potentially far graver environmental crisis. In 1999 cars and trucks accounted for half the poisonous carbon monoxide released into our atmosphere, as well as for 30 percent of the hydrocarbon and nitrogen pollution, according to the Environmental Protection Agency.[16]

It gets worse. "Nationwide, mobile sources represent the largest contributor to air toxics" that can cause cancer, the EPA added. In 2007 in America, cars and trucks were responsible for a third of the greenhouse gases that contribute to global climate change, the State Department reported.[17]

There's a flip side to Moore's lament and to the car's undeniable impact on the environment. It's true that the automobile propelled its own industry's flight to the suburbs and left crumbling cities and jobless workers in its wake. It's true that cars burn nonrenewable oil resources that pollute the planet. But for those who rode along with the carbon-emitting automobile migration, the move meant a big step up in the world.

In 1900, just before the car revolution, only 40 percent of Americans owned their own homes. Part of the problem, according to Randal O'Toole, a thin, gray-haired, bolo-wearing fellow at the Cato Institute, a libertarian think tank based in Washington, D.C., was transportation costs. The members of the working class couldn't afford urban home prices—nor could they afford the cost of commuting between outlying neighborhoods, where houses were cheaper, and their jobs that were at the time still located downtown. "Henry Ford made the affordable car," O'Toole says. "Workers began to move to the suburbs to buy homes. Home-ownership postwar shot up." In 1940, just 43 percent of American households owned a home, according to the Census Bureau. In 1950, 55 percent did.

"If you kill the car, you kill the suburbs," O'Toole says. And if you kill the suburbs, you kill home ownership for the millions of Americans who managed to escape the cities. Our domestic prosperity hitched a ride to the 'burbs in a gas-guzzling automobile, whether we like it or not.

"Over the course of the 20th century, the auto industry remade modern America—and indeed the world," Sugrue wrote. "The auto industry grew explosively in the early and mid-20th centuries, scattered and decentralized and reconstituted its work force. The impact on everyday life—from where people live to what kind of work they do—cannot be underestimated."[18]

The end result is the bifurcated American auto culture in 2010: on one side, a highly suburban, mostly white-collar population that still holds much of the country's wealth and, like most everyone else, depends entirely on the cars it makes to get around; on the other side, an admittedly smaller poor, urban, and largely car-less population that missed its chance to flee, in cars, to where most of the jobs have moved. The depth of America's car dependence means there's no easy way to change up. As much as we own them, our cars also own us.

"We are still a nation of cars, of highways, of sprawl, of industrial decentralization," Sugrue concluded. "We still live in the automobile nation."[19]

■ ■ ■ ■

Or do we? A trend one hundred years in the making suddenly reversed itself in 2009. That was the first year ever that the number of private cars in America dropped compared to the year before. In 2008 America owned 250 million cars; in 2009 just 248 million.[20]

Not only did we own fewer cars in 2009, we also drove our remaining cars less. In January that year, Americans drove seven billion fewer miles than they did in January 2008. In fact, from late 2007 on, American drivers have logged fewer miles each month than in the same month the year before.[21]

We might still have been the world's biggest drivers in the world's most auto-dependent country, but for some reason we were driving less and less in fewer cars.

The recession that began in 2008 most likely caused the drop in car ownership, as marginal drivers switched to alternative modes of transport, and the scrapping of old cars outpaced new auto sales. "When we have more money, we buy cars. When we have less, we buy bicycles," concluded Peter Bregman, from consulting firm Bregman Partners, Inc.[22]

The mileage reduction, on the other hand, was harder to explain. Nate Silver, a columnist and statistician, built a mathematical model that blended historical driving habits, employment figures, and gas prices, and came to surprising conclusion. Higher unemployment and underemployment resulting from the deepening recession would normally mean drivers putting fewer miles on their cars, on average. But the same tough economic conditions forced down gas prices, which would encourage more driving and should have more than compensated for the employment-related mileage drop.[23]

That's not at all what happened. "Americans should have driven slightly more in January 2009 than they had a year earlier," Silver wrote in a column for *Esquire*. "But instead, as we've described, they drove somewhat less. In fact, they drove about 8 percent less than the model predicted."[24]

"Could it be that there's been some sort of paradigm shift in Americans' attitudes toward their cars?" Silver asked. He then pointed to a seemingly related set of statistics: average home prices were falling in the U.S. cities traditionally most dependent on cars. In cities where commuters could walk, ride their bikes, or catch a subway or city bus, houses were getting pricier, presumably as demand increased. However belatedly, and modestly, we Americans were drifting away from our cars.[25]

Lester Brown, founder of the Earth Policy Institute, pointed to the car's evolving cultural significance. In the 1950s, "getting a driver's license and then getting a car of some sort or a pick-up [truck] in the rural community was sort of a rite of passage," Brown told Voice of America. In that era, driving and owning a car meant growing up. But in the 2000s, "young people are socializing over the Internet and 'smart' phones and not in automobiles."[26]

We still overwhelmingly rely on our cars to get us from point A to point B, but fewer of us buy cars for emotional reasons, and that means fewer cars at the margins of day-to-day, practical need. More and more, people only buy cars they actually need, rather than cars they simply want. That was Brown's explanation, at least. He predicted American would shed 10 percent of its cars in ten years, even with steady population growth.[27]

Brown even pointed to an historical precedent. In the 1990s Japan underwent a similar change of heart with regard to the car. In part due to environmental concerns, the automobile lost its iconic status. Car sales in the island nation dropped more than 20 percent in just a few years. Japanese automakers were forced to rely on foreign markets—the U.S., for one—to keep up sales.[28]

It was easy to overstate the American driving decline. Even after three years of driving fewer and fewer miles, in 2010 Americans were still the world's most enthusiastic drivers, logging some seven hundred miles per person, per month—compared to just five hundred miles a month in 1980 and fewer than two hundred in 1950. Even so, critics of American car culture—environmentalists, especially—practically danced on the automobile's grave.[29]

"Auto sales have plummeted not merely because of a bad economy, but because the technology no longer makes sense. . . . [T]hey all consume unsustainable resources to manufacture, operate and terminate," wrote Greenpeace adviser Harvey Wasserman. To Wasserman and his compatriots, the car's terminal decline could not come fast enough. The death of the car might even save the world, they claimed.[30]

"The products built in the factories of GM, Ford, and Chrysler are some of the greatest weapons of mass destruction responsible for global warming and the melting of our polar icecaps," Moore chimed in. "The things we call 'cars' may have been fun to drive, but they are like a million daggers into the heart of Mother Nature. To continue to build them would only lead to the ruin of our species and much of the planet."[31]

Our cities, too, would benefit from the absence of cars, the critics added. "There are people in this city who believe, in spite of an abundance of opposing evidence and logic, that cars belong. They are dead wrong," wrote Kevin Monahan, a member of Break the Gridlock!, a Chicago nonprofit devoted to "reduc[ing] dependency on the private automobile."[32]

"It doesn't take 200 horsepower to carry 200 pounds of humans and baggage 25 miles per hour," Monahan spat. "Cars are oddly over-engineered for city transportation. They are colossal wastes of energy when compared to the amazing efficiencies of walking or riding a bicycle."[33]

Or traveling in a supposedly low-pollution high-speed train. Moore proposed that the federal government—which in 2009 briefly bought a controlling share in General Motors in order to rescue the company from total liquidation—rejigger the company's workers and factories for producing trains.

"We need to dig up roads, not build more," Wasserman wrote. "We need rails and coaches, bio-diesel buses and self-propelled trolleys, Solartopian super-trains and in-town people movers."[34]

In a major report on the car's decline, Brown imagined that fewer cars would mean "reduced outlays for oil imports and thus more capital retained to invest in job creation within the United States. As people walk and bike more, it will mean less air pollution and fewer respiratory illnesses, more exercise and less obesity. This in turn will also reduce health care costs."[35]

Brown also anticipated less need for new roads, highways, parking lots, and garages, saving money that could invested in public transit and high-speed rail. "The United States is entering a new era, evolving from a car-dominated transport system to one that is much more diversified."[36]

"After their century-long love-affair with the car, Americans are turning to mass transit. There is hardly a U.S. city that is not either building new light rail, subways, or express bus lines or upgrading and expanding existing ones."[37]

"As a dominant form of transportation, the automobile is dead," Wasserman crowed.[38]

■ ■ ■ ■

To be sure, the recession and heightened environmental awareness stirred interest in alternative modes of transport. But there was a small problem.

Actually, a huge problem. The technologies that Wasserman and Brown mentioned—and that dominated media coverage of U.S. transportation—are mostly immature. And many of those that aren't immature are more hype than substance.

Trains, for instance, are a great way of getting heavy stuff, especially raw materials, across America on broad but low-density networks. But they're not all that great for anything else, such as passenger service. Not in America. Not today.

Edward Glaeser, a Harvard economist, built a mathematical model based on a theoretical passenger rail between Dallas and Houston, cities that today are connected only by airlines and highways. Turns out trains could replace airplanes, albeit at a big premium. "I estimated that if the rail link had the same ridership as all airlines now connecting the two cities—1.5 million—then annual costs would exceed the direct benefits to riders by $546 million," Glaeser reported.[39]

As for trains replacing cars: forget about it. Cars are easily the best way of getting Americans to and from home and work, and handling all those little trips we take every day for shopping, fun, and everything else.

One of the biggest problems is that most people don't live or work within walking distance of a train station—and never will, unless we build literally tens of thousands of stations *tomorrow* or promptly bulldoze our suburbs and crowd everyone into downtown apartment blocks. What's more, at least 60 percent of all jobs are more than ten miles from the city centers where train stations would be concentrated, Glaeser pointed out.[40]

Most rail passengers would have to drive to the train station and pay to park their cars while they ride the train, then catch a cab or a bus at the far end in order to cover those last few miles to the workplace. In essence, commuters would shell out for one mode of transportation in order to take advantage of another, ostensibly more efficient mode. It would be pretty inconvenient, at the least. "For these reasons, driving will continue to be extremely attractive" even with new rail lines, Glaeser wrote.[41]

Whether we like it or not, American society has evolved in a way that can't easily be reversed. Since World War II, we've settled on cars for our short-distance, daily travel and airplanes for long-distance trips between cities. To reshape the country in such a way to make trains viable for our daily commutes, we'd have to build so much new infrastructure that the net energy cost, over any imaginable period of time, would actually exceed the cost of simply keeping our cars.

Even if someone magically gifted tens of thousands of miles of new rails and thousands of new trains to America, it's not clear they would save anyone money, cut energy consumption, or decrease pollution.

Amtrak, a government-owned and -operated rail network with some twenty thousand miles of track, is America's only major inter-city passenger rail. It "spent more than $3 billion carrying people about 5.4 billion passenger miles in 2006," according to O'Toole. "This works out to 56 cents per passenger-mile, more than four times the cost of flying."

Bus service is no more efficient than rails, O'Toole adds. "Also in 2006, America's urban transit agencies"—that is, public bus operators—"spent about $42 billion on 49.5 billion passenger-miles, for a cost of 85 cents per passenger mile, or more than three times the cost of driving."

The bottom line is that driving is still the most cost-effective way to get most commuters from A to B. One reason is the flexibility inherent in personal ownership. You only drive your car when you need to, ensuring it almost always operates at fairly full capacity, whereas public transportation, including trains and buses, run even when they have few passengers, resulting in the overhead costs frequently being spread over fewer riders.

Another reason is that automotive technology is still making big energy-efficiency gains compared to other, more staid, forms of transport. It's possible cars only *appear* to be huge energy hogs because we pump the gas into them ourselves. We see the energy source go in. As our cars get lighter over the course of a trip, we feel the energy—and the money we paid for it—disappearing.

Trains, on the other hand, are fueled up out of sight of passengers or run on electrical grids that are powered by huge power plants that might be miles and miles away. When it comes to energy efficiency, cars have an image problem. But rail systems can actually be bigger fuel-guzzlers. "Many light-rail operations use more energy per passenger-mile than the average sport utility vehicle, and almost none uses less than a fuel-efficient car such as a Toyota Prius," O'Toole claims.

Energy efficiency has environmental implications, of course. And cars in 2010, again despite the popular conception, can actually be modest polluters—especially compared to cars just a few decades ago and even compared to many trains, buses, and other modes of transport.

A large SUV with just one person inside is still a big carbon-junkie, emitting around 500 grams of carbon per passenger-mile, according to a 2007 report from the American Bus Association. Most passenger trains emit around 200 grams per passenger-mile, the report revealed, while planes coughed out 250 grams and city buses a whopping 300. A hybrid car, by contrast, is one of the cleanest modes of transportation, at just 120 grams of CO_2 per passenger-mile, assuming an average passenger load of slightly more than one person.[42]

Hybrids, never mind purely electric cars, are cleaner than most trains under many circumstances. But even many gasoline-powered cars can rival trains' perceived low emissions. With two people aboard, the average gas car emits roughly the same amount of carbon per passenger-mile as any typical train would over the same route carrying the same two people. This efficiency is a fairly recent phenomenon—and quite accidental. It happened without anyone really trying, as a happy side effect of better design.

Traditional gasoline-powered cars are 50 percent cleaner than they were thirty years ago, but the average emissions have held steady since around 1991. What has changed is the performance of the typical car. In 1975, cars averaged two tons and 140 horsepower, with a zero-to-sixty acceleration time of fourteen seconds, while emitting 680 grams of CO_2 per passenger-mile. In 2009 the average car weighed the same but sported a 230-horespower engine and accelerated to sixty miles per hour in less than ten seconds. It emitted 420 grams of carbon, assuming just one passenger. All this, according to EPA statistics.[43]

The remarkable thing is that the efficiency improvements were incidental, according to the EPA. "From 1987 through 2004, on a fleet-wide basis, this technology innovation was utilized exclusively to support market-driven attributes"—acceleration, for instance, or speed, size, or appearance. Even so, better engineering resulted in lower-polluting cars, even if lower-polluting cars weren't the point. Only in 2005 did a large number of car designers start intentionally making their vehicles cleaner, the EPA noted. Big emissions cuts are sure to result in coming years as that work bears fruit.[44]

Cars aren't as dirty as people think. They're also cheaper to operate than many critics allow. Those are both strong arguments in favor of the automobile. But there's one argument that's even more compelling, which is that most people simply want cars and like them.

■ ■ ■ ■

There might have been slightly fewer cars in America in 2009 than there were in 2008, but Americans were still the world's biggest drivers. There are fewer teen drivers than there were just twenty years ago, but most kids still turn sixteen and immediately get their driver's licenses.

There are lots of good reasons for that, explained Greg Cohen, the young, sideburn-wearing president of the American Highway Users Alliance, a pro-highway advocacy group based in Washington, D.C. "There's opportunity you have because of the highway system," Cohen says. "If you only could go where the rail line goes or where weather is amenable because you're biking, you'd be pretty limited. Look back in history to when we didn't have automobiles and highways. Most people never got outside their town in their whole lives. That's not the way progressive people want to live their lives."

Anti-car advocates want to take away Americans' transportation choice, Cohen contends. "Some people are ideologically opposed to allowing people to live as they wish to live." In light of Americans' continuing, overwhelming preference for cars, building, say, high-speed rails or more bike paths represents a form of "socially reconstructing" America by people who trying to "create a Utopian community in the eyes of people who feel this is what Utopia is: no one needs cars."

If new rails, bike paths, and other "green" transportation means more choice for travelers, Cohen said he is in favor. "I'm all for choice, but it's a shame the one choice some have deemed unacceptable is the choice that 99 percent of people make. We can always do more to provide alternatives where they make sense and are cost-effective."

But so few alternative modes of transportation actually meet those criteria. Instead, they require government subsidies in order to operate. As often as not, the subsidies are funded by—you guessed it—cars and highways. "If you drive a car or truck, you pay gas taxes meant to keep roads in good shape, but increasingly those are diverted to other forms of transportation. I don't see anybody riding their bike saying, 'Let's tax ourselves so we can have better roads'" for our cars. "Frankly, none of these other modes support themselves in terms of paying their own way."

Transportation expert Bruce Mulliken, writing for *Green Energy News*, was upbeat about trains but realistic about the tax implications. "There's no doubt that a high speed rail system like a national bullet train network would be good for the country and good for the planet. Yet it would require government funding to build it and keep in running."[45]

Even if we all started working from home, gave up all recreation save television, and did all our shopping online, our highways would still teem with vehicles. The reason is that roads make for efficient, flexible delivery of finished goods in small quantities—and Americans demand huge quantities of that stuff. Every day some 42,000 FedEx delivery trucks, 90,000 UPS trucks, and 260,000 U.S. Postal Service vehicles crisscross the country delivering around 50 million packages, not counting letters, which number in the billions daily even in the age of e-mails, cell phones, and social-networking websites.

Including consumer goods that move between distribution centers via highway, some 80 percent of all freight in America, by value, travels on our roads, according to Cohen. Unless people want to start picking up all their packages at central cargo hubs that might be miles and miles away, we'll still need highways for delivery. Even if people were willing to pick up their parcels themselves, how would they get there? And how would we shop, if our predominantly suburban retail stores were cut off from their daily truck deliveries?

Again, the only answer would be to totally reshape American society by essentially bulldozing the suburbs and crowding everyone into the cities, with neighborhoods built around passenger rails and retail outlets concentrated close to freight rails.

There's a better way to improve American transportation—one that doesn't involve social engineering, cost trillions of dollars, or require huge new taxes. It's a two-pronged approach: tweak the U.S. highway system to smooth out the worst bottlenecks while directing private and public research funds into improving our cars and trucks.

■ ■ ■ ■

It's clear to Cohen that most Americans want to keep driving and have good reasons for doing so. Cohen has crunched the numbers. He knows that highways are our only mode of transportation that is not only self-funding, by way of fuel taxes, but also generates revenue that is used to underwrite transportation alternatives such as buses and trains. He knows what many Americans believe but won't say: that highways are good for us.

Despite Americans wanting highways, we have essentially stopped building them. An army of laborers forged the greater part of our highway system in a feverish bout of backbreaking labor between 1950 and 1980, at a rate of more than a thousand miles a year.[46] Between 1980 and 2010, the U.S. population grew by nearly a third, to more than 300 million people; our national car fleet ballooned from 150 million to 250 million. But over the same three-decade period, highway construction ground nearly to a halt, papered in by lawsuits and starved of capital by governments unwilling to underwrite anything as ugly as a new highway.

For years it was a cliché of American local politics and a trope of sitcom and movie plots. British sci-fi author Douglas Adams even inflated the concept to galactic proportions in his novel *The Hitchhiker's Guide to the Galaxy*, which is popular in the United States. Some faceless bureaucracy wants to build a highway through your neighborhood. Object all you want, file petitions, and hold rallies: that road is going in whether you like it or not, even if it means bulldozing your house and your neighbor's. In *Hitchhiker's*, evil space developers called the Vogons demolish the whole Earth to make way for a "hyperspace expressway."

"There are folks that legitimately raised concerns over decades of major highway-building, when things weren't done right," Cohen admits. "Unfortunately, a lot of folks are convinced that something like the Cross-Bronx Expressway"—the first freeway to be built *through* urban neighborhoods, largely destroying many of them—"is coming to their neighborhood every time there's a proposal to improve roads or widen roads."

"Mistakes were made," Cohen says. It's hard to tell whether or not he's deliberately using the classic bureaucratese admission of guilt. "There were projects built many decades ago that could have been better or more sensitive to their communities. I don't see that happening today." All the same, there's just no political will to build the roads we all know we need.

"Since 1980 we've only added 3 percent capacity to our highways"— fewer than 2,000 miles—"but traffic has doubled," Cohen says. Today, interstate highways account for just 1 percent of America's roads, but carry more than 15 percent of the traffic. That proportion is growing as the suburbs expand and our average daily commute—and the distance that shippers must travel to deliver parcels and goods—steadily grow. "We're not really meeting the needs of people," Cohen laments.

It's not that all our roads and highways are always packed headlight to taillight with idling cars. A lack of capacity means bottlenecks at key points. There, you *will* find cars idling headlight to taillight, going nowhere, burning gas, pointlessly belching carbon and other pollutants, and wasting everyone's time. The Texas Transportation Institute reported that road bottlenecks cost us $87 billion in 2007, up from $17 billion in 1982.[47]

"We want to fix those bottlenecks that cause needless pollutants and impact quality of life and enable people to have that free access in an efficient way and thoughtful way," Cohen explains. "That's pretty much all we can do, but we even have trouble with that."

Cohen and his people conducted an exhaustive survey. "Our study found that the worst two hundred or so bottlenecks, if you could fix those—and pick your fix, whether through widening or better approaches—that would reduce carbon emissions by over two-thirds in the vicinity of those bottlenecks and would save an enormous amount of wasted fuel and time."

"Number one in our survey," Cohen adds, "was the intersection of the 710 and 101 in L.A. In D.C., you could look at the American Legion Bridge or the 495 and 270 interchange. It used to be that the Springfield interchange was the worst, but they've been doing lot of work on it and should be pretty much done now. That one was costing the economy in the area of billions of dollars."

The two hundred worst bottlenecks, if you fixed them, would pay for themselves with gas and productivity savings in a decade's time, Cohen insists. He believes that if average Americans truly understood that, they'd demand more and better highways and get them. "Folks who don't like highways are an incredibly vocal and organized bunch, but they don't represent the majority view." Everyday commuters "still expect government to fix the problems they face on the roads on a daily basis."

Even with the recent small decline in the number of cars on our roads, we're still burning close to a $100 billion a year idling at highway bottlenecks. And those bottlenecks get worse by the year as old highways crumble with age. If we don't demand improvements soon, Cohen says, "It's going to get a lot worse."

Mixed Breed

In late 2008 and early 2009, the U.S. auto industry was in freefall. Sales in America had dropped by a third across the five biggest automakers: General Motors, Ford, Honda, Toyota, and Chrysler. Of the Detroit-based "Big Three," only Ford turned a profit in 2009—and a slim one at that.

Layoffs and cost-cutting lay at the heart of the companies' turnaround strategies. But there was also huge investment in new technology, with an eye toward coming out on top when the world economy recovered. For most of the automakers, in the short term that meant hybrids: cars and trucks combining the proven performance and low purchase price of a traditional gasoline-powered car with the lower pollution and reduced long-term costs of an electric model.

President Obama summed up the state of affairs during a March 2009 tour of a Californian car-battery factory. "So we have a choice to make," Obama said. "We can remain one of the world's leading importers of foreign oil, or we can make the investments that would allow us to become the world's leading exporter of renewable energy. We can let climate change continue to go unchecked, or we can help stop it. We can let the jobs of tomorrow be created abroad, or we can create those jobs right here in America and lay the foundation for lasting prosperity."[1]

Washington bet on hybrids to lead the U.S. auto industry, and to a lesser extent the whole U.S. economy, to a brighter future. But hybrids' reality is more complex than the government's all-good-news assessment of the technology. In truth, hybrids offer advantages only in certain scenarios. In some situations, certain types of hybrids are actually worse for the consumer, and for the planet, than a totally gasoline-powered vehicle.

Washington, D.C.'s city government illustrated this problem in 2006. To encourage commuters to switch to supposedly fuel-efficient hybrid cars, that year Washington legislators passed an ordinance allowing hybrid owners to use high-occupancy lanes, even when driving alone. That meant scores of hybrids speeding along at seventy miles per hour on the area's freeways.

"That makes no sense to me," said Tom Ryan from the Society of Automotive Engineers. At high speed, Ryan explained, hybrids burn gasoline just like old-fashioned cars—and sometimes even burn it faster. It's only at lower speeds, especially during stop-and-go driving that captures braking energy for an electrical charge, that gasoline-electric hybrids run on battery power, saving gas, cutting emissions, and preserving both the environment and their owners' bank accounts.

D.C.'s backwards incentive reflects widespread misunderstanding about the real costs and benefits of the different types of automobiles on the market. Typical consumer-model hybrids only help if you're a traditional city commuter, driving short distances at low speeds with lots of stops—and then only if you plan on keeping your car for several years. Other driver "profiles"—highway speedsters, long-distance trekkers, and anyone hauling a big load, plus anybody who likes to buy a new car every couple years—won't benefit at all from making the switch. They'll gobble just as much gas, and a lot more money, with a commuter hybrid.

The reasons are under the hood. Hybrids generally have two motors. The car switches between them depending on what you're doing. For consumer hybrids—your commuter models—there's a gasoline motor and an electric one. The small electric motor in a commuter hybrid is emissions-free and saves you gas, but it doesn't provide the same oomph you get from a full-size gas engine. For slow driving, like in a city, electric works just fine—with the added bonus that the electric motor can siphon off energy from frequent braking, "recycling" it back into propulsion through a process called "regenerative braking."

For long-distance cruising and for any high-speed travel, however short the dash, a commuter hybrid switches to its gas motor, which is most efficient at sustained high-speeds. Carrying two motors gives you the benefits of both. The downside is that one of them is always dead weight that can actually *increase* gas consumption under certain conditions.

And besides all that, in 2008 commuter hybrids—indeed, most types of hybrids—were more expensive than traditional vehicles, owing to the extra motor. Just how expensive depends on who makes the hybrid. Toyota builds more commuter-type hybrids than GM and Ford and can sell them cheaper. All the companies use a term called "payback" to refer to how long the average city-dwelling consumer will have to drive a hybrid before typical gas savings pay back the extra cost of buying the hybrid.

For Toyota Prius hybrids in 2008, it was just two years. For GM's hybrid Tahoe SUV, it was around five. Ford's payback for its new hybrid models was a staggering eleven years. In 2009 gas prices were lower—and the payback periods even longer.

For a certain class of driver, the gas vehicle is still the best bet. That said, there are hybrids to fit most people. But to benefit from hybrid technology, non-city drivers and any non-commuters—commercial truck and delivery drivers, for instance—need a different mixture of propulsion technologies than the typical city commuter needs. In many cases, they need their own kind of hybrid.

For Detroit's engineers and researchers, that means devising not just one new technology, but a whole slew of them, all falling under the loose rubric of "hybrid." What consumers understand to be one, monolithic notion— combine a gas engine with an electric one and make a better car!—is in fact a bewildering mix of technologies that is stretching the auto industry's R&D culture to its limits, with some amazing results.

■ ■ ■ ■

In the 1990s, research into hybrids branched into two broad channels: one aimed at developing consumer vehicles suited to the driving patterns of typical, middle-class office workers, the other targeting the fringes of the vehicle-buying public that need something bigger and tougher than a compact car or light SUV.

These heavy hybrids might also replace commercial and government logistical fleets, including military trucks. At more than million vehicles combined, these fleets are a big deal. Factor in the top-down, centralized management of most fleets, and you've got a gigantic pool of conventional vehicles that, in theory, can be swapped out for hybrids in short order—*if* the technology is available.

That's a big "if."

As is often the case with new technologies, especially in the transportation sector, the military was first out the gate. The late 1990s and early 2000s saw a dramatic blossoming of military hybrid research programs, with the shared goal of building a more efficient breed of diesel truck. In military service, diesel hybrids promised better fuel economy, a reduced fuel burden, and the ability to "export" power. That meant you could plug your appliances—computers and battery chargers, for instance—directly into an outlet built into the vehicle.

But the promise ran headlong into contrary reality. Temperamental technology and disappointing test results dampened the military's initial enthusiasm for hybrids. And in 2006, the U.S. Army's top hybrids expert all but declared the military diesel hybrid dead. "Right now we do not have a current hybrid program that is targeting fielding," said Gus Khalil, a senior researcher at the U.S. Army's TARDEC, headquartered in a collection of blocky buildings on a roomy campus in Warren, Michigan.

Khalil, a thin, almost stern-looking man, and other TARDEC engineers have been developing military hybrids since 1992. In those early years, their work seemed to pay off fast. By the mid 2000s, the Pentagon had no fewer than thirty different, electric-hybrid demonstrator vehicles in some form of testing.

These demonstrators ranged from hybrid models of existing vehicles, such as Humvees, M-113 armored personnel carriers, and M-2 Bradley infantry fighting vehicles, to new designs such as the Marine Corps's Reconnaissance, Surveillance and Targeting Vehicle, or RST-V—a high-tech, air-transportable all-terrain vehicle sized to squeeze inside a V-22 Osprey tilt-rotor aircraft.

Some of these demonstrators were more promising than others. Some even offered new niche capabilities. But all failed to achieve the combination of performance, toughness, price, and utility that the military demanded of its vehicles. One problem was that Khalil and his team had been following all the same basic design processes as the civilian automakers, which were hard at work on hybrid versions of existing cars and trucks.

It was a summer day in 2006, and Khalil and some of his top engineers had gathered in a nondescript TARDEC boardroom to discuss the state of their hybrids research. "We found out way back when that you cannot just take what is being developed out there for commercial cars and put it in military vehicles," Khalil said. "The space available on military vehicle platforms is extremely tight and the demand of the user is different than that of the average driver on the road."

"Hybrid technologies may seem like an easy undertaking, especially with the automotive industry making headway to reduce commercial [gasoline] consumption by way of hybrid platforms," TARDEC announced separately from the meeting. "It is not so easy for the military. Our vehicles have larger electric- and use-loads than standard commercial vehicles, so adopting commercial technology for military use is not always possible. Additionally, our vehicles operate in conditions that most commercial vehicles do not."

"Generally speaking, size and weight are challenges for everything we do," Khalil said. The engineer's skinny build and generic, business-casual attire belied the respect, almost deference, his fellow engineers showed him. "The weight is limited and that is dictated by how you transport the vehicle from one place to another," he continued. "And there are definite limits on volume. You need components that deliver very high power but fit in the vehicles and are light enough not to exceed weight [limits]. Another area is cooling."

"The area under vehicle armor is a very hot environment for all electronics," the TARDEC statement continued. "So, in order to make hybrid technology survive, the Army needs to cool the components. In order to properly cool the components, you have to add some type of cooling system—which then adds more weight to the vehicle."

Khalil was visibly irritated as he recounted the all dead ends his team has discovered after years of apparent progress. He seemed like a man who was ready to give up.

But he didn't. The military continued pursuing hybrids research. More to the point, the armed services gained a realistic sense of the challenges they faced in improving the efficiency of classes of vehicles that were already highly efficient in their expected duty cycles. A blanket approach simply wouldn't work, for the margins of potential improvement for each class of vehicle were just too slim for anything but a focused, almost surgically precise solution.

To make a more efficient infantry fighting vehicle, the army would need to assemble a hybrid power plant specifically suited to infantry fighting vehicles. To field a less fuel-guzzling medium supply truck, the Marine Corps would need a combination of technologies meant just for the supply truck. The military learned an important truth about hybrids long before the civilian automakers did, because the civilian companies had bigger margins into which to fit blunt improvements.

In that sense, the Pentagon was ahead of the curve and blazing an important new trail that the broader auto industry would later follow, as it began migrating new technologies into America's enormous truck fleets.

■ ■ ■ ■

In the early 2000s, TARDEC was on the cusp of codifying some important truths that would guide the development of hybrid designs across the country. But that wasn't always clear to the engineers in Warren whose work seemed to be leading nowhere. Many of them saw only failure. The enormous challenges facing military hybrids had discouraged some manufacturers from investing much in demonstrators. Other companies were gambling on hybrids that were, at best, compromises—that met some military requirements while falling far short of others.

Michigan-based AM General, which builds the ubiquitous Humvee, eased up on military hybrids after several years of serious investment. "We were developing a hybrid Humvee, but the army canceled the contract a couple years back after some prototypes were built," said one company official, who asked to remain anonymous. The official said the limitations of batteries were a major factor in the army's decision to cancel the contract. "Now there isn't a clear direction from the army or the Department of Defense on hybrid programs. Besides, the focus these days is on armor, not alternative fuels."

AM General spokesman Craig McNabb, speaking on the record, was more diplomatic. "We are exploring all the alternative fuels options, which is to say, bio-diesel, alcohol, hybrid-electric, and fuel cells," McNabb said. "We're looking at all of them, but none of them are quite soup yet."

Both Oshkosh, based in Wisconsin, and General Dynamics Land Systems, based in Michigan, pressed on with hybrids despite the technological problems and despite the military's cool interest. They hoped for, and ultimately found, civil applications for technologies that were forged in Warren under Khalil's supervision.

Oshkosh pinned its hope on a hybrid development of its successful Heavy Expanded Mobility Tactical Truck, or HEMTT. The hybrid HEMTT's development was jointly funded by Oshkosh, the army, and the Department of Energy, which was interested in commercial and civic applications of large hybrids, such as municipal garbage collection.

The army deploys the HEMTT for heavy battlefield transport. The hybrid HEMTT, which entered testing in February 2005, uses ultra-capacitors, rather than batteries, to store diesel-generated AC power, effectively skirting the problem that doomed other military hybrids. Ultra-capacitors are safer and more efficient than batteries but store less energy per unit of weight than batteries and are more complex.

When a driver is riding the brakes to slow the vehicle, small motors attached to each of the hybrid HEMTT's four axles switch modes and start functioning as generators, capturing the braking energy that would normally radiate as waste heat. The energy gets stored in a dozen ultra-capacitors. "They can store 1.5 mega-joules of energy," Gary Schmiedel, Oshkosh's vice president for advanced products, said of the ultra-capacitors. "With that energy, I can add 190 horsepower to the truck for ten seconds or 19 horsepower for a hundred seconds. That saves fuel. And when I'm all done at the end of the mission, I can take whatever energy is still stored in the capacitor and export it."

The hybrid HEMTT's design favors missions that involve a lot of starting and stopping to provide that regenerative braking that tops off the capacitors. But when cruising at a steady speed over a long distance, as is common during convoy missions in war zones such as Iraq, the hybrid HEMTT is little better than a conventional truck. And the hybrid model is more expensive than straight diesel models.

"We're not just doing hybrid-electrics to save fuel," Khalil stressed. Hybrids offer all sorts of other advantages over conventional vehicles that made them worth exploring. Where the hybrid HEMTT is most improved is in its physical profile. It's true that hybrids must fit a greater volume of components into a given space than traditional vehicles. But many of a hybrid's subsystems function independently of each other. That means they can be positioned more flexibly than large conventional drivetrains can be. Like many hybrids, the HEMTT uses individual induction motors instead of a driveshaft, torque converters, and axles. This allowed the A3 designers to adapt the HEMTT to better facilitate cargo transfer from aircraft such as the C-130.

"We came up with a strategy that gets the load-handling system of the truck to the same elevation as the C-130['s cargo hold]," Schmiedel explained. "We were only able to do that with a hybrid system. A conventional truck has some significant drivetrain components in the center of the truck, but by going with the hybrid approach, we were able to embed the load-handling system within the profile of the airplane."

In addition to layout advantages, Oshkosh touted its demonstrators' power-export capabilities. The hybrid HEMTT can export as much as 100 kilowatts of power.

As of 2010, all these new capabilities still hadn't warranted a production contract from the army. For the time being, the military seems content to just study and test hybrids while holding off on issuing formal requirements for a particular mission need that hybrids might fill. Khalil stressed that for any of the current hybrid demonstrators to make a quick transition to production, the military would have to write requirements tailored to the vehicle's strengths.

In the meantime, he seemed to stay positive by telling himself, rightly, that his work is not in vain. "[A demonstrator] in 1992 and a 2005 demonstrator are two different vehicles in terms of performance. The whole community knows a lot more about how to integrate hybrid-electric technology into military platforms than it did fifteen years ago. And acceptance has grown based on the experimentation."

For Oshkosh, the benefits of working with Khalil were clear. With funding from the U.S. Department of Energy, the company took the hybrid HEMTT's power plant and, in 2006, squeezed it into a new garbage truck design. "During extensive customer field tests, it has shown improved fuel efficiency of 20 to 50 percent over the typical refuse trucks," said Don Verhoff, Oshkosh's executive vice president for engineering technology. Considering that Oshkosh is the world's biggest manufacturer of garbage trucks, the savings could really add up for agencies that buy the truck.

Oshkosh's new garbage truck will be a direct competitor with another kind of hybrid truck produced by Bosch-Rexroth. The Bosch-Rexroth truck followed pretty much the same development path as the Oshkosh truck: from military experimentation via federal funding to a commercial application.

■ ■ ■ ■

Zoran Filipi has a neatly trimmed beard and moustache, small eyes, and angular eyebrows that give him a highly focused, almost dangerous look. He stands out among his softer, gentler-looking colleagues at the University of

Michigan's Automotive Research Center, housed in an aging, blocky building on the hilly, bustling campus. On a morning in early January 2010, Michigan is deep into its typically cold, snowy winter. Outside ARC, intrepid students pull their coats closed against a driving snowstorm while plow and salt trucks barrel past, primed to do battle with snowdrifts.

Filipi, dressed in the age-old professor's uniform of white shirt and tweed jacket, sits in his cluttered office shuffling piles of paperwork to find brochures on ARC and its many programs. The brochures are outdated; Filipi attacks one of them with a pen, crossing out names of departed faculty and penning in the names of their replacements.

ARC is one of many of similar institutions scattered across suburban Detroit. When the American automotive industry moved to the suburbs beginning in the 1950s, so too did its intellectual class. The University of Michigan in Ann Arbor, today a town of around 100,000 people, became a nexus for automotive research. Here, on the southern fringes of the Michigan's industrial heartland, public and private support for American carmakers intersect.

In addition to its heavily automotive-focused undergrad and graduate engineering programs, by 2010 U of M boasts two major agencies jointly funded by auto companies and the federal and state governments. The $15-million-a-year UMTRI, Jim Sayer's group, is focused on safety technologies, in close cooperation with the U.S. Department of Transportation.

ARC, with an annual budget of around $5 million, devotes the bulk of its efforts to modeling new heavy vehicle designs on behalf of the U.S. Army. UMTRI and ARC both act as technology bridges spanning the gulf between the government—especially the military—and civil transportation culture.

Filipi came to ARC in 1995 after receiving his bachelor's, master's, and doctoral degrees at the University of Belgrade in Serbia. He had escaped Serbia just in time. International sanctions in the wake of the bloody Balkans War had crippled the Serbian economy, particularly its automotive sector. In 1993 Serbia's industrial output fell by 40 percent. Two-thirds of the industrial labor force lost their jobs. The Yugo Motor Company's Zastava plant laid off almost all of its 15,000 employees.[2]

ARC, with its catalog of army programs, was a good fit for immigrant Filipi. He says he's always been interested in the military side of logistics and transportation. He recalls watching the 1965 war movie *Battle of the Bulge* and realizing that the 1944 clash the film depicts was essentially a "battle for logistics." The Germans, low on gas, launched a massive attack in a bid to seize Allied fuel depots.

At ARC, Filipi specializes in developing military engines that would use less fuel, potentially preventing a future Battle of the Bulge for U.S. troops. More fuel-efficient engines would reduce the total quantity of vehicle fuel required by U.S. troops in Iraq and Afghanistan.

In Iraq that could mean fewer convoys organized by units like the 1052nd Transportation Company. "Maybe you just need twelve trucks instead of fifteen," Filipi says. Considering that roadside bombs are the biggest killer of U.S. troops, a smaller convoy "saves lives."

In Afghanistan lives *and* vast amounts of money are at stake. In that conflict, fuel reaches U.S. forces two ways: either tanker trucks travel from Pakistan's port of Karachi a thousand miles through Taliban-controlled territory, or American military planes haul the fuel into Bagram Airfield. Either way, it's pricey. The airlift option adds a $700 premium to every gallon of fuel. Filipi's mission, he says, is "saving fuel that costs you a lot on the battlefield."

It has taken two wars to inject a true sense of urgency into army automotive research. But the basic programs are a decade old. "We were for many years at the cutting edge of hybrid research," Filipi says. Even before Iraq and Afghanistan—and before "hybrid" had become a household word—ARC was exploring different hybrid engine combinations on TARDEC's behalf.

The reason the army led the Detroit automakers in the race toward hybrids is simple: the army has trucks, lots of them—the biggest fleet in the world, in fact. And whereas cars in the 1990s still had lots of room for efficiency improvements—in fuel type, aerodynamics, and weight—traditional, non-hybrid trucks had pretty much reached the apex of their development.

"The huge difference between trucks and passenger cars is that the truck already has an efficient diesel engine," Filipi says. "You can't make it much more fuel efficient," unless you install a totally new type of engine. "Cars can go from gas to diesel and there's a huge difference. But trucks? No. Also, you can't do much with a truck's aerodynamics. There has to be a huge box in the back."

Nor can you just shave weight off a truck. "If you can afford to spend $20 million per truck, then you can use composites," Filipi scoffs. Otherwise, a truck is bound to stay heavy. It occurred to ARC, TARDEC, and the army in the 1990s that the only way to improve a truck was to make it a hybrid.

They got to work. ARC did the basic research. The center would take some engineer's idea—say, a diesel-electric hybrid engine for a particular model of heavy-duty truck—and build a mathematical model to predict the engine's performance. ARC's engineers and student assistants might even tinker with engine components or, less likely, a whole engine prototype. If the theoretical hybrid engine seemed worthwhile, ARC would pass the data to TARDEC for further experimentation and, perhaps, the production of full-scale demonstrator vehicles.

ARC's research can result in all kinds of surprises. Some technologies end up being less than ideal for military applications but perhaps worthwhile for certain civil uses. ARC gets some funding from nonmilitary government agencies—the EPA, for instance—and is allowed to "hand off" promising technologies to U.S. automakers. In that way, both the military and the private sector benefit from ARC's mostly military research. ARC and other research institutions represent a great part of the common source from which America's civilian and military logistics spring.

As the wars in Iraq and Afghanistan heated up, the army settled on diesel-electrics as its preferred hybrid. ARC crunched the numbers while TARDEC partnered up with military vehicle-makers to build a slew of diesel-electric demonstrators, including hybrid versions of the Humvee plus several hybrid supply trucks—in essence, smaller versions of the tan big rigs the 1052nd drove in Iraq. While the army and the main part of its research base charged full-tilt toward its electric-hybrid future, Filipi had split off in a curious direction.

Filipi sensed that the army, in its fixation on diesel-electrics, had missed out on a kind of hybrid that was potentially more efficient in certain scenarios. He was right: by 2006, the army had given up on quickly developing a production-ready electric hybrid. Meanwhile, Filipi pressed ahead, believing he could always find a commercial user for his hybrid. The army's loss would be the civilian sector's gain.

On that snowy morning in early January, Filipi walks downstairs from his upper-floor office, into the basement of the ARC building. Offices and cubicle farms give way to huge, open spaces subdivided by metal grates. Machines and parts of machines rest in orderly stacks. Engineering students wearing protective goggles shout at each other over the mechanical din of some mysterious power-train experiment taking place out of sight.

Filipi enters a control room occupied by a solitary engineer—a towheaded young man—sitting at a computer workstation. Through a thick window, Filipi regards an adjacent laboratory. Installed in the center of the lab's floor is a heavy-duty truck engine manufactured by Navistar, the same company that makes many of the Pentagon's MRAP bombproof trucks. Wires and tubes snake from the engine, feeding it fuel and channeling performance data to the young engineer's computer.

This is ARC's "engine-in-the-loop" test bed, one of the few such installations in the world, the first place where Filipi's ideas meet the reality of steel, fuel, motion, and friction. With the Navistar engine as a foundation, Filipi and the other ARC engineers can build models of future engine designs that blend virtual, digital components and real ones.

The engine might be real, but the transmission exists only in cyberspace, accepting data from the engine and turning it into different performance data, according to the simulated transmission installed. ARC can add real electrical components and batteries plus a simulated transmission to mimic a diesel-electric hybrid, for instance. Test data flows to the computers, helping ARC refine its designs.

At the moment, the test bed is configured with an odd-looking tube the width of a two-liter soda bottle but much longer. It looks like a large piston tube, the kind that you might fill with fluid to build a hydraulic shock absorber. In fact, that's exactly what the tube is. But instead of just *absorbing* force, this device is meant to *apply* it. It lies at the heart of Filipi's vision for better automobiles.

■ ■ ■ ■

When most people use the term "hybrid" to refer to a car or truck, they usually mean a vehicle propelled by a combination fuel-and-electrical engine. The motor uses fuel when fuel is most efficient—say, during high-speed cruising—and battery power when battery power is more efficient. As a bonus, brake-pad friction from the car's stop-and-go motion recharges the battery while you're driving.

But there are other types of hybrids. The one that most intrigued Filipi swaps the battery for a hydraulic "accumulator" that stores potential energy like a water piston does. It's called a "hydraulic hybrid," and Filipi sees a bunch of ways it can make our trucks better, cheaper and cleaner.

The hydraulic hybrid has three major components. Fluid is stored in a reservoir. When the vehicle slows, brake energy powers a pump that forces the fluid from the reservoir into the accumulator, where it gets compressed to 5,000 pounds per square inch, representing "a huge amount of potential energy," Filipi points out. As the vehicle falls below a certain speed—say, twenty miles per hour—the fuel engine cuts off and the accumulator releases its pressure in the form of a concentrated gas shot directly into the drivetrain, propelling the vehicle. A fully charged accumulator can also start the vehicle from a full stop, like a blast of water whipping a garden hose around the yard.

The energy you can squeeze out of today's accumulators is modest. Batteries are still better, in energy terms. But hydraulic hybrids have other advantages. They're cleaner, since there's no need to dispose of a toxic spent battery. Also, batteries degrade when exposed to frequent, small recharges; a battery wants to be fully recharged over a fairly long period of time, then fully drained. "A hydraulic accumulator takes almost any rate of recharge," Filipi points out.

Filipi completed his first comprehensive analysis of a hydraulic hybrid in 2002. Around the same time, there appeared in the U.S. auto market an Australian company called Permo-Drive, which billed itself as "a world leader in parallel hybrid hydraulic regenerative energy technology for urban commercial vehicles." On the strength of Filipi's work, Permo-Drive approached U.S. auto-part maker Dana Corporation with the idea of building a prototype army supply truck with a hydraulic-hybrid engine.

The army tested Permo-Drive and Dana's 6x6 hydraulic-hybrid truck at Aberdeen Proving Ground in Maryland and found it 30 percent more fuel efficient than a traditional truck. But that wasn't enough to convince the army to keep exploring hydraulic hybrids. The military prefers diesel-electrics, not the least because it likes to have all that spare battery power for a vehicle's weapons and sensors. A hydraulic hybrid isn't really electrified. Any batteries you install for weapons don't contribute to a truck's propulsion; they're dead weight.

Filipi, Permo-Drive, and Dana were undeterred. "We are looking forward to extending the contract and introducing this technology into other markets, both military and commercial," said Mike Laisure, a Dana executive.[3]

But then Dana admitted to massive "accounting errors" and, in early 2006, said it had just lost more than a billion dollars. U.S. car sales were slipping, a preview of the coming recession, and Dana with its sloppy accounting was an early casualty. The company, which had 80,000 employees, declared bankruptcy in 2006 and gave up any plans for hydraulic hybrids.[4]

Dana's finances might not have been sound, but Filipi's hybrid still was. When Dana offered to sell it a hydraulic-hybrid unit, German firm Bosch-Rexroth—a huge global auto-parts maker with 35,000 employees—quickly snapped it up.

The trick now was finding the right applications. After all, hybrids even more than traditional cars are each highly adapted to a narrow range of circumstances—again, their "duty cycles." A gasoline-electric engine, for instance, is great for vehicles that stop often—but not *too* often—and have lots of installed electrical equipment can benefit from a big, rechargeable onboard battery. For its part, a hydraulic hybrid likes to stop and start a *lot* but can't help out with electronics.

To Bosch-Rexroth, that meant delivery trucks and garbage trucks: big, fairly simple vehicles that might stop every few dozen yards—stop, go, stop, go—all day, every day. All that starting and stopping would be a solid day's work for a hydraulic accumulator. Every time the driver braked, the accumulator would recharge. Every time to hit the accelerator, the accumulator would spurt compressed gas into the drivetrain, giving the truck a fuel-free, no-emissions boost. For an urban garbage truck, Bosch-Rexroth estimated its hydraulic drive would save a gallon of fuel every two hours of operation.

In the summer of 2009, Bosch-Rexroth teamed up with the New York state government for a yearlong test of a pair of hydraulic-hybrid garbage trucks in New York City. If the hybrids worked out, the city said it might replace all twenty-two hundred of its sanitation trucks with hybrids over a decade's time.[5]

The potential for fuel, emissions, and cash savings was huge. And if the hydraulic hybrids caught on in New York, other cities were sure to follow. "This is an important step toward achieving the commercialization of heavy-duty hybrid hydraulic vehicles," said Rocco DiRico, a deputy commissioner from the New York City Sanitation Department.[6]

Delivery operations were next, according to Bosch-Rexroth engineer Michael Conrad, speaking at a 2008 engineering conference in California.

UPS, FedEx, the U.S. Postal Service, and countless other organizations—from major global firms like Coca-Cola to local florists, bakeries, and other small businesses—together operate hundreds of thousands of trucks that match the ideal duty cycle for hydraulic hybrids.[7]

Early adopters might pay a premium—UPS estimated its first handful of hybrids would take three years to pay for themselves through fuel savings—but as production ramped up, prices would drop and even the smallest operator would be able to afford them. The market was simply huge. "Hydraulic hybrid vehicle technologies are gaining momentum," Conrad assured his audience.[8]

Bosch-Rexroth stood to make millions, even billions, of dollars. "It's the best thing that ever happened to them," Filipi says of his hydraulic hybrid.

First, some refinement was in order. New York City's hydraulic garbage trucks represented an early incarnation of Filipi's and Bosch-Rexroth's concept. They're "parallel" hybrids that essentially bolt the hydraulic components onto an old-fashioned diesel engine. So-called "series" hybrids build the hydraulics into the drivetrain from the start. Parallel hybrids are okay for brute-force applications such as garbage trucks, but for passenger cars and delivery trucks, which are much lighter, series hybrids work much better.

In 2008 UPS ordered up five prototype series-hydraulic hybrids from the automotive division of Eaton, a $15 billion, seventy-thousand-person technology company based in Ohio—and one of Bosch-Rexroth's main competitors. The trucks hit the road in Minneapolis in 2009. Filipi watched the results closely. He didn't care about Bosch-Rexroth's market share, really. All he cared about was the basic technology and whether it worked in the real world. "They're seeing very high fuel-economy improvements," he reported a year later, still pleased.

The New York tests, UPS's experiment, and other small-scale hybrid operations, combined with ongoing research at ARC and other Detroit-area laboratories, "should lead to a product," Filipi says—one that could transform American commercial road transport. Better trucks would burn less fuel and emit fewer pollutants, proving to skeptics what automotive engineers have long known: that America's logistical future is still road-bound.

■ ■ ■ ■

It's not hard to imagine automobiles that go farther, more cheaply, and sustainably while polluting less—all without costing much or any more than they do today. At government, industry, and university labs scattered across the country, researchers are laboring to create the car of the future, one that will make us wonder why we were ever so enamored of trains, buses, bicycles, and the absurd notion that fifty years of suburbanization might be undone overnight.

"I don't know whether the future means hybrids, advanced diesels, fuel cells, electrics, a combination of all four, or some other system we haven't even thought of yet—but I don't need to know," Arthur St. Antoine wrote for *Motor Trend*. "All I need to know is this: Cars will continue, and they'll continue to wow us. How can I be so sure? Because mankind has always risen to the challenge. Always."[9]

6
Parsing Parcels

For most Americans, Valentine's Day equals cards, candy, roses, and scrambling for dinner reservations. For a 103-year-old company based in Atlanta, it means double shifts, overtime, and a 60 percent increase in volume, processing all the gifts that people are too far apart to hand-deliver. "Everybody loves mama," says Clarence Lanham, air operations manager for United Parcel Service's Southeast regional hub. And that means parcels. Lots and lots of parcels.

In early February 2010, Lanham, looking two decades younger than his forty-three years, stands on a polished concrete floor, 252,000 square feet in all, surrounded by conveyer belts on the floor and dangling from the ceiling, and heaps of packages—lots of pinks and reds between them—piling up on conveyers, bulging from bins and containers.

At this hub, located on a leafy campus adjacent to the metropolitan airport just a few miles outside Columbia, South Carolina, six hundred employees receive, by air, West Coast packages bound for South Carolina, North Carolina, and Georgia—and process West Coast–bound packages from the same states. The fourteen-year-old facility also serves a stopover for parcels originating locally and with local destinations. In early 2010, the hub handles around seventy thousand packages every day.

It's one of seven regional UPS hubs and a critical node in a network of overlapping public and private distribution networks. You want to get something from point A to point B? Depending on who you are, whom you're shipping to, the nature of the material to be shipped, and how urgent it is, you'll use UPS, FedEx, DHL, or a some smaller logistical company; the U.S. Postal Service; or a military transportation system.

Each method has its strengths and weaknesses. Each method competes with the others for the patronage of nearly the full range of customers. Sure, military transport never handles strictly civilian parcels, unless you count mail addressed to deployed troops from their friends and families back home. On the other hand, civilian operators routinely handle both civilian and military parcels. Even in war zones, you can find UPS, FedEx, and DHL offices. This marketplace free-for-all is one of the great advantages of American logistics. Our demand is great enough to sustain many competing shipping enterprises. Two in particular stand out.

"Few companies are as dependent on the efficiency of their [supply] chains than [sic] international courier operations," *Rethink IT*, a trade publication, proclaimed in 2004. "This has put arch-rivals Federal Express and UPS in the forefront of technological innovation." The whole United States benefits from this innovation. As the bigger of the two firms, UPS in particular functions as a sort of incubator for techniques and technologies that have a direct shaping effect on our prosperity at home and our power abroad.[1]

■ ■ ■ ■

Lanham walks across the floor at the Columbia hub. He begins in one of two corners with identical sets of more than a dozen bays, where trucks outside can back in and plug their rear ends into elevated garage-door-style openings. For incoming shipments bound for the West Coast, workers shove the parcels individually out of the trucks, sort them on large tables, and spill them onto one of several conveyers, one for each of several destination regions. The conveyers terminate at more sorting stations. Parcels are progressively grouped by destination and by size and shape as they move across the facility toward the opposite wall.

Small packages, once grouped with others headed to roughly the same place—the same city, say—are packed around a dozen apiece into nylon sacks, then crammed into outhouse-size metal containers shaped to fit the curved interior of a 767 or Airbus freighter. Bigger parcels that don't fit in the bags get tossed into the containers—"cans," the workers call them—on their own.

An empty can weighs 570 pounds. Full up, it can top the scales at more than two tons. A 767-300 can carry up to thirty cans. Including 767s, UPS flies some three hundred air freighters.[2] That makes UPS one of the world's biggest air forces, in terms of its potential for daily ton-miles. Only the U.S. Air Force can haul more. Every day, seven freighters land in Columbia, drop off their cans, and pick up new cans bound for the West Coast. Meanwhile in Columbia, eighty drivers in the company's signature brown trucks drop off local parcels for onward delivery and pick up inbound parcels for local delivery. Planes and trucks, coming and going, all day every day, all packed to the brim with packages.

Parcels flow from the airplanes to the trucks and the trucks to the planes and to other trucks in what amounts to a set of mirrored processes. The Columbia hub organizes the broad flow of parcels by side. One wall of the hub is for incoming packages coming off the planes. The opposite wall and its identical bays is for packages going out on the trucks. Parcels meet in the middle, heading in opposite directions.

To keep track of thousands of packages per hour tumbling through the Columbia hub, workers carry scanners just like those you find at a supermarket checkout. At every step of the sorting process they scan barcodes affixed to each parcel. A computer registers the parcel's location with every scan. Throughout the cavernous hub, the beeps of scanners successfully reading barcodes comprise a subtle electronic symphony.

Thanks to relentless scanning, it's rare to lose a package. "Our missort goal is one in three thousand," Lanham says as he strolls through the facility. "We're now at one in thirty-two hundred."

The hub is busier today than during most shifts, owing to Valentine's Day. But it's nowhere near as busy as during Christmas, when Columbia might sort 105,000 parcels in a single shift. The facility's basic infrastructure—the bays, the conveyers, the scanners—is adequate for that level of activity, but the usual staffing is too low. So for the holidays, Columbia roughly doubles the number of sorters, to 120, and puts two people at stations that normally have just one. All those extra employees—many of them part-timers—know in advance that they'll be needed.

"We try to stay in front of unexpected surprises," Lanham says. That might sound paradoxical. What Lanham means is that big, periodic boosts in demand are routine parts of any logistical operation. Over time, the ebb and flow of materials over distance begins to fall into patterns that can be modeled and predicted. Tending to those models is the job of UPS's industrial engineering department, with offices at all the hubs. "They set plans on how we run," Lanham explains.

The Columbia planners might start with the day's incoming flight schedule and derive from this the number of workers needed and where they should stationed along the conveyer system, in order to get parcels sorted and out the door in time. At the same time, the branch must fill the planes with outgoing cans.

Lanham opens a door into an office segmented into cubicles to say hi to the planners. Rashida Bridges, the engineer responsible for the hub's Valentine's Day plan, is glad to see him. She pulls Lanham aside. "We've got a contingency"— aka a problem. A plane got delayed in Orlando and will be late arriving in Columbia. Her challenge, and Lanham's, is twofold: how do they get the parcels off the late-arriving plane in time to meet the delivery deadlines the customers paid for? And what about parcels waiting at the Columbia hub to fly outward on that plane? "We'll have to plan alternative movements," Bridges says.

The effects will expand outward like ripples from a splash. Alternative movements mean planes carrying cargo they weren't anticipated to carry just a few hours earlier. That might require additional sorters at UPS facilities across the country, wherever the planes are bound—or fewer, if parcels are being diverted along different paths to their ultimate destinations.

Drivers will have more parcels to deliver, or fewer. Sudden slack in drivers' loads means they should fill that slack in order to keep working at peak efficiency. Every flight, every sorting shift, and every truck load incurs a cost and a benefit weighed against UPS's total overhead, its customers' expectations for when their packages should arrive, and the projected performance of rival companies. That's a lot of numbers to crunch.

■ ■ ■ ■

Lanham is a twenty-two-year veteran of UPS. He started out as a part-timer while attending the University of South Carolina's Aiken campus back in the eighties. His experience is not unusual. Julie Myrick, another Columbia hub manager, recently promoted, got her start as a truck loader and driver eleven years ago. "We all started at the lowest level," Lanham explains as he leans against a wall in Myrick's office. "We like to promote from within."

That makes sense for the company, Myrick explains. Every job at UPS relates to every other job in a tangible way. "It's all the same process," she says.

"I've loaded package cars, I've unloaded package cars." Now as a manager, she gets to "move around, see all the aspects. I love it."

Myrick means it when she says she sees everything. In her office at the Columbia hub, Myrick can track every truck and driver under her supervision, thanks to two new pieces of technology that together comprise a small step toward the computer-assisted cars that Jim Sayer at UMTRI is working on, and the fully automated vehicles the army envisions one day crawling across distant battlefields. For delivery drivers, UPS's DIAD system—that stands for "Delivery Information Acquisitions Device"—is like having an invisible supervisor riding shotgun for your entire shift, day after day, your whole career.

When DIAD first appeared in 1990, it was essentially just an electronic notepad to record customers' signatures and note delivery times. It had storage of less than a megabyte. In its fifth version in 2010, DIAD is a multipurpose handheld computer and tracking device. The one-pound tablet can record signatures, take pictures to help settle disputes, and scan documents. It also functions as a cell phone and GPS device.

The addition of GPS means managers such as Myrick can track brown trucks everywhere. "We can look at a screen and see with just a ten-minute lag where all our drivers are."

In addition to each driver carrying a GPS tracker with him or her, more than 10,000 UPS trucks, out of a global fleet of around 100,000, are fitted with "telematics"—in essence, digital gauges that each track a particular aspect of a vehicle's function. Braking, say, or idling or acceleration. All that data gets dumped into a log, where a team of UPS PhDs can access it. "You don't know what it means, so you have to do the data mining to figure [it out]," Jack Levis, UPS chief analyst, told CNET. "We plug it in, and then go off looking for another nugget, another piece of information [and] another relationship we didn't know existed."[3]

The analysts try to ask the right questions, then look for telematics data to answer them. Is a driver spending more or less time at stops than his peers? Is he accelerating too hard, potentially burning more fuel than necessary. Is he buckling up? Are the mechanics replacing parts that really need replacing? How much maintenance is actually necessary to keep the trucks healthy?

Since the telematics program began in 2008, UPS analysts have made some big improvements. They discovered that drivers were, on average, idling fifteen minutes longer than they needed to every day, wasting a million and a half gallons of fuel per year. They caught one mechanic overhauling an engine that only needed a single O-ring replaced. The analysts were also able to boost seatbelt usage from 98 percent to 99.8 percent and reduce backtracking by a quarter.[4]

Needless to say, some drivers have resisted all this monitoring. They particularly object to some remote manager telling them to buckle up. But Myrick had one driver, a habitual nonbuckler, who changed his tune. Two or three months after the telematics tattled on the guy and Myrick ordered him to buckle, the driver got into an accident, flipping his truck—and his seatbelt saved his life.

"The dividends pay for themselves," Myrick says of the new technologies. And such automation will only expand. It's a relatively small step to go from passive monitoring to active intervention to a full, robotic autopilot. After all, telematics is the foundation of the kinds of "active safety" initiatives Sayer is involved in, and active safety is a very basic form of automatic driving, like DARPA and Perceptek are advocating.

Systems such UPS's DIAD and telematics already have much of the situational awareness they needs to play an active role in driving a truck. It won't be long before UPS drivers are really just copilots, and parcel handlers, for their computerized coworkers. Sometime in the next decade, that innovation could dovetail with a separate initiative to convert UPS's truck fleet to alternative propulsion. At UPS, hybridization is well under way, meaning it could be the first organization to unite the two most important technological developments in ground transportation today.

■ ■ ■ ■

UPS, like all logistical operators, must surge with demand while remaining overall lean enough that excess overhead doesn't sink them during the slow periods. That means finding efficiencies where efficiencies can be found. Vehicles, for one. For UPS and other logistical firms, having the most efficient trucks isn't a luxury—it's a matter of survival. But even company as big as UPS can't absorb the R&D costs to develop super-efficient vehicles.

For that, the company relies on the U.S. military with its huge slice of the federal budget. UPS is one of the many civilian logistical operators that directly benefits from military research. It's hardly charity. The military benefits in return by releasing new, immature technologies into the marketplace where civilians can work out the kinks before the military readopts them.

UPS made the decision to go hybrid long before most consumers considered it a viable prospect for their own personal vehicles. Development work began in 1998, when UPS decided to piggyback on Gus Khalil's military hybrids research. UPS contracted with PEI Electronics, a Texas-based company working on the electric-hybrid Humvee, to build a diesel-electric version of UPS's ubiquitous brown delivery truck. PEI delivered the demonstrator in 2000, and in 2001 UPS put it through its paces in Huntsville, Alabama.

"It went okay," Robert Hall, the director of UPS automotive fleet, recalls. By "okay," he means it didn't go well at all. "Obviously, we didn't hit some of the targets we wanted to hit with the prototype." If they had, it's possible that by now the majority of the UPS fleet would be hybridized. Instead, UPS went back to the drawing board.

Looking back, it should have been obvious that PEI was the wrong contractor to handle hybridizing the UPS truck. The company was focused on military programs, and the military has always had unique needs. For one, the normal driving profile of a Humvee is nothing like that of a UPS truck. UPS trucks stop and start frequently while carrying fairly light but bulky loads.

Humvees, by contrast, cruise for longer periods at higher speeds and higher weights. In fact, the Humvee's duty cycle doesn't lend itself very well to any sort of hybridization. A diesel-electric Humvee probably wouldn't offer any fuel efficiency improvement compared to the purely diesel model. The only good reason to hybridize a Humvee is to enable it to export useable power—and even that comes with liabilities. Namely, giant lithium batteries don't respond well to gunfire.

Which is why the military still hasn't fielded a hybrid Humvee as of 2010—and might never. Hitching their future to that unlikely star was a bad move for UPS. Shortly after the disappointing test in 2001, UPS refocused its hybridization efforts. "We decided to move over to an automotive-type supplier versus a military one," Hall says. That meant a new partner, in the form of the Eaton Corporation, a rival of Bosch-Rexroth, the company to which Filipi had handed off his groundbreaking hydraulic-hybrid research.

UPS got its first prototype hybrid delivery truck—a diesel-electric—back from Eaton in 2004, and by April 2010 the company had more than two hundred electric hybrids in its fleet. The electric hybrids-are a flexible, albeit partial, solution to UPS's problem, Hall explains. "Hybrid-electrics can run on virtually any route in the country we need them to." But their efficiency improvements over diesel trucks are often marginal.

What UPS wants is a bunch of different types of hybrids, each tailored to a particular job across a specific duty cycle. "We'd be able to put very specific vehicles into specific routes" in different parts of the country, Hall says. Within its niche, a tailored hybrid might cut energy usage by 30 percent.

Around the same time the first electric hybrid arrived, UPS asked Eaton to also begin developing a hydraulic hybrid like Bosch's. Eaton brought in Navistar, maker of the MaxxPro MRAP and other large trucks, to build the hydraulic hybrids' chassis. The U.S. government was also a formal partner in the program, as the EPA holds many of the patents related to Eaton's hydraulics design.

The first truck to come out of the UPS-Eaton-Navistar-EPA program joined the UPS fleet in Minneapolis in 2009. Hall and his team had picked Minneapolis for a reason. By analyzing telematics from across the company fleet, UPS had been able to map the typical duty cycles of trucks in particular cities. Los Angeles, for instance, has a duty cycle with lots of nonstop, high-speed cruising, since the UPS hub for that city is located outside downtown and connects to most delivery areas by way of an interstate. San Francisco and Las Vegas are the same way. But Minneapolis, Cleveland, Chicago, Austin, and Houston all have downtown distribution centers, and their duty cycles are all stop-go, stop-go.

Among the eligible cities, UPS prioritized those with air-quality problems. So Minneapolis got the first two hydraulic hybrids. Cleveland got the third. Hall and his team designed a training course for drivers. "We have to train the driver to allow the technology to operate. No heavy starts, no heavy stops. The hybrid needs to be feathered on acceleration and braked slowly so it gets regenerative braking."

Mechanics also needed training. "We're a little surprised about how well they've adapted," Hall reports. "They've taken on learning about the technology as much as possible to ensure these things operate as flawlessly as possible." Good maintenance prevented any early breakdowns. "We expected to have many minor issues, but really—knock on wood—these things have performed really well."

So are the hydraulic hybrids resulting in any savings? Hall says he does-n't know yet—and at this stage that's actually beside the point. The EPA covered much of the R&D cost. That helped reduce UPS's risk. Discounting development costs, the first three hydraulic-hybrid brown trucks were priced just $7,000 higher than a standard diesel truck. Hall says he would be happy to make up that premium through energy savings in three years.

More broadly, he just wants to begin laying the groundwork for a new approach to designing, fielding, and using trucks. In the past, UPS mostly took a one-size-fits-all approach, using the same diesel-fueled brown trucks in all markets. In the future, if the company's hybrids programs are any indication, every market might have its own, unique suite of truck technologies: cruising electric hybrids for highway markets, for instance, and hydraulic hybrids for those stop-and-go urban locales. Technologies still in the pure research stage might find their own niches.

That's the direction automotive technology is and should take across the board in the United States: UPS is just a few years ahead of the curve in developing a menu of logistical technologies. As Americans, we have no single solution to our transportation needs, because there's no single need. It's easy for self-proclaimed reformers to latch onto some attractive technology—high-speed trains come to mind—and declare it answer to all our problems. Never mind that a diverse mix of hybrid cars and trucks would probably do better, faster, and without forcing us to live in ways we don't really want to live.

And for some of our logistical needs, the answers aren't technological at all. In some fields, the technology is already "perfect," in the sense that there's no obvious way to make big improvements. Sometimes we just need to preserve the highly refined systems we've already got, rather than try to revolutionize something that can't really change. The venerable old freighters that haul our steel and coal across the Great Lakes are the perfect example.

PART **THREE**

7

The Greatest Lakes

It's two days after Christmas 2009 on Lake Superior. The freighter *Paul R. Tregurtha*, all 1,013 feet of her, is waging war with ice and wind. A thirty-mile-per-hour gust coming out of Canada, combined with the spray from the ship's natural, rhythmic heaving, sends water sweeping across the deck, where it freezes on contact with metal and wood.

Every crew member who can be spared is up on deck, bashing ice with tools, fighting a slowly losing battle to keep the ship from freezing over. The *Paul R. Tregurtha* is headed east toward St. Clair, Michigan, where a Detroit Edison–owned power plant on the banks of the St. Clair River burns coal and fuel oil to generate fifteen hundred megawatts of power for regional industry, including several auto plants.

On a typical day, the St. Clair plant might burn thirty thousand tons of coal, an 80-20 blend of Western and Eastern coals from Montana and Pennsylvania, respectively. The Montana coal comes by train to the port of Superior, Wisconsin, and takes the shortcut across Lake Superior in the holds of ships like the *Paul R. Tregurtha*. The ships tie up on the riverbanks and offload their cargo straight into the power plant's yards, using long, arm-like conveyers built into the vessel's structure.

The *Paul R. Tregurtha* and her beleaguered crew, the port of Superior, the St. Clair power plant, the coal it burns, and the auto plants it powers are all nodes in a time-worn logistical network that underpins America's industrial heart-land. We might build fewer cars than we did just a few years ago, but manu-facturing—cars, in particular—still accounts for 12 percent of the U.S. gross domestic product and around 10 percent of American jobs. Manufacturing as a percentage of GDP hasn't much changed in almost thirty years; it's not likely to budge any time soon. We will keep building lots of stuff, and we'll build much of it in the historically industrial states ringing the Great Lakes.[1]

We'll do it because of the Great Lakes and the fast, cheap transportation the Lakes afford.

There's a downside to our enduring reliance on the Great Lakes—and that's winter. Every year between late December and late March, the lakes mostly ice over, rendering most ship movements impossible. Global climate change hasn't yet altered the frigid clockwork of the traditional nine-month shipping season.

That means that customers like Detroit Edison, owner of the St. Clair power plant, must plan ahead. Every fall, St. Clair stockpiles more than two million tons of coal to see it through the winter. The *Paul R. Tregutha*'s December 27 run across an icy Lake Superior is one of the last coal deliveries of the season. Without her vital cargo, Detroit Edison might run dry. The power would fade, the factories would go dim, and thousands of workers would be out of a job. To call the ship's work important is a gross understatement.

■ ■ ■ ■

In the comparative comfort of the *Paul R. Tregurtha*'s bridge, Capt. Tim Dayton watches his crew attacking ice buildups on the deck below. Days like today are about as bad as it can get on the lakes from the perspective of the lower-ranking crew, Dayton says later, after his ship has reached St. Clair and successfully offloaded its sixty thousand tons of coal. "You have ten-degrees-below-zero temperatures. It's cold. You fight ice; you fight snow."

Dayton, a round-faced man with arched eyebrows that give him a perpetually surprised expression, laughs. His high Midwestern accent gives him a mischievous air. "I don't do that—I don't even go outside. I sit up in the pilot house and say, 'Wow, that's a cold day.'" To the fifty-five-year-old Dayton, the worst days aren't the icy, windy ones; they're the days with "high wind and low water-level," because ships as big as the *Paul R. Tregurtha* usually won't sail, for safety reasons. "You're stopped somewhere," Dayton gripes. "You're not moving or accomplishing what you need to do."

After thirty-six years on the lakes, Dayton still has a measure of the restless energy that drew him into this life in the first place. He grew up in

Danbury Township, Ohio, which lies on a thumb-shaped peninsula jutting eastward into Lake Erie, just north of the tiny island that today is home to Cedar Point amusement park, which with its bright lights, noise, and roller coasters is the Midwest's somewhat more modest answer to Disney World.

The Great Lakes freighter *Paul R. Tregurtha*.

For the boy Tim Dayton, the lakes were a constant presence—and so was the sprawling industry that they supported. In the 1950s the American auto industry was at its peak. Millions of soldiers who had returned from World War II sank their savings into new cars. Downtown factories churned out millions of new vehicles a year for markets at home and abroad. The Great Lakes, with their veins of connecting canals and rivers and their borderlands rich in coal and iron ore and dense with cities and workers, were at the heart of it all.

More than a hundred ships crewed by several thousand captains, engineers, and deckhands crisscrossed the lakes and their near waterways, hauling coal to the power plants, iron ore to the steel mills, and finished steel to the car factories. Slow, capacious Great Lakes freighters and sleek, speedy automobiles became permanently bonded, fraternal twins at opposite ends of a muscular industrial process that remade America. Dayton's father, like so many other boys' fathers, was part of that process. The elder Dayton, a farmer most of the time, also worked for Ford to supplement his income.

The fifties auto boom forged the steely seeds of its own destruction. Suddenly millions of Americans had cars and, thanks to the federal government under President Dwight Eisenhower, thousands of miles of highways leading out, out into the abandoned farmland that would become American suburbia. Factories followed migrating populations. Cities collapsed. The auto industry began a long, slow contraction in the number of workers it employed, thanks in part to the management-optimized suburban prosperity it had helped pay for.

Car design would remain an indelibly American function for many, many years, but dirty, dangerous, and expensive car production would increasingly find cheaper places to root: Canada, for a while, then Mexico, and ultimately China. The outflow of factory employment was an arguably inevitable consequence of economic development, but for the workers it rendered jobless, it was nothing short of tragic.

The Daytons didn't have much money. Looking around him after high school, Dayton realized he didn't have many options for college. "I didn't have enough money to go to Ohio State for agriculture," he recalls. Really, the only price he could afford was free. And the only places to get a free education was ROTC or the service academies: the army's West Point, the Naval Academy, the Air Force Academy.

And the Merchant Marine Academy in King's Point, New York—another peninsula, this one jutting into Long Island Sound. Next to studying agriculture, this was the best fit for Tim Dayton. At the Merchant Marine Academy, he would learn to operate ships like those that plied the waters around his childhood home.

■ ■ ■ ■

The Merchant Marine Academy, sometimes just called "King's Point," was born in fire. On September 8, 1934, a blaze broke out in a storage locker aboard the American-owned luxury line SS *Morro Castle*, bound for New York City from Havana with 549 passengers and crewmen. In just half an hour, the fire spread throughout the ship. In the heat, smoke, and pandemonium, 135 people died.[2]

An inquiry pointed out poor safety practices and crew training. The ship was coated inside and out with thick layers of flammable paint. Fireproof doors were compromised by wooden openings installed over them to boost air circulation. Water pumps were too weak. There had been no organized firefighting efforts by the crew.[3]

The *Morro Castle* incident "convinced the U.S. Congress that direct federal involvement in efficient and standardized training was needed," according to the Merchant Marine Academy's website. Congress passed the Merchant Marine Act in 1936. The act established a federal merchant marine and an academy to support it. Workers broke ground at King's Point in 1942, and the school opened in September 1943, in the middle of World War II.[4]

The Merchant Marine Academy had a busy war, supplying officers to the thousands of U.S.-flagged vessels that carried war supplies from America to far-flung Allied forces. In all, the academy graduated more than sixty-six hundred officers before war's end. One hundred and forty-two graduates died in Axis attacks on their vessels.[5]

After the war, King's Point evolved along with the world shipping system. To avoid the high cost of abiding by U.S. laws and regulations, more and more shipping companies, even wholly American-owned ones, registered their vessels in less legally stringent foreign countries—Liberia, for instance, or Panama. As the U.S.-flagged shipping fleet shrank to its current size of just a couple hundred vessels, so too did the demand for merchant mariners.

Today, there are fewer than a thousand midshipmen at King's Point—and many of those, when they graduate, take government-approved jobs in the commercial shipping industry's shore infrastructure. Others enter the navy, the coast guard, or the National Oceanographic and Atmospheric Administration. Just a third actually go to sea—or to the lakes—as U.S. merchant mariners.

The Great Lakes shipping fleet accounts for around half of the U.S.-flagged vessels. There's a good reason for this. An earlier version of the Merchant Marine Act that founded the academy at King's Point required that all waterborne shipping between U.S. ports be carried in U.S.-owned, U.S.-flagged, and U.S.-crewed vessels. Nicknamed the "Jones Act" for its sponsor Wesley Jones, a Washington senator, the 1920 law is both a protectionist measure and a pillar of national defense, for it preserves an industry that is especially vital in wartime.

The Jones Act shaped American logistics in a way that few laws have. The law protects the U.S. shipping industry from total destruction at the hands of foreign firms. It also ensures that the Navy's Military Sealift Command always has sufficient sailors to call on in times of emergency.

The Lake Carriers Association summed up the problem, and the justification, for the Jones Act, in a 1997 position paper. "When a vessel operator builds his ship to lesser safety standards, registers it in a country with virtually no safety and environmental oversight on shipping and employs crew members for $15 a day (with no benefits), it's obvious the freight charge will be less than a U.S.-flag vessel built to the world's highest safety standards, operated in compliance with U.S. Coast Guard regulations, and crewed with American citizens who receive wages and benefits in line with other modes of transportation in this country."[6]

Lower freight charges mean foreign companies can easily underbid American shippers for contracts, barring protectionist measures. Without the protection afforded by the Jones Act, American shippers would go out of business. That would put tens of thousands of Americans such as Dayton and his crew out of work. It would be equally disastrous for Military Sealift Command.

When MSC mobilizes its Ready Reserve Fleet, a collection of fifty government freighters meant to support major military operations, just short of three-quarters of the required crew members come from Jones Act shippers. Since the 1990s, Ready Reserve ships have hauled cargo for operations in Iraq, Somalia, Bosnia, and Latin America. In just the second year of the Iraq War, the RRF activated nearly two dozen ships. Without the Jones Act, there wouldn't have been sailors for these ships.

Our national security depends on sealift. Our sealift depends on Military Sealift Command. MSC depends on U.S. shippers. The shippers depend on the Jones Act. You can draw a straight line from one, nearly century-old piece of protectionist legislation, and America's ability to shape world events in the twenty-first century.

■ ■ ■ ■

Dayton first set sail aboard the fifty-year-old freighter *Benson Ford*, owned by the Ford Motor Company and assigned to haul raw materials to riverfront and Lakefront Ford facilities scattered across the Midwest. It was 1974. Dayton was a second-year midshipman at King's Point.

The now-retired *Benson Ford* was an "old clunker," Dayton says. But he didn't mind. He was eighteen years old, the son of a farmer and factory worker, working the world's biggest lakes hauling raw materials for one of the world's most powerful corporations. The seminal moment in his first cruise came when the *Benson Ford* was chugging across Lake St. Clair, which is between Lake Huron and Lake Erie, just east and northeast of Detroit, when three other vessels intersected the *Benson Ford*'s path.

On the high sea, a close encounter between four ships each displacing tens of thousands of tons of water and carrying cargoes worth millions of dollars would cause some serious alarm among the crews. But lakefaring culture is different from seafaring culture. Dayton had the *Benson Ford*'s wheel at the time. At sea during such an approach, a captain would almost always pull a midshipman off the wheel and replace him with a more experienced officer. But the *Benson Ford*'s captain let Dayton stay and steer the freighter through the tangle of vessels and into the clear. "Nobody got excited," Dayton says.

"On the lakes, even as a third mate, you do a lot more ship-handling than even as a captain down on the coast," Dayton says. "I love ship-handling. It's the best part of the job. All the other stuff sucks. Dealing with the office, dealing with personnel problems, dealing with the coast guard, dealing with Homeland Security, dealing with Customs—that stuff I could erase from the slate."

But steering a mammoth vessel across the world's greatest lakes, supplying one of the world's greatest industrial heartlands—"That's what drives you to do the job." And that's exactly what Dayton found himself doing his first season on the lakes. His main assignment with the *Benson Ford* was hauling raw materials to Ford's sprawling facility on the Rouge River, where it met the Detroit River just a few miles south of downtown Detroit.

The Rouge plant is among the most famous factories in America. It was founded to manufacture navy patrol boats in World War I, but the war ended before the so-called Eagle Boats could begin assembly. In the war's aftermath, Ford founder Henry Ford converted the Rouge first for making tractors, then for producing parts for the company's world-changing Model T car. Rouge made the components, then shipped them off for assembly at other factories.[7]

The Rouge reflected Henry Ford's obsession with owning all facets of car production. He bought up iron ore mines, forests, and limestone quarries. He owned the ships and trains that hauled the raw materials. The Jones Act certainly encouraged Ford's entry into waterborne transport, as vessels hauling materials directly to the Rogue had to be U.S.-owned anyway. For a time, Ford ships were among the most sophisticated in America. The freighters *Henry Ford II* and *Benson Ford* were the first diesel-fueled vessels on the Great Lakes.

At the Rouge, Ford built what was the world's biggest steel mill, to supply the parts production—and later final assembly—at the same complex. In time the cost of this "vertical integration" outweighed the benefits, and Ford began relying on outside suppliers. But for a time, the Rouge was vital node in a sophisticated logistical enterprise. Raw materials flowed into the Rouge from all over the world and emerged as partially or fully complete automobiles— thanks in no small part to the crews of ships like the *Benson Ford*.

Dayton stayed with the *Benson Ford* and the Ford Motor Company after graduating from King's Point. It was 1976, and already "things were really tight," Dayton said. Fewer factories meant less need for ore, coal, limestone, and steel. The Great Lakes freighter fleet shrank with the shrinking demand. The changing marketplace dashed Ford's dream of total vertical integration. In the late 1980s, Ford sold off its Rouge steel operation. The new company, Rouge Steel, then sold off its two freighters to Interlake Steamship Company.

Dayton followed the ships to their new owner. More than a decade into his Great Lakes career, he was still a subordinate officer. His first chance at command came in 1993, when he was tapped as the master of the *Mesabi Miner*, one of the flagship vessels of the lakes fleet.

■ ■ ■ ■

In many ways, the Great Lakes are like small oceans. Looking across Lake Erie from a beach in eastern Michigan, you can't see the opposite shore. The vessels that ply the lakes look a lot like their oceangoing sisters and can rival them in size. But there's a critical difference in the Great Lakes, compared to the ocean, that has big effect on the economics of lakes shipping. The lakes, unlike the oceans, contain freshwater.

Freshwater is far less corrosive than saltwater. That means the steel hulls of freighters last much longer on the lakes than they do at sea. Few saltwater vessels last more than thirty years, but it's not uncommon for lakes freighters to last more than a century. There are vessels on the Great Lakes that were built when Theodore Roosevelt was president.

The longevity of lakes freighters means extremely low demand for new vessels. Great Lakes shippers build new vessels only when the overall industrial market expands. Unless there's more ore, coal, and steel to haul, there's little need for more ships. The only other reason shippers would build new ships is if some new technology comes along that renders existing ships obsolete.

The 1970s was the last time that both happened. In the middle of the decade, when Dayton was still a midshipman at King's Point, the Great Lakes shipping industry was still in an "expansion mode," says Glen Nekvasil, an Ohio-based shipping advocate. "The industry was expanding because the American steel industry was expanding." There were new coal mines in Pennsylvania, new steel mills in Ohio. A single new mill might require five

new ships just to haul the thousands of tons of ore it gobbled. Not coinci-
dentally, in the mid-seventies the Great Lakes fleet—around two hundred
strong at the time—was adding four or five vessels a year.

At the same time, the lakes shipping industry saw its first fresh technology in fifty years. In studying the economy of lakes shipping, companies identified the biggest bottlenecks. When it came to loading and unloading, ships
were essentially just inert, floating barrels: helpless on their own, they relied
on shore-based stevedores using cranes to load and unload their cargoes once
they had tied up pier-side.

Shippers realized they could save themselves and their customers time and
money by designing ships that didn't rely on all this expensive, manpower-
intensive infrastructure. The ideal ship would carry along with it all the gear
it needed to load and unload its cargo. That type of vessel would be able to unload on no notice at any stretch of shoreline that provided some place to tie up.

With shipping demand still on the rise in the mid-seventies, a slew of shipping companies ordered up thirteen new, larger ships—each a thousand feet
long—that would be the biggest ever to sail the Great Lakes. The "thousand-
footers," including the *Paul R. Tregurtha*, would also come equipped with
new self-loading/unloading equipment that would also be retrofitted to existing ships. The self-loading/unloading gear, a Great Lakes invention,
amounted to a telescoping arm cradling a conveyer system hundreds of feet
in length that terminated in a ship's cargo hold and could swing laterally to
reach ashore. Cargo would trundle down the conveyer into the customers'
waiting arms.

Between the thousand-footers and the new equipment, the Great Lakes
fleet "got a tremendous increase in efficiency," says Nekvasil. A thousand-
footer carrying seventy thousand tons of ore could unload in just ten hours;
before, a typical ship carrying just twenty-five thousand tons needed as many
as eighteen hours to empty its hold.

But for Great Lakes crews, the efficiency increase couldn't have come at
a worse time. Just as the thousand-footers were entering service, the U.S.
auto industry was entering a period of decline that would culminate in the
recession that lasted from 1980 to 1982. The demand for Great Lakes shipping fell with overall industrial output.

"We went from building ships to scrapping them," Nekvasil recalls. In
the decade from the mid-seventies to the mid-eighties, the Great Lakes fleet

shrank by a third, to just 150 vessels. That put hundreds of sailors out of work. In 1983 Dayton got his pink slip. "It certainly screws up your personal finances," he says of getting laid off. "But that's what you end up with in this business."

Part of the problem is structural. When demand for shipping falls, fleets get less busy, but individual ships don't. Since each ship comes with significant overhead costs, it's more efficient for shipping firms to lay up whole ships and keep the remaining vessels busy, rather than retaining the whole fleet and simply reducing each vessel's cargo volume. In every economic downturn, a big swath of the lakefaring workforce gets pink slips. Great Lakes employment is binary: you're either busy as hell or totally unemployed.

Luckily for Dayton, he had a decade's experience under his belt by the 1980 recession. He eventually got hired back. And by the mid-nineties, Dayton was assigned exclusively to thousand-footers that, owing to their relative newness, were unlikely to ever get idled. Dayton says that in recent decades, he's spent more time on the lakes than he has at home. "My wife reminds me of that constantly."

He has job security—or at least as much job security as one could have in such a volatile industry. But for many other lakefarers, unemployment always hangs over their heads like a thousand tons of iron ore. It's just one of the risks in an industry that can be dangerous, uncomfortable, and not a little maddening.

■ ■ ■ ■

Just as the overall size of the Great Lakes shipping fleet has contracted, so has the number of crew aboard each ship. The addition of automated systems has steadily displaced flesh-and-blood sailors. In mid-century, a "laker" might have had thirty people aboard. Today even the thousand-footers have just twenty or so.

That makes for ships that sometimes feel empty, even when they're at their busiest. On the plus side, they don't stink. Military ships with their big redundant crews—hundreds or even thousands of people—"have a certain odor," Dayton says. "Merchant ships don't."

Big, lonely boats. Long cruises. A nine-month working season that allows for few breaks. For sailors, the list of hardships is a lengthy one. "Working in damp and cold conditions often is inevitable," according to the Bureau of

Labor Statistics. "While it is uncommon for vessels to suffer disasters such as fire, explosion, or sinking, workers face the possibility that they may have to abandon their craft on short notice if it collides with another vessel or runs aground." Sailors also risk death or injury from malfunctioning machinery, toppling cargo, and even falling overboard.

On the plus side, most American vessels are now air-conditioned, sound-proofed against machinery noise and fitted with better living quarters than sailors had access to just a generation ago. "These amenities lessen the difficulty of spending long periods away from home," the BLS reports.

Still, it's a solitary job that Dayton describes as "singular" for the highly experienced sailors who tend to sail with today's diminished, super-efficient Great Lakes fleet.

"Everybody is sort of prideful in their job, and everybody knows you have to do what you have to do." That strict utilitarianism means rank and status mean less than they do on naval vessels and in office workplaces ashore as well. Dayton says that applies even to a ship's skipper. "While I, as captain, have a certain amount respect accorded to me, I don't run around with a shirt that says 'captain.' Mostly I'm dressed in jeans and a sweatshirt. People know who you are and what you need to do."

The captain's perks are minimal: "I have an office, and that's about it." Beyond that, Dayton is assigned the same spartan, but relatively spacious, living quarters as everyone else. "It's kind of like living in a hotel."

For decades, lakers were highly isolated from life ashore. To talk to your wife, you'd have to dash to a shoreside payphone whenever you could grab a few minutes during loading or unloading. It might be three in the morning and below freezing. Then came the affordable, portable digital technology of the 1990s. "Satellite TV made a huge difference," Dayton breathes, almost sighing with recalled relief. "Now we have cell phones, which have made an even bigger difference." Today's sailors stay in touch with their families and the world around them, even while battling ice in the middle of Lake Erie, beyond sight of land.

Still, "it's a work environment," Dayton stresses. The only luxury—and it's a big one—is the food. Laker crews, like sailors on many ships, eat better under way than they do ashore. A Great Lakes freighter usually has two cooks on board for a crew that might top out at twenty. Meals are a "morale issue," Nekvasil says.

For his crew, food is "part of the pay," Dayton says. As captain, he's highly sensitive to his sailor's stomachs. If a cook slacks off and the food suffers, it can affect the whole ship and, by extension, the performance of an entire logistical chain. "I make sure the cook's putting out what he's paid for," Dayton stresses.

He describes a typical day's meals. "A sandwich tray for lunch plus a hot meal and some soup, and in the evening you may have some kind of fish, some steak, or chops. But the cook better know how to put it out so it tastes good. It's tough being cook because everybody looks forward to meal hour."

Feeding twenty Great Lakes gourmands for every ship can be pricey for shipping companies. But skimping isn't an option. Nekvasil recalls when one shipping firm fired its cooks in the 1980s and replaced them with microwaveable meals. "The crews basically mutinied," he laughs.

The company should have known. Sailors cling to their meal privileges as one of the last perks of a job that rarely rewards them financially. The boom and bust cycle for shippers means many junior sailors spend months or years at a time unemployed. Even when they are working, the pay isn't exactly great. Median income in 2008 was just $32,000. Median pay for captains is just a thousand dollars more.[8] "It's not something you jump into and make a fortune then jump out of," Dayton cautions. On the Great Lakes, he says, "There's no fortune." Just honest work that matters.

And often, not even that. The recession that began in 2008 cut deep into a Great Lakes shipping fleet that still hadn't fully recovered from the accumulated strain of previous economic downturns.

■ ■ ■ ■

Glen Nekvasil slumps in his chair as though an invisible burden were weighing him down. It's a snowy day in January 2010 at the nondescript Cleveland offices of the Lake Carriers Association, an advocacy group for some of the larger Great Lakes shippers.

Nekvasil is a small, weary-looking man. He got his start doing PR for an iron-ore supplier before moving over to the association in 1983. He thumbs through reports, looking for figures to illustrate the impact of the eighteen-month-old recession on his friends and clients. He seems to grow more depressed as he rattles off the numbers.

In 2004, lakers hauled 40 million tons of limestone. Five years later, that figure shrank to just 23 million tons. Coal was down 25 percent from 2008 to 2009. Iron ore contracted 50 percent. In 2008, lakers hauled 101 million tons of cargo of all types. In 2009, it was just 66 million tons. With the reduction in volume, shipping companies laid up whole vessels. Seven of the Lake Carriers Association's fifty-five freighters didn't sail at all in 2009.

In other transportation and logistical sectors, lean times often spur innovations. The carmakers have turned to fuel-efficient hybrids and automation. Parcel companies added more automation to their distribution processes. But for the laker fleet, innovations are hard to come by. Freshwater freighters, Nekvasil says, "are a pretty mature technology." With few opportunities for countering a downturn with new technologies, Greak Lakes shippers can only suffer through. "I don't see any silver lining," Nekvasil sighs.

But the lean times have added urgency to efforts by Nekvasil and other laker lobbyists to improve the legal and physical infrastructure surrounding their clients' ships. First, they must redouble their defense of the Jones Act as competing transportation sectors "chip away" at the U.S. shipping fleet's legal protection. In 2009 and 2010, the American Petroleum Institute argued for a looser interpretation of the Jones Act in order to allow cheap, foreign-owned vessels to haul oil-rig components around the Gulf of Mexico.

Keeping foreign ships out of the oil-rig trade "could have a very significant impact," said Sara Banaszak, an API representative. "What the [oil] companies end up doing is they get a project and they're trying to line up all of these pieces and they get a window with a very expensive ship to do this very complicated work," Banaszak said. Requiring oil companies to use only U.S. vessels would create "choke points in the projects."[9]

Jones Act defenders rejected that assessment. American shippers and shipbuilders would quickly meet any demand from the oil companies, Ken Wells, from Offshore Marine Service Association, told the Louisiana *Times-Picayune* newspaper. "I think that this industry has always met the customers' needs, and we will meet them in this regard."[10]

That's the whole point of the Jones Act, Wells added. As Nekvasil points out, most countries have Jones Act–style laws protecting domestic shippers. It's those laws that in part fuel the highly competitive world shipping and shipbuilding industries. The Jones Act doesn't give American shippers an advantage, globally: it simply gives them a chance. Nekvasil calls the Jones Act "good maritime policy." "We need a level playing field where the laws that are designed to protect American vessels and American mariners are enforced," Wells said.[11]

While fending off attacks on the Jones Act with one hand, with the other shipping lobbyists were busy defending against attacks by truckers, air freighters, and railroads. Even with the Jones' Act protection against foreign shippers, "we still have to compete with rail and air and trucks." "They want our business," Nekvasil says. "The industry cannot sit back and say we got a lock on this."

For guys like Nekvasil, that means touring the country to visit government and industry officials, constantly making the case for Great Lakes shipping. Nekvasil recites one of his favorite comparisons: "You'd have to have a convoy of trucks two thousand trucks long to equal one of our thousand-footers." With figures like that in their quiver, and with the Jones Act providing top cover, laker advocates have managed, so far, to protect the vital Great Lakes transportation network.

But there's no letting up. In lean times, competition escalates—and so, too, does pressure on public finances. The latter is particularly vexing for Great Lakes shippers, as they rely on the Army Corps of Engineers to maintain the public waterways that vessels use to reach inland ports.

Drawing on a fund supplied by taxes on Great Lakes shipping, army engineers are supposed to fix locks and dredge channels. In recent years that fund has taken in around $1.5 billion annually, but the Corps of Engineers spends only $700 million on average. The balance, in theory, remains in the fund, but just as fuel taxes fund trains and buses, the federal government habitually draws on the Great Lakes maintenance pot for nonmaritime projects, promising to eventually pay back what it has taken. That has left the fund with $5 billion in IOUs.

In the meantime, Great Lakes shipping infrastructure is deteriorating. Old locks need repair. New locks are called for. The lock that connects Lake Superior to the rest of the Great Lakes is a dangerous choke point in the system. If it were to fail, shipping on the lakes would fall by 70 percent, Nekvasil says. Congress approved construction of a second lock, and workers even broke ground. But they can't finish until the government ponies up $500 million in promised funding.

Channels are silting up. Nekvasil says there's 15 million cubic yards of sediment awaiting removal. Clogged channels means ships must carry lighter loads to reduce the depth they draw. Lighter loads mean lost revenue. "The money is there" to fix the problem, Nekvasil points out. It's just a matter of spending the money for its expressed purpose.

And then there's the ice that nearly defeats Dayton and the crew of the *Paul R. Tregurtha* on their December voyage. On the cold edges of the shipping season, icebreakers zigzag across the lakes, breaking channels for ships making their last or first deliveries of the season. Just eight coast guard icebreakers support a more than one-hundred-strong freighter fleet. Five of those icebreakers are more than thirty years old and badly in need of rehabilitation or replacement. Again, it's a matter of funding. The House of Representatives voted to buy new icebreakers, but in 2010 the measure died in the Senate. As of mid-2011, Congress had yet to reconsider buying new icebreakers, though not for a lack of lobbying by Great Lakes shippers.

As the icebreaker fleet deteriorates, winter damage gets worse. In 2008, ships in Nekvasil's association suffered $1.3 million in ice damage. In 2009 several of LCA's shippers delayed the commencement of their seasons because the spring icebreaking campaign was behind schedule. Mother Nature is slowly winning the battle for the Great Lakes.

■ ■ ■ ■

To work the Great Lakes is to battle the weather, the brutal economics of a boom-bust cycle, and voracious competition from overseas and at home. It's cold, hard, unforgiving work with few tangible rewards. But it's honest work and important. And after that first chilled taste of life on the lakes, it's rare for a young sailor to just give it up. Great Lakes sailors tend to stick around for thirty, forty, even fifty years.

"I'm not looking at retirement in any less than two, three, or four years," Dayton says. One reason is the economy. "My retirement account has taken some wonderful hits, as with everyone else's." He laughs. "I'm not working for a bank handing out million-dollar bonuses." But there's more to it than that. Dayton likes his job—even loves it. It all started when he was just eighteen, went to sea, and found he really liked it.

The old laker sighs. And with a hint of tranquility in his voice born of decades of worthwhile labor, he says, "I'm going to be here a while." That's good news for the Midwest's regional economy and the national economy it girds. And it's good news for an emerging national-security strategy that relies heavily on ships and the skilled men and women who crew them.

8

Medical Care, Anywhere

Since the age of four, Ches Lacollo, now eleven, has had an abnormal growth on the inside of his right eyelid. The growth partially blocks his eyesight, makes reading impossible, and is so disturbing to look at that his friends and family avoid looking at him, he says.

Removing the growth requires a straightforward surgery. But in Puerto Cabezas, Lacollo's hometown on Nicaragua's remote eastern coast, doctors and medical facilities are scarce. For most surgeries, patients fly hundreds of miles to Managua, the capital. But the flights from Puerto Cabezas cost $100—more than most local residents can afford. So for seven years, Lacollo has endured and hoped for a miracle.

That miracle takes an unusual form. On August 11, 2008, USS *Kearsarge*, an 840-foot U.S. Navy amphibious assault ship, appears in the haze a few miles from Puerto Cabezas's seaweed-strewn beaches. Four days later, Lacollo lies on a bed in the *Kearsarge*'s fluorescent-lit medical ward, being prepped for surgery to remove the growth. The operation will be quick and, more importantly, free of charge.

"Even though it's a simple surgery, it will have a big impact on this child's life," says Cdr. Brian Alexander, a navy optometrist from Virginia. Mere hours later, his colleague Lt. Brian Barber begins unwrapping the bandages from Lacollo's head to give the boy his first view of the world through "new" eyes.[1]

Lacollo is just one of around forty-seven thousand patients who pass through the *Kearsarge*'s ward and onshore health clinics during the vessel's four-month, six-nation cruise in the fall of 2008. Designed to launch marines on bloody beach assaults, the *Kearsarge* has been emptied of her combat troops and pressed into service as a floating hospital. In doing so, she has become a symbol of a profound new application for America's most capacious and underappreciated logistical system: her naval ships.[2]

■ ■ ■ ■

The *Kearsarge*'s deployment was actually the second of its kind by a navy assault ship: earlier in 2008, its sister ship, USS *Boxer*, saw twenty-four thousand patients while along the Pacific side of Latin America. The ships, in turn, modeled their work on an epic, four-month humanitarian cruise by the hospital ship USNS *Comfort*, which treated nearly a hundred thousand people in twelve countries. And that's just Latin America. All over the world since 2007, navy ships have fanned out on missions of mercy, aiming to "influence generations to come" through sheer force of goodwill, according to Capt. Frank Ponds, senior officer for *Kearsarge*'s deployment.[3]

The Pentagon has a name for this humanitarian strategy. It's called "soft power." Harvard professor Joseph Nye coined the term back in the 1980s. He described it as "the ability to attract people to our side without coercion." The Pentagon's is an approach that hinges entirely on deft logistics.[4]

The basic theory is simple: it's easier, and in the long run cheaper, to win over people with friendship and gifts than it is to fight them into submission when a crisis flares. At the cost of a few thousand dollars plus a couple hours of labor, someone like Lacollo becomes a lifelong ally of the United States, and so do his friends and family. Multiply that by a hundred thousand, and you've "conquered" a country without anyone dying—and the allegiances, presumably, are stronger than they'd ever be from a defeated enemy.

It took the wars in Iraq and Afghanistan—both decidedly "hard" conflicts—for soft power to find strong adherents inside the Pentagon. In late 2007, as Iraq in particular seemed headed for total societal meltdown, Secretary of Defense Robert Gates appeared willing to try anything to avoid another bloody, endless war. "I am here to make the case for strengthening our capacity to use 'soft' power and for better integrating it with 'hard' power," Gates said in a landmark speech at Kansas State University in November 2007. "One of the most important lessons of the wars in Iraq and Afghanistan is that military success is not sufficient to win."[5]

It was a lesson that two powerful naval officers took to heart. In 2007, when Adm. James Stavridis rose to the top position at Southern Command, the Defense Department's regional headquarters for Latin America, he quickly decided that traditional military forces simply weren't going to be terribly useful—at least not in their usual roles. "We can't solve the problems down here with tanks and ships and high-priced aircraft," he said.[6]

Instead, with Gates's encouragement, Stavridis took Nye's soft-power theory, and paired it with the world-beating logistical potential represented by the navy's underutilized assault ships. "It carries a lot," Ponds said, when asked about an assault ship's greatest strength. What it carries, is left to commanders' imagination. Stavridis saw an opportunity to fill assault ships and other vessels with something other than their usual lethal cargos. "Whenever he can get an amphibious ship, he takes it," said Bob Work, a naval analyst who eventually rose to the rank of navy undersecretary. And instead of marines, armored vehicles, and attack helicopters, Stavridis filled the ships with humanitarians.

Two years earlier, in another hemisphere, another navy admiral had had the same idea—to take leftover big-box ships and fill them with different cargos for soft missions. In 2005, before anyone in the Pentagon had really embraced Nye's soft-power theory, Sixth Fleet vice admiral Harry Ulrich decided the navy needed to boost its operations along West Africa's coast. But there, as in Latin America, traditional military forces were worse than useless—they might raise fears of renewed colonialism and win America more enemies than friends.

Ulrich needed to go in soft. He tapped the repair ship USS *Emory S. Land* for a four-month deployment, delivering trainers and maintenance personnel to several African nations, like a full-service, mobile, charity mechanic's shop. The *Land* helped fix African navies' old boats and gave African sailors refresher maintenance training. Cdr. Chris Servello, who served under Ulrich, called it a "test case" for soft power. "It was well received."

On the backs of Ulrich's and Stavridis's experiments, naval soft power was born. By 2009 the navy had institutionalized the experiments. Every year, in every hemisphere, amphibious, hospital, and other big-box ships sail on missions of charity, aiming to conquer the world without anyone firing a shot.

Now, soft power isn't without its complications. For one, medical outreach like the *Kearsarge*'s and charity repair work like the *Land*'s only work when there's a need. And the kinds of dire medical and material need that might justify a major, U.S. military deployment tend to be in remote, isolated communities in poor, nearly inaccessible countries. After all, it's these conditions that create the need in the first place.

But getting a ship from its homeport to some impoverished village thousands of miles away is easier said than done. And once it's there, it has to interface with land—another daunting task, considering how small and shallow are many countries' ports and how big and deep-drawing are most of the navy's ships.

However "soft" the power, the techniques for exercising that power are hard, heavy, grimy, and dangerous. It's all about big ships pumping fuel through giant hoses during high-seas rendezvous, lubricant-leaking helicopters, and rusting landing craft hauling tons of supplies through hot, hazy skies and surging, seaweed-clogged surfs. More than anything else, soft power is a muscular expression of skillful logistics that only the United States has mastered. And sometimes it even requires *brand-new* logistical procedures that few militaries have the intellectual and technological resources to develop.

For the *Kearsarge*, it all begins with a deceptively light-footed dance at sea.

■ ■ ■ ■

Like prehistoric amphibians, the two giant U.S. Navy vessels yawn toward each other across the two-hundred-foot chasm of water separating them. The *Kearsarge* and the tanker USNS *Laramie* plod on precisely parallel paths across the Atlantic, the afternoon sun high to starboard, saltwater spraying their gray-painted flanks, dolphins leaping alongside.

It has been just under a day since the *Kearsarge* departed her homeport of Norfolk, Virginia, with nearly seventeen hundred people in her staterooms and enlisted berths and thousands of tons of supplies in her holds. She's headed south, down the East Coast, around Florida, and into Latin America. For the next six months, she will hail at a succession of austere ports in six of the Southern Hemisphere's poorest nations. First up: Puerto Cabezas.

At each port, the *Kearsarge* will serve as a sort of military Habitat for Humanity combined with a mobile, full-service surgical hospital. Her engineers will come ashore to build schools and fix roads and bridges, while her doctors, dentists, nurses, corpsmen, and veterinarians treat tens of thousands of patients—human and animal alike—for everything from toothaches to severe cleft palates, parasites, and nearsightedness, for free.

It will be thirsty work for the gigantic, fifteen-year-old ship. With her flat, rectangular flight deck, nearly nine hundred feet from bow to stern, the *Kearsarge* is similar in shape and size to a World War II aircraft carrier. In addition to space for scores of helicopters and AV-8B jump jets, the *Kearsarge* has what's called a well deck—a floodable ramp area in her stern that opens to the ocean, so landing craft and amphibious tractors can climb in and out. The *Kearsarge* and the navy's nine other assault ships are *built to deliver things*, in even the most dangerous environments. While the navy considers them combat vessels, they also represent a logistical capability that no other navy can equal.

Usually assault ships haul choppers and landing craft plus a battalion of combat marines and their supporting troops—more than a thousand extra people, in addition to her crew of a thousand. For her Latin American venture, the *Kearsarge* is packing humanitarians instead of infantry, and medicine and construction equipment instead of combat gear. But it's still a lot of work.

In her cavernous tanks, the *Kearsarge* can carry around 2 million gallons of fuel to fire her two massive steam boilers, but she might burn through that in as little as a week, depending on how fast she sails. Her top speed is around twenty knots, or twenty-five miles per hour.

Many of the ports that the *Kearsarge* will be visiting in Latin America lack the facilities to resupply a ship of her size. To keep fuel tanks full, her lubricants fresh, and her galleys and workshops stocked with food and spare parts, the *Kearsarge* requires the *Laramie*'s special attention.

Tankers like the *Laramie* provide logistics to the logisticians.

Planning for the two ships' rendezvous began weeks ago. The tanker, forever traveling a long, circuitous path up and down the East Coast, calculated a rendezvous with the *Kearsarge* that accommodated the assault ship's tight schedule.

With a series of maneuvers that is among the most deceptively simple in the whole field of transportation, the *Laramie* will top off the *Kearsarge*'s tanks and holds while both ships are still moving, then veer away to continue her seemingly random wandering. Wandering that is, in fact, not random at all, rather carefully planned to allow the tanker to cross paths with as many thirsty ships as possible before her own supplies are exhausted and her crew bleary with overwork.

The Military Sealift Command tanker USNS *Laramie* refuels the assault ship USS *Kearsarge* en route to Nicaragua in August 2008. DAVID AXE

The vessels' rendezvous on August 6, 2008, is a scene straight out of the age of sail, when rival warships would take up station side by side and exchange withering cannonball broadsides. Only now the vessels are fifty times larger than any nineteenth-century man-of-war—and the only weapons in evidence were the ships' defensive machine guns, now shrouded to ward off corrosion, plus modified M-14 rifles wielded by sailors wearing red hardhats.

Instead of bullets, these rifles fire slugs towing a thin nylon cord. Other sailors standing by, around the red-hat-wearing, rifle-wielding line-throwers, wear their own colored headgear: purple for winch repairers, orange for supply inspectors, blue for line handlers, green for signalers, yellow for captains, and white for safety and medical personnel. Together, they will perform a muscular, industrial dance that is no less elegant than a ballet and about a thousand times more dangerous.

The line throwers, standing on the catwalks running along the sides of the *Kearsarge*, take aim at the 450-foot *Laramie* and fire. The sounds of the waves and of the wind whipping down the steel canyon formed by the ship's tall flanks make it impossible for observers to hear the rifles' reports, but by squinting you might just make out the slugs arcing over the churning water, trailing their whipping nylon tails: lines, anchored to the *Kearsarge*'s steel bulk.

The slugs strike the *Laramie*'s deck. Deckhands, all wearing the same colored hardhats, pounce on them. Thus secured, the lines form a spiderweb-delicate connection between the two vessels. That fibrous link is the first stage of one of the human world's most understated feats of logistical prowess: what the Navy calls an "underway replenishment," or UNREP.

Over the following hours, the *Kearsage*'s crew—teenagers and kids in their early twenties, mostly—will pass heavier and heavier lines across the span of water separating the vessel from the *Laramie*. By using each cord to tow a slightly larger one, eventually the two ships will be connected by crisscrossing cords, ropes, and wires.

Last to cross: rubber hoses, four inches in diameter. Through those hoses, the *Laramie* will pump up to forty thousand gallons of fuel per minute into the *Kearsarge*'s fuel bunkers, while MH-60 helicopters, painted gray with special saltwater-resistant paint, buzz between the two vessels' flight decks dangling boxes of food, medicine, parts, and ammunition from hooks fixed to their aluminum bellies.

The ships' elephantine ballet began more than an hour earlier, when the *Kearsarge*'s lookouts spotted the *Laramie* on the horizon afore, holding a steady course. Sidling an assault ship displacing forty thousand tons of water alongside a tanker that displaces almost as much is to tease catastrophe. The ships have to be just 180 feet apart for the *Laramie*'s hoses to reach the *Kearsarge*, and they have to maintain that distance for the entire two hours the crews needed to top off the *Kearsarge*'s tanks and fill her storerooms.

With each vessel traveling at twelve knots—around fifteen miles per hour—it will take them just a minute to cross the span of water separating them, in the event either helmsman flinches.

To avoid a disastrous collision at sea—tens of thousands of tons of metal, wood, and rubber, and hundreds of bodies shattering—the sailors have to steer their respective vessels on exactly the same course, deviating by no more than one degree while compensating for the heaving ocean and the suction effect of the other ship.

An assault ship the length of a sixty-story building can hardly be considered sprightly. When it takes many seconds for your vessel to respond to course changes, you've got to be almost prescient to steer her true, especially during an UNREP. A huge electronic monitor mounted on the *Laramie*'s superstructure flashes the distance between the vessels in a bloody shade of red, as if to remind the helmsmen of the lives depending on their steady hands.

■ ■ ■ ■

Underway replenishment is one of those vital practices, poorly understood outside a handful of the world's most professional navies, that truly underpin a nation's military power. While sheer numbers of tanks, fighter jets, and warships make for impressive treaty declarations and breathless news reports, it's the militaries that master tricky logistical skills, such as the UNREP, that truly shape world events.

China might have more airplanes and tanks lined up on its military's tarmacs and vehicle parks than, say, the United Kingdom. But China only recently began refueling its ships at sea, whereas the British have been doing it since before World War I. Conducting UNREPs allows your ships to sail beyond your own national waters. It allows them to travel anywhere, at the time of their choosing, to fight any enemy or maybe just threaten to do so. You might have the biggest navy in the world, but if it can't get to where the action is, it's useless.

The U.S. Navy recognized that important truth more than a hundred years ago in a period of rapid expansion. During the Civil War, the Union had built hundreds of wooden and ironclad warships, but many of these were rush jobs too rickety to last beyond the war years, and those that were solidly built were technologically obsolete by the 1880s.

With an eye to expanding American influence in Latin America, in 1883 Congress authorized construction of four modern, steel vessels that would represent the core of a renewed U.S. fleet. In 1898 America mobilized for war with Spain. Cuba and the Philippines were the prizes, and the war would be fought mostly at sea. The War Department envisioned a blockade of Cuba by dozens of fast cruisers to intercept Spanish ships, while America's six battleships and fifteen armored cruisers sailed to meet the Spanish fleet head-on.[7]

One little problem: there was no way to get coal to this big, and busy, fleet. For all its investment in warships, the navy had not thought to build colliers to haul coal for the combatants. Naval theorist Capt. Alfred Thayer Mahan had only begun lecturing about naval logistics the year prior.

Assistant Secretary of the Navy Theodore Roosevelt changed all that. He drew up plans to purchase or lease civilian colliers. With congressional support and funding, scores of auxiliaries entered the fleet. From that point on, the U.S. Navy would always maintain a large force of logistical ships and stay ahead of the curve in logistical practices.

In 1899 the collier USS *Marcellus* and the battleship USS *Massachusetts* performed the very first underway replenishment, when the battleship took the collier in tow while sailing at six knots and the crews shuttled bags of coal along a line strung above the tow cable.[8]

Four years later, the U.S. Navy would experiment with underway replenishment while two vessels were lashed side by side. That method was less successful, as waves heaved the ships into each other. "About the roughest proposition I ever stood up to," one sailor called it. But it was a worthwhile experiment that, at the very least, underscored the astern method of replenishment that remained standard through World War II, long after coal had given way to liquid fuel.

The UNREP is just one of these "secret" logistical practices that separates showy armies from those that are only interested in genuine capability. It has its equivalents on land and in the air. Ground forces practice on-the-move logistics, coordinating thousands of cargo trucks, tanker trucks, helicopters, and light aircraft—and the activities of countless warehouse clerks, crane operators, and port cargo handlers—all in an effort to keep tanks and combat helicopters fueled and armed, and infantry formations fed and watered, over a shifting battlefield that might expand a hundred miles in any direction, every day. For fliers, there's aerial refueling: the art of plugging a fighter, cargo plane, or helicopter into an orbiting tanker plane.

The United States isn't alone in mastering these logistical operations, but it is alone in combining skills and scale. Lots of militaries resupply ships, aircraft, and ground forces on the move, over long distance. But only the American military does these things every day, hundreds of times per day, in every hemisphere. China's military is big. Britain's is skilled. But only the U.S. military is big *and* skilled.

To support roughly 280 combat ships, the navy in 2008 had eighteen tankers, including the *Laramie*, plus another sixteen replenishment ships carrying mostly "dry stores," such as ammo and food. China, by contrast, had only eleven replenishment ships, most of them smaller than the U.S. Navy's. The British Royal Navy had ten.[9]

Bob Work, the former marine who spent several years as a naval analyst before becoming a navy undersecretary in 2009, put into perspective what it means to have the "largest and most capable" naval logistical force.[10] "[T]he U.S. Navy operates globally twenty-four hours a day, seven days a week, 365 days a year," Work wrote in a 2008 report. "At any given time, approximately one third of the fleet is underway. Many of these ships are on operational deployments that last six months or longer. . . . [O]nly a few navies can match the U.S. Navy's high operational tempo, which translates directly into superior real-world training, operational experience, and tactical expertise."[11]

The chest-thumping rhetoric belies an important point: that logistical prowess boils down to a lot of hard, wet, patient work by young sailors aboard ships like the *Laramie* and the *Kearsarge*. Two hours after threading together with those first, delicate nylon cords, the assault ship and the tanker finish their August 2008 UNREP. The assault ship's tanks and holds are full. The tanker has given away all she can spare. The *Kearsarge* releases the *Laramie*'s lines and hoses, and the tanker's weary crewmen, in their blue coveralls, hardhats, and leather gloves, reel them back in.

Before the crimson sun touches the purple horizon, the two vessels part ways: the *Kearsarge* to continue south toward Nicaragua; the *Laramie* to make an imminent rendezvous with another, equally thirsty warship—and perhaps even take fuel for herself from a larger tanker. For the *Kearsarge*, the modest miracle that is the UNREP is a regular but infrequent occurrence. For the *Laramie*, it's an almost daily affair. That something so difficult could become downright quotidian is testimony to the unrivaled logistical capability that underpins U.S. military operations.

It took a century of practice for the U.S. Navy to perfect the UNREP. So it should come as no surprise that the navy suffered a few setbacks when it began crafting brand-new logistical procedures to support soft-power missions. Amphibious ships such as the *Kearsarge* were designed to support World War II-style amphibious assaults—another world-class logistical operation that, tragically, also represents one of the bloodiest classes of military maneuver in history. Thankfully, amphibious assaults have all but gone extinct as helicopters have allowed "vertical envelopment" of shore defenses. The last time the U.S. military invaded an enemy shore under fire was during the Korean War.

It was this absence of a dedicated mission that freed up the *Kearsarge* and her sister ships for soft-power missions in the first place. But adapting the navy's amphibious fleet to soft power's peculiar demands takes hard work, creative thinking, and not a little learning-by-failing. Well before the first soft-power cruise set sail, the navy began imagining ways to build at-sea supply bases for army and marine land forces, in order to fight major ground wars in places without any nearby friendly countries to offer up logistical bases.

Essentially, that means lashing together a bunch of cargo ships and finding some way to ferry lots of stuff between the island of ships and the nearby undefended shore. The navy calls this "seabasing." It's an idea that moldered, for lack of any real-world application, until soft power caught on.

In that way, sailors assigned to soft-power missions have become the first serious seabasing practitioners. "It's a learning experience," muses Capt. Walter Towns, the *Kearsarge*'s commanding officer.

■ ■ ■ ■

The *Kearsarge*'s first full day ashore in Nicaragua goes off without a hitch. On the morning of August 12, the helicopters and landing craft ferry personnel to their sites. The biggest and most important—a temporary health

Marine Corps CH-53E helicopters land aboard USS *Kearsarge* during operations off Nicaragua in August 2008. DAVID AXE

clinic situated on the grounds of a high school—boasts stations for doctors, dentists, and optometrists, plus a makeshift pharmacy.

At dawn, hundreds of Nicaraguans begin lining up outside. The doors open around 10:00 in the morning and, by lunchtime, the clinic is seeing patients at a rate of one every couple minutes. Around 3:00, the weary humanitarians board the choppers and boats for the short trip back to the *Kearsarge*.

For Captain Ponds, the day's success is a huge relief. The next day, he will meet his boss, Rear Adm. Joseph Kernan, at the high school for an unofficial inspection of the *Kearsarge*'s operations. It's his chance to prove that he can turn Stavridis's soft-power strategy into reality.

But when Ponds and Kernan step out of their respective helicopters on the morning of August 13, they find hundreds of angry Nicaraguans mobbing the clinic's gate as Nicaraguan cops and soldiers hold them back. Inside, the medical stations are deserted. Not a single humanitarian has made it ashore from the *Kearsarge*.

Ponds is mortified. "I've never seen anyone reach for a cell phone so fast," says one young sailor who accompanied him.

It turns out that a problem with one of the *Kearsarge*'s CH-53E helicopters pushed back the day's whole flight schedule, stranding people on the ship. The delays were compounded when the Nicaraguan soldiers assigned to escort the *Kearsarge* teams to their work sites were themselves hours late.

In military operations, delays are expected. But running a health clinic isn't like fighting a war. Civilian patients can't be expected to understand the mechanical complexity and maintenance demands of a Super Stallion heavy-lift helicopter.

Worse, no one bothered to set up a communications link to the main medical clinic. Again, in the military, people expect to wait and don't necessarily expect to be told why they're waiting. But the *Kearsarge*'s patients aren't soldiers or sailors. They waited without any explanation for several hours as the temperature rose. By the time the first doctors finally arrive around noon, they are met by an angry mob. Ponds watches from a distance as his people scramble to set up their stations and make up for lost time.

Late in the afternoon, the harried clinic staff finally catches up to the day's patient quota and makes plans for a radio link to keep patients informed of future delays. If any of the *Kearsarge*'s people relax, it's premature, for the day's snafus are only beginning. Because they've stayed late to make up for their tardiness, the weary humanitarians have missed the last chopper flight of the day. So they trek to the beach to catch a ride on a World War II-style landing craft making supply runs between the *Kearsarge* and the beach.

It takes an hour to load the flat-bottom boat. The last aid worker has just boarded when the boat's navy crew tells everyone to get off and board a different boat. The first one, they say, is supposed to carry only equipment.

Loading the second landing craft takes another hour. The doctors, nurses, corpsmen, and engineers have to wade from beach to boat with their backpacks held over their heads, like an amphibious assault in reverse. Soaking wet, hungry, and tired, they probably feel just like their scorned patients did that morning.

The landing craft is just a couple hundred yards offshore when there comes a call over the radio: the other boat, the one carrying the equipment, has lost an engine and will need a tow. More delays are in the cards. Instead of groans from the heaps of weary people, there is only sardonic laughter. It might be easier to simply attack and conquer Puerto Cabezas. That, at least, the navy can do at the time of its choosing.

As the *Kearsarge*'s people work out new sea-basing procedures, "there will be efficiencies" over time, Ponds says. Still, he's furious over the failures of August 13. The planning meetings that night aboard the *Kearsarge* reflect his obvious rage. So does the next day's performance. On August 14, all the helicopter flights leave early—an almost unheard-of achievement in any military operation.

Kearsarge's crew has learned an important lesson not only for their own Latin American operation, but for the whole navy, as the world's largest sea service tries to figure out how to build a logistical base at sea. The lesson is that connecting the ship to shore is the riskiest aspect of sea-basing: helicopters and landing craft don't always work. For future soft-power missions, the navy will need a better way.

■ ■ ■ ■

Over the next few days, the *Kearsarge*'s people develop a routine. Every morning they wade or fly ashore and head for the clinic in rented buses. On their return trips, the helicopters carry surgical patients like Lacollo to the ship for in-patient care. Back in Puerto Cabezas, the shore teams work until they're exhausted, often seeing hundreds of patients a day. In the evening aboard the *Kearsarge*, they discuss the day's events over coffee and cookies in offices and the ship's well-appointed wardroom. Then they grab a few hours of sleep. The next day, they repeat the whole process.

For the *Kearsarge*'s nearly two thousand doctors, nurses, corpsmen, engineers, sailors, and pilots, soft power is hard work. It's forgivable that their conversations over dinner or while waiting for a chopper ride are about the little things: supplies, paperwork, the softball game scheduled for next week. Few seem to care that their daily toils, snafus notwithstanding, are contributing to a fundamental shift in U.S. military strategy, one emphasizing logistics over firepower.

But thousands of miles away, on the bank of the Anacostia River in Washington, D.C., a little-known organization is riding that shift to unprecedented levels of influence. To regular navy sailors, Military Sealift Command and its civilian seafarers are known for operating the *Laramie* and other tankers and supply ships. But the command does so much more.

The $3 Billion Maritime Operating Company, with Guns

Around midnight on July 26, 2007, a two-hundred-ton naval engine slides off a tractor-trailer on a road outside the National Steel and Shipbuilding Company shipyard in San Diego. The engine punches straight through the two-lane road, opening a ten-foot water main and pulverizing one car parked on the shoulder. Another car is partially crushed; a woman sleeping in the back is slightly injured. She was waiting for her husband, a late-shift shipwright, to get off work.

While police and company investigators probe the water-filled crater, NASSCO briefly closes the shipyard. By the next day, work is back in full swing, as forty-six hundred employees race to complete a $7 billion order for fourteen *Lewis and Clark*–class logistical ships. The seven-hundred-foot-long vessels, named after the famous explorers, represent the flagships of the new, improved U.S. Military Sealift Command. The command is expanding and adapting to a changing world hungry for more and more stuff, faster.

The Lewis and Clarks, also known by their navy code T-AKE, are some of the biggest—and certainly the most technologically advanced—military cargo ships ever built. And they are in high demand. MSC is shoving them out to sea as fast as NASSCO can build them. Which is pretty fast, by shipbuilding standards. Every six months, on average, a complete T-AKE slides into the ocean from its construction slipway, a sort of drainable, water-filled furrow opening directly into the ocean, where ships are built from the keel up.

For all its speed by today's reckoning, NASSCO's construction pace is glacial by World War II standards. After the Japanese attacked Pearl Harbor in

December 1941, Japan's ally Germany was obliged to declare war on the United States. While Pearl Harbor still burned, an initial wave of five German submarines set sail across the Atlantic, bound for the largely unprotected U.S. East Coast and America's rich supply lines. In six months, U-boats sank nearly four hundred ships totaling some 2 million tons displacement. Around five thousand American seafarers died.[1]

To make good these losses and to ensure that America could feed and supply itself and its wartime allies, Washington launched the world's greatest shipbuilding program. From the British, the U.S. government borrowed a simple design for a fourteen-thousand-ton cargo ship, swapping slow, traditional riveting for fast, cheap welds. Eighteen shipyards all over the U.S. built the so-called Liberty Ships.[2] At peak production in 1943, three Liberty Ships were completed every day. The fastest was the *Robert E. Peary*, which as part of a government PR campaign came together in less than five days.[3]

In all, Americans built more than twenty-seven hundred Liberty Ships by 1945. Their sheer number, plus improved convoy tactics and Germany's inability to build and crew sufficient U-boats, kept the sea lanes open and helped ensure Allied victory.[4] Six decades later, war has changed and instant fleets composed of thousands of fast-built ships are no longer necessary. After all, nobody is sinking ships.

But sealift and sea-based logistics are no less important. Despite the size and sophistication of the U.S. airlift fleet, the vast majority of war supplies for Iraq and Afghanistan still travel by sea, and naval forces are busier than ever on logistically demanding soft-power missions.

The T-AKEs are the spiritual descendents of the Liberty Ships. But they aren't strictly cargo-haulers: lugging bulk supplies is just one thing the new ships are capable of. In addition, they serve as underway replenishment vessels for far-flung warships, as humanitarian vessels carrying doctors and aid workers to impoverished countries, and, in one famous case in 2008, a prison ship for Somali pirates captured by the U.S. Navy. T-AKEs are the logistical jacks-of-all-trade for a country more dependent than ever on the sea as a medium for exerting its influence.

In July 2007, the third T-AKE, named *Alan Shepard*, is ready to be handed over to MSC. Numbers four and five—*Robert E. Peary*, named for the Liberty Ship, and *Amelia Earhart*, respectively—are under construction. Materials are beginning to arrive for number six. Money is already flowing, from

Congress to the navy to NASSCO, to pay for the next eight. Naval analyst Work is proposing the navy buy even more T-AKEs, potentially keeping NASSCO busy for another decade.

It's not hard to see why MSC loves its new ships. Each T-AKE can carry roughly seven thousand tons of dry cargo including munitions, two thousand tons of refrigerated provisions, three thousand tons of cargo fuel, and two hundred tons of potable water—plus some deck space could be used for cargo. A fully loaded *Lewis and Clark*–class ship displaces forty thousand tons fully loaded, versus just twenty thousand tons empty. MSC officials say a single T-AKE can carry six thousand tons more cargo than any two of its older stores ships.

As UNREP ships, the T-AKEs are also a huge improvement. Unlike older UNREP ships with all their gear on just one side, T-AKEs feature hose stations on each side, allowing the simultaneous resupply of two warships.

T-AKEs are built to be flexible. They have space to spare, all over. Their decks are bigger than previous logistical ships. Their internal corridors are wider and taller. Their elevators are bigger and stronger. Their cargo holds—some refrigerated, others meant for dry stores—feature thousands of holes in their floors, so that walls mounted on pegs can be erected and removed on short notice. Each hold is a "reconfigurable space," like a warehouse made of giant Legos.

"It's all about moving cargo," says Art Diaz, MSC's representative at NASSCO. "We have the capability of moving cargo rapidly within the ship and vertically. There's unprecedented elevator and crane capacity plus eight replenishment stations to move cargo off the ship. Also, we have aviation facilities." Huge aviation facilities, to be more precise. The T-AKE has the biggest flight deck of any logistical ship.

The vessels' cutting-edge design is matched by the most modern construction processes, although the slipways in which the new T-AKEs take shape are a throwback. At every other shipyard in the United States, vessels are built in giant cradles on land and dragged into the water when mostly complete.

But everything else about NASSCO is super-modern. Raw materials and machinery—such as the engine that nearly smashed the shipwright's wife— arrive by truck or train. Workers bolt and weld together house-size slices of a new T-AKE deep in the yard before giant cranes lift these sections into the slipway, where they are assembled inside the vessel's steel-frame skeleton.

NASSCO workers are proud of their handiwork. On July 26, NASSCO spokesman Karl Johnson climbs into a golf cart, dons a hard hat, and leads a tour of the shipyard, weaving between cradles where slices of ships are being assembled, braking to avoid trucks trundling through with fresh components, and darting around teams of workers coming on or off their shifts.

Most of the yard activity on this day is directed at constructing T-AKEs for MSC. But parts are also beginning to arrive for the first of nine six-hundred-foot tankers, costing $100 million apiece, for U.S. Shipping Partners, an oil hauler based in New Jersey. The tankers are so-called Jones Act ships—in other words, vessels built in the United States in order to comply with the Jones Act's requirement that ships hauling material between U.S. ports be built in the U.S.[5]

Most of the Jones Act shipping in the United States is on the Great Lakes. These freighters suffer little corrosion from the Great Lakes' freshwater—and that means they can last a century or more. For that reason, lakers don't do much to sustain the U.S. shipbuilding industry.

But some Jones Act shipping occurs between U.S. seaports. For one, a fleet of tankers hauls oil from Alaskan ports to refineries in California. In the Pacific's salty waters, these Jones Act vessels *do* corrode and must be replaced every couple decades. NASSCO is the "leading builder of ocean-going Jones Act ships in the nation today," according to NASSCO president Frederick Harris. That reliable demand helps keep the company afloat.[6]

That's good for NASSCO's workers and also for the U.S. Navy, which buys essentially all of its cargo ships from NASSCO. In the same way that the Jones Act preserves the human resources—the experienced ship's crews—required whenever MSC mobilizes for a large sealift, the act also preserves the industrial base that builds MSC's vessels.

Seen from a figurative distance, the shipyard is as much a machine as the machines it produces. Feed materials, skills, and labor; six months; and a few hundreds of millions of dollars at a time into one end. Out the other end come the gigantic, high-tech ships that are among the most vital instruments of American power—and the tankers that help keep the lifeblood of oil flowing into our economy.

It's a machine resting on a firm foundation of policy. Without the Jones Act, there would be no American-built tankers. As a consequence there would be no NASSCO. And that would mean no T-AKEs for MSC and the navy, an outcome that would threaten our ability as a nation to exert our influence upon the world.

■ ■ ■ ■

MSC has its headquarters on the Anacostia River, along the southern edge of Washington, D.C. Established in 1799, the Washington Navy Yard is the sea service's oldest facility. For 160 years, the navy built ships and munitions at the Yard, steadily adding slipways, factories, and warehouses until there were more than 150 buildings at the site.[7]

In the 1960s, as naval shipbuilding consolidated at a handful of commercial shipyards in Virginia, the Gulf Coast states, and California, the navy began converting the Navy Yard into office space. Today it anchors the redevelopment of southern D.C. New construction flanks the Yard's jumble of restored buildings. Military Sealift Command's headquarters lies just outside the white brick wall marking the Yard's original boundaries.[8]

Unlike bigger and more martial military commands, MSC's headquarters in 2007 is a fairly modest operation. It takes just a quick check-in at the front desk and a couple ninety-degree turns to arrive in the small office of MSC commander Rear Adm. Robert Reilly. Few large-scale U.S. military operations are possible without MSC, and the command is the focal point of some of the most important military innovation of the early twenty-first century. Despite this, Reilly sees few visitors. He eagerly clears an hour to sit down and discuss cargo, cargo ships, shipping schedules, and life at sea for his seventy-five hundred mariners.

The tall, pale, red-haired Reilly took the helm of Military Sealift Command in 2006, at a time when it was already running at surge capacity to support the wars in Afghanistan and Iraq, in addition to scores of smaller deployments and exercises.

"Consider the fundamental laws of physics," Reilly says. "Ultimately, 95 percent of equipment to support the Department of Defense goes by sea." The reason is clear: ships are more energy-efficient than airplanes, by a huge measure—and that translates into huge cash savings. Hauling one of the army's thirty-ton MRAP trucks by air costs $135,000 to Afghanistan. By sea, it costs only $18,000.

MSC ships even haul certain types of aircraft to Iraq because it's cheaper and safer than flying them there directly. "We looked at a number of cost op-

tions and figured out a scheme by which we could sealift a number of aviation assets to places like Rota [Spain], then take them out, put fluids back in,
and they were flown the last distance into theater, so they were fully ready
and available when they arrived," Reilly explains in a smooth monologue
laden with military jargon.

"That's part of MSC's distribution process ownership," he says, now slipping into the diction of a youngish business executive. "Let's find out what
the customer needs, when they need it, and how much it costs, then decide
the best way to get it to them," he recites, as though he's said it before. Which
he has.

It's no accident that Reilly is fluent in boardroom biz-speak. While technically part of the navy, these days MSC is more accurately described as a hybrid of a naval fleet and a civilian logistical company such as UPS, FedEx, or
DHL. MSC does essentially the same thing as the shipping companies. The
only difference is that MSC serves just one customer: the U.S. government.

Plus, MSC's ships, unlike UPS's brown trucks and air freighters, carry machine guns for self-defense. That might seem unusual for a cargo vessel. But
for naval vessels, MSC vessels "don't possess a lot of combat systems," Reilly
says. "What's the threat?" he asks rhetorically.

Well, pirates, for one. And terrorists, for another. In September 2008, off
the pirate-infested Somali coast, the crew of the MSC tanker *John Lenthall*
fired shots to ward off two small boats that appeared to be vectoring for an
attack. "This incident is clear proof that all mariners must remain vigilant,"
MSC's Capt. Steve Kelley says.[9]

But the command's crews can also be *too* vigilant. In March 2008, sailors
on the cargo ship *Global Patriot* shot and killed an Egyptian bargeman while
the *Global Patriot* was waiting to pass through the Suez Canal with around
a hundred MRAPs on board. The shooting occurred after the bargeman
failed to heed warnings not to approach the ship. The *Global Patriot*'s crew
might have feared a suicide attack, like the one on the destroyer USS *Cole* in
Yemen in 2000 that killed seventeen sailors.[10]

The *Global Patriot* incident was a sobering one for Sealift Command. In
May 2009, Somali pirates attacked the *Lewis and Clark*, the lead vessel of
the T-AKE class, off the East African coast. The 700-foot hybrid cargo ship
and tanker, which ironically had been resupplying warships deployed to
fight pirates, fired back, this time with a so-called nonlethal weapon—a

sophisticated loudspeaker called a Long Range Acoustic Device that fires a tight beam of ear-splitting sound as far as three hundred yards. After sweeping the pirates with the sonic beam, *Lewis and Clark* poured on the speed. The pirates pursued for an hour but couldn't catch up.[11]

Machine guns, pain rays, and tragic killings aside, every day MSC looks more and more like its civilian counterparts. Gone are the days when military shipping meant evading German U-boats on the North Atlantic or throwing up a wall of gunfire to destroy Japanese kamikaze planes. Today's conflicts grow out of religion, politics, and what the army calls "human security"—that is, everyday people's struggles with disease and starvation. War has become increasingly rooted in nonmilitary problems. And waging war increasingly is within the purview of nonmilitary agencies.

"Most of us who grew up in the navy envision Military Sealift Command as the oiler that showed up over the horizon to provide you fuel to top off your tanks and food for your reefer decks and occasionally some new ordnance," Reilly said in a 2008 speech before the Navy League. "Our mission set has expanded dramatically over the last three decades. One of the reasons it has, is that we have continued to embrace the commercial maritime model that is reflective of our national maritime industry."

"Military Sealift Command is essentially a $3 billion maritime operating company," Reilly continued. "On any given day, I have one hundred ships in full operational status across twenty-two different times zones. They are government-owned and -operated ships, they are government-owned, contractor-operated ships, and some of them are leased to me and those are contractor-operated ships."

In addition, Reilly said, his command keeps around eighty ships in reserve, with skeleton crews and basic maintenance. These ships are for rare emergencies, like the intensive build-up periods preceding a major overseas war.

More and more, Sealift Command doesn't even send its own ships for many missions. Instead, it subcontracts. During the 2006 Israeli invasion of Lebanon, the navy ordered Sealift Command to evacuate Americans from Lebanon, stat. No U.S. Navy or MSC vessels were available, Reilly said, so Sealift Command turned to its charter contract office.

"They responded by doing a rapid survey of the market for vessels that meet U.S. Coast Guard safety standards. There weren't any U.S.-flag vessels, so we hired a small Lebanese-flag cruise ship and a Saudi Red Sea passenger ferry—and a high-speed ferry from Italy." The three vessels ultimately evac-uated fifteen thousand people and demonstrated Sealift Command's diversi-fying missions, and its increasing reliance on commercial practices to perform those missions.

Becoming more commercial means becoming more efficient—something the military rarely worried about before. "Redundancy is inherently a virtue in war," Fred Kagan pointed out.[12] But as the line between war and peace has grown blurrier, and the same techniques and technologies increasingly un-derpin both, the military has begun to look more and more like a commer-cial enterprise that can't afford inefficiencies.

At UPS, industrial engineers use sophisticated number-crunching to model changes in demand for their services. That's how the company knows how many extra package sorters to hire right before Valentine's Day or another holiday. These models allow them to forecast future demand: this in turn helps the providers scale their capacity to the bare minimum required, thus cutting overhead costs.

Reilly says Military Sealift Command is just beginning to improve its fore-casting. Better forecasting means doing more work, more efficiently, with fewer ships and people—and at lower cost. It's the "lean" business model, adapted for military logistics.

■ ■ ■ ■

Contrast this to history's biggest, sustained sealift campaign, which was any-thing but lean. During World War II, U.S. military ships carried 7.3 million passengers and 270 million tons of cargo to overseas destinations on more than five thousand vessels. So vast, sprawling, and—frankly—disorganized was the six-year shipping effort that the army, navy, and U.S. Maritime Commission between them oversaw no fewer than four separate sealift agencies.[13]

It wasn't until after the war that the Pentagon was finally able to take a deep breath and sort through the tangled mess that was its gargantuan, and overly complex, sealift infrastructure. In December 1948, Defense Secretary James Forrestal decreed that "all military sea transport including Army trans-ports would be placed under Navy command." Seven months later, the navy formed the Military Sea Transportation Service, renamed Military Sealift Command in 1970.[14]

At its inception, the new organization had just ninety-four ships, all transferred from other navy commands—and stark testimony to the speed and extent of postwar disarmament. Within a year, ninety-one former army ships had chopped to MSTS. Over time, old World War II–era vessels retired and new ships—generally larger but fewer in number—took their places. Through it all, MSTS/MSC remained the world's biggest logistical force.[15]

Arguably, MSC's finest hour after World War II was in 1990 and 1991, during the buildup to Operation Desert Storm and the liberation of Iraqi-occupied Kuwait. Some two hundred ships owned or chartered by Sealift Command hauled the majority of the roughly 12 million tons of cargo and fuel to U.S. troops in Saudi Arabia. At the supply operation's peak, ships landed around forty thousand tons of supplies per day—a rate nearly three times the peak rate during the Pacific campaign in World War II.[16]

But the sheer scale of the sealift effort belied its ultimate inefficiency. Poor planning meant that Sealift Command shipped too many of some items and too few of others. MSC hauled some four hundred thousand antitank shells, for instance, but in lightning-fast ground combat the army and marines fired only forty thousand, according to Gary Mears, an air force general, and Ted Kim, an army colonel, in a 1994 article.[17]

Mears and Kim recommended swapping vast, static stockpiles of supplies for "just-in-time" delivery. Instead of filling whole ships with armor-piercing shells just in case somebody needed them, logisticians would quickly provide only what was clearly needed. It would be a smart, adaptive, and uninterrupted trickle, rather than a dumb, clumsy, and sporadic surge.[18]

This smart trickle would rely on careful tracking of every item in the supply chain. Mears and Kim compared their imagined "smart" logistical force to FedEx, but it would be equally similar to UPS, which tracks packages at every step of the distribution process, using scanners in the hubs and the drivers' DIAD terminals during delivery. From its monolithic origin in World War II, MSC is evolving into a strictly sea-based version of UPS, serving just one customer instead of millions.

■ ■ ■ ■

There's another side to MSC. In addition to handling the bulk of the military's long-range transport needs, Military Sealift Command also owns most of the Pentagon's special-missions ships. The salvage ship USNS *Grasp*.

Aviation support ships loaded with spare parts for fighter jets. Crane ships. Repair ships.

But it's not all hardware. MSC also maintains two hospital ships, each a forty-thousand-ton former tanker ship with surgical bays and hundreds of beds inside, plus a helicopter landing pad up top and boats along the sides for bringing patients on board. USNS *Mercy*, home-ported in San Diego, sails the Pacific. USNS *Comfort*, in Baltimore, covers the Atlantic.

The *Comfort* and the *Mercy* were converted from a pair of NASSCO-built tankers in the 1980s. They were meant to sail behind marine amphibious forces and receive the battle casualties flowing from a beach assault. But the Cold War passed without the marines ever having to retake Norway from Soviet occupiers, and the hospital ships lay mostly idle. There was talk of retiring them.

Then in the early 2000s, soft-power doctrine began percolating inside navy headquarters. Soft power intersected with sea-basing concepts. The result was a model for sustained, naval, medical outreach—delivering health care to sick and impoverished communities in developing nations, all in an effort to make friends and influence people. Amphibious ships like the *Kearsarge* can do it, but hospital ships can do it even better.

In the span of just a few years, the *Mercy* and the *Comfort* went from navy has-beens to some of the busiest ships in the fleet. The *Mercy* spent much of 2005 helping victims of the 2004 Indian Ocean tsunami and part of 2008 touring some of the poorest communities in Southeast Asia. The *Comfort* assisted with relief efforts after Hurricane Katrina in 2005, then focused her efforts on Latin America.

■ ■ ■ ■

In the spring of 2009, the *Comfort* sails from Baltimore, heading south with nine hundred doctors, nurses, corpsmen, support staff, and crew members aboard. In four months she will visit seven nations and see a hundred thousand patients, continuing the work that the *Kearsage* started six months earlier.

"We have huge capability here on *Comfort*, averaging around seventeen thousand patient encounters ashore per day, and twenty-five to thirty surgeries per day, some pretty significant," says Cdr. James Ware, chief medical officer on the ship. "In terms of capability, we have the equipment and supplies to do all types of procedures—everything a normal hospital of one thousand beds does, except three procedures." They are open-heart surgery, total joint replacement, and organ transplant—all of which require specialized equipment that the *Comfort* does not carry.

Treating so many people with so many different ailments every day, day after day, requires some deft logistics. It's hard enough supporting a ship for four months, thousands of miles from home. But when that ship doubles as a full-service hospital, the difficulty compounds.

No one knows that better than Thomas Finger, the *Comfort*'s master at the time of her Latin American mission. Finger supervises a crew of sixty-four experienced MSC seafarers, many of them with decades on the water.

"Our day starts at five o'clock, when we get up to launch the boats," Finger says mid-way through the *Comfort*'s deployment, while the vessel is anchored off the Panamanian coast. "At daybreak, we embark the medical personnel and engineering teams going ashore. Depending on where we are, that can be as many as six boat runs. Once we get that done, we normally start setting up for moving cargo ashore."

The cargo includes any equipment the ashore medical personnel might need to set up and service an outpatient clinic. One of the clinic's jobs is to identify patients who might need inpatient care; these the boats shuttle to the ship. If the boats are busy, the ship's two helicopters might take over.

Lt. Landon McKinley commands the helicopter detachment and its fourteen people. "We transport a great deal of cargo and move a lot of VIPs. Our main purpose now is patient transfer, both from shore to the hospital, and once fully recovered, we take them back home."

"Our bread and butter is moving people and things from point A to point B. This is much different than normal," McKinley adds. "Usually we're flying soldiers, sailors, and cargo from point A to B in the Persian Gulf, or we're stationed on supply ships." In Latin America, the cargo is civilians. Sick civilians. And the equipment to care for them.

Hauling sick civilians and the supplies for them means flying into some unusual places compared to the steel decks and concrete landing pads the aviators are accustomed to. "We've seen a lot of incredible places," McKinley says—remote villages all but hidden by lush forest, seaside communities perched on water's edge. "They're perfectly good landing zones—a little more difficult to get into and out of. They're not better or worse, just . . . different."

"I'm not sure of the ship's capability to move large cargo [to shore]," McKinley continues. "So we'll move wheelchairs and other large cargo from ship to shore. Our advantage is our ability to move this cargo. If the ship is in port, there are no issues, we can bring the cargo to the deck and crane it off. But getting supplies off the deck and onto a boat—I'm not sure how feasible that is."

Not terribly feasible, is Finger's answer. The *Comfort*'s boats handled passenger movements, shuttling medical personnel and patients between the ship and the shore clinics. But as for cargo, most of what the *Comfort* moves on its own, without the help of helicopters, is its garbage—and that's headache enough. "With nine hundred people on board, we generate a lot of trash," Finger says. "One of the biggest things is, how are we going to, in an environmentally safe manner, get trash ashore for disposal? In Panama, we were generating thirty cubic yards of trash on a daily basis. We can compact that, to get it down smaller." But it's still a lot.

"Normally, a barge comes from the beach, and we lower trash by hand or by crane into the barge and get it moved ashore." But for safety reasons, no boats can move when the helicopter is flying. That complicates garbage disposal and personnel transfer. The *Comfort*'s people have to schedule boats and choppers in a complex dance. "We're constantly working with the mission staff, the hospital staff, and the helicopter staff to keep things flowing," Finger says.

"This is a relatively challenging environment, going to ports where we have very little support, that aren't used to handling ships of this size," Finger adds. "There's a lot of coordination required. We have to do a lot of things ourselves, where we might be able to count on shore support if we were going into fully developed ports. We have them all pretty much IDed ahead of time. For example, in Haiti, which is relatively undeveloped, we had to take special steps for making water there, because we had no access to potable water from an approved facility."

Perhaps the worst ports are the ones where the *Comfort*, nine hundred feet long and one hundred wide, simply won't fit, by virtue of her size. In Latin America, that's most ports. "The only site could get pier-side was here in Panama," Finger says. In the Dominican Republic, Haiti, and other countries, "there was just not enough water, not enough piers, not enough tugboats to get us alongside." So the *Comfort* had to anchor some distance offshore.

"The big challenge, then, is how to get mission personnel where they need to go," Finger continues. "The patient and crew launches are run by ship's crew. If the weather picks up, is it still safe to run boats? What steps can we take to mitigate that risk? I'm proud to say, we've anchored at exposed ports and still been accident-free."

All that overhead—the people, the processes, the equipment—exists for one reason: to get patients the care they need. The patients are the best evidence that the logistics is working. "We've done seven hundred surgical procedures, including general surgeries on hernias and plastic surgery," Ware says. "The emergency surgeons have done some dramatic life-changing surgeries. One patient hadn't seen for ten years, then the optometrist brought sight to her eyes. One grandmother here hadn't seen her grandchildren. Her grandchildren had to cook for her. After three days, she had sight in both eyes and looked forward to cooking for them."

"One of our first patients in Haiti, I was able to see her pre-surgery," says Elie Malloy, a volunteer civilian nurse. "She had a huge uterine fibroid"—a benign tumor—"and looked nine months pregnant. She had been like that for two years. We were able to take that out with a hysterectomy. I was able to care for her for two days in the ICU, as well. And I saw her on shore, the day she went ashore. It was lucky for me to interact with her that way and see her joy at being a relatively normal person again, not carrying around that fibroid any more. Her gratitude was amazing."

"This is the third mission I've been on and the capstone of my career," Finger says. "From a personal point of view, this is the most rewarding ship I've been on. To see the looks in the little kids' eyes. . . . "

■ ■ ■ ■

Today the *Kearsarge* and the *Comfort* represent the state of the art for urgent humanitarian operations in austere environments. But the navy is looking ahead to new technologies that might allow humanitarians to get to disaster zones faster and do their work more efficiently.

One option is to break the monolithic relief platforms—giant hulls like the *Kearsarge* and the *Comfort*—into several, much smaller ships capable of getting closer to shore. It's not that the big ships aren't good at their jobs, MSC boss Reilly says. "They are very capable platforms but were designed and built in the 1980s to handle Cold War casualties." That is, battle-injured marines, mostly requiring trauma care and who usually arrive by helicopter.

"As medicine has evolved over twenty years, we're finding that some of these capabilities are in excess," Reilly says. Humanitarian cases—say, people suffering from long-term illnesses or hungry and dehydrated disaster survivors—don't need so much trauma care and don't necessarily justify the expense of a speedy helicopter ride. They might as well come by boat. But the boats need to be more reliable than the rugged-duty landing craft assigned to ships like the *Kearsarge*.

Today's humanitarian patients require a broader range of "softer" treatments. Pediatric care, for instance. Cataract surgery. Nutritional counseling. It's not all about patching up bullet and blast wounds.

Plus, with the shift away from battlefield medicine toward humanitarian operations, it's less important to concentrate your medical resources in a single location where they can be easily protected. It's more important to scatter them widely, for quicker access to patients living ashore.

Reilly says he envisions a smaller, more flexible approach to seagoing hospitals. "Take a mobile field hospital. It's already modularized. Maybe you could break it down and put it on a High Speed Vessel." The vessels Reilly refers to are a new type of fast catamaran ferries, similar to those formerly owned by civilian shuttle operators that were rented by the navy in the early 2000s, painted gray, and pressed into service hauling troops, equipment, and humanitarian supplies off the coast of Iraq and, less often, in Latin America. The army and navy began building purpose-built military catamarans, formally known as Joint High Speed Vessels, or JHSVs, in 2010. Several JHSVs might do the job of a single amphibious or hospital ship—and probably do it cheaper and with greater flexibility. Distributing the operating rooms and clinics across three or four hulls instead of cramming them into just one— and placing these hulls just a few yards offshore instead of miles away— would help alleviate bottlenecks and reduce the patient waits that nearly capsized the *Kearsarge*'s efforts in Nicaragua and complicated Finger's job getting the *Comfort* to its patients during that ship's 2009 cruise.

Joint High Speed Vessels are one option. Another is to forgo ships entirely. In late 2009, one navy analyst proposed building gigantic airships to haul aid workers and their supplies, up to five hundred tons at a time, directly into afflicted communities. These "Angel Ships" would travel faster than any ship while carrying much, much more than any normal aircraft. They would have their own water purification, power generation, and lodging, and would require just an open field for landing. An Angel Ship would be like a sea base without the sea.

The proposal represents just one facet of a new way of conceptualizing aerial logistics. In the late 2000s, the U.S. military refined airborne transportation to something approaching an art form. Plans for giant airships were just one outgrowth of this advancement. Just as the Iraq War propelled huge leaps in ground-based logistical technologies and soft-power operations drove new concepts for seaborne logistics, the War in Afghanistan forced Americans to find new ways of moving things by air.

PART **FOUR**

10

Big Blimpin'

The fire began around the airship's fins. It spread quickly, fueled by the vessel's cotton skin and the hydrogen gas contained in sixteen cotton bags fixed to its metal skeleton. In just over thirty seconds, the *Hindenberg*, the largest aircraft in history, was a smoking ruin, smoldering on the landing field at Lakehurst Naval Air Station in New Jersey. Of ninety-eight people on board, thirty-six died.[1]

The disaster on May 6, 1937, was the end of an important era for human flight. Wind-driven hot-air balloons were the very first aircraft: Chinese warriors rode giant "sky lanterns" on spy missions as early as the third century. Powered balloons called "airships" preceded airplanes by more than a century. In 1784 French inventor Jean-Pierre Blanchard fitted a hand-cranked fan to a hot air balloon and flew across the English Channel, making him the world's first true aviator.[2]

By the turn of the twentieth century, huge airships crisscrossed the globe. The most sophisticated models packed gas balloons inside a rigid hull that might be hundreds of feet long. German dirigibles manufactured by the Zeppelin Company were so successful on transatlantic passenger flights that the firm's name became synonymous with large airships. In World War I, the German air force pressed zeppelins into service as long-range bombers.

After the war, large airships again hauled passengers across the Atlantic while military models patrolled the oceans. The troubles started in 1921. A 695-foot British airship purchased by the U.S. Navy crashed before delivery, killing forty-four Americans and Britons. Four years later, in September

1925, the 680-foot navy airship *Shenandoah* was caught in a storm in Ohio and crashed with the loss of thirteen of her forty-two crewmen.[3]

The accidents came one after another, like a tragic staccato. The 785-foot USS *Akron* crashed in poor weather off the coast of New Jersey in April 1933, killing seventy-three of her seventy-six crewmen. A smaller navy blimp sent to help also crashed, killing two. In February 1935, *Akron*'s sister ship *Macon* lost her tail fin in a storm off the California coast and settled into the ocean. Two crewmen drowned.[4]

The *Akron* and the *Macon* were among the most sophisticated airships ever built. They had been modified to carry four biplane fighters apiece inside their hulls, like airborne aircraft carriers. The fighters launched and recovered by way of a complex trapeze system that lowered the fighters into the airstream and later snatched them from it. With their fighters as scouts and escorts, the *Akron* and the *Macon* were the most capable naval reconnaissance vessels fielded in their day.

But for all their innovation, the *Akron* and the *Macon* were unlucky vessels. The *Akron* suffered several accidents prior to crashing for good. In May 1932, she strayed into a rising column of warm air while moored in San Diego harbor. Someone cut the *Akron*'s main cable to prevent the airship from standing on her end. Three young sailors handling her lines on the ground were yanked into the air as the *Akron* shot upward. Two fell to their deaths as news reporters watched and filmed; a third held on until he could be hoisted into the hull. The *Macon* nearly crashed into mountains in Texas while crossing the continent from west to east in 1934.[5]

While airships were falling out the sky like lead weights, airplanes were becoming safer and more capable by the day. People's preferences were already shifting from airships to airplanes in the months leading up to the *Hindenberg*'s fiery destruction. The German vessel's dramatic demise, covered live on radio and later shown in newsreels, hastened the airship's comeuppance.

As the 1930s waned, airplanes replaced most of the world's airships for anything but niche roles. The U.S. Navy flew patrol blimps in World War II and even modified a few as radar platforms after the war. One of these radar pickets crashed in 1960, killing eighteen people. Two years later, the military ended all airship operations. For the next four decades, the only airships in regular service in the United States were a couple dozen minimally manned models—usually with just a pilot aboard—used for advertising. The collectively named Goodyear blimp is the most famous.[6]

Then came GPS and major advances in weather forecasting. If weather-related accidents killed the airship in America, weather-related improvements might also resurrect it. The result could be a new way of moving around lots of stuff, more cheaply than with aircraft and faster than by ship. Airships could provide a big boost to cargo firms, military logisticians, and, according to one navy study, even humanitarians trying to deliver aid faster and without the snafus that have plagued ship-based relief work.

■ ■ ■ ■

The fog is a problem. For several days running in late February 2010, the pilots at Airship Ventures stare up into the Northern California sky, scrutinizing the haze shifting beneath layers of gray clouds. It has been an unusually cold and unpleasant winter across the United States, even in California where sunny days are the norm. For an airship operator, unpleasant weather isn't just a nuisance—it costs money. Yesterday Airship Ventures had to cancel a scheduled sightseeing tour of the San Francisco area. Ten paying customers went home disappointed, rain checks in hand.

Airship Venture's Zeppelin NT, *Eureka*, comes in for a landing at Moffett Field in February 2010. DAVID AXE

For hundreds of years, men have traipsed the skies under giant bags filled with hot air or expansive gas whose mass is lighter than a comparative volume of air. For hundreds of years, bad weather has been the biggest danger to lighter-than-air flight. Balloons' envelopes can be delicate, sensitive things. Unexpected gusts have crashed many airships and killed many airship occupants. Clouds and fog limit an airship pilot's visibility. Since airships fly visually, rather than by instruments, bad weather renders them blind.

Airship Ventures understands these risks. They don't take chances. After all, they're primarily a tour operator. A single crash, a single injury—these could destroy the company's reputation among tourists and force it to close.

But prudence is costing Airship Ventures. Every flight means several thousand dollars in revenue. The company aims to complete several flights per flying day. What does a wisp of fog cost? To Airship Ventures, up to $15,000 per day.

In the end, California's traditional sunny disposition wins out. The clouds thin. The sun burns through the fog. Airship Ventures pilot Jim Dexter makes the call: today, America's only passenger airship will fly.

■ ■ ■ ■

Airship Ventures is the child of an aeronautical marriage. Growing up, Brian Hall spent summers in Upstate New York, near the Old Rhinebeck Aerodrome, an aviation museum with a collection of more than fifty World War I–era airplanes, including a 1909 model that is the second-oldest intact flying machine in the world. Some of the Old Rhinebeck airplanes are still flyable, and the museum offers rides to paying customers and stages mock dogfights for guests. "Watching dogfights there got him hooked on aviation," Airship Ventures' website says of Brian. As an adult, he took a job with a company that developed flight-planning software and later founded his own software company.[7]

Brian's wife Alex wanted to be an astronaut when she was a little girl growing up in Bedford, England, the site of some of England's massive, old airship hangars. Alex figured getting her commercial pilot's license was the best first step, but she was too short to qualify. She never lost her love of space and aviation, and she later found work in England's National Space Centre and the Chabot Space & Science Center near Oakland.[8]

In 2005, Brian attended a software conference in Cologne, Germany, then home to the world's only passenger airships—a fleet of three Zeppelin NTs (for "new technology") that had entered service in 2001. Brian booked a flight and was amazed at what Airship Ventures later described as the NT's "precise handling, and quiet, spacious cabin with oversized windows and restroom . . . designed for luxurious passenger operations. . . . Realizing that there was no experience like this, and no such airship technology in the U.S., Brian immediately embarked on his next business venture." He e-mailed the Zeppelin Company with a proposal to launch airship passenger service in San Francisco, using one leased airship.[9]

Brian and Alex married in February 2007. They founded Airship Ventures in March. With their sole Zeppelin NT under construction in Germany, the Halls needed a base for the 250-foot, $7 million craft. That meant a hangar. Alex worked some old contacts in NASA, which had taken over Moffett Field after the navy abandoned it, and arranged a meeting for Brian. NASA loved the idea of returning airships to the historic airfield with its three massive airship hangars. It took a year to process all the paperwork, recruit investors, and train staff and crew. The American zeppelin *Eureka* completed construction in Germany in May 2008. She was promptly packed into crates for sea shipment to the U.S. The *Eureka* made her first American flight the same month.[10]

■ ■ ■ ■

Military air travel can be one of the most exciting things in the world: catapulting off an aircraft carrier in the middle of the Pacific Ocean, churning low over the Afghan countryside in a twin-rotor CH-47 helicopter, spiraling down for a tactical landing in a C-130 bound for Baghdad. By comparison, an airship ride is almost tranquil.

The *Eureka* lifts off from an expanse of tarmac outside one of Moffett Field's three huge airship hangars. Belted into airline-style seats installed along the huge windows of the underslung gondola are nine tourists: an elderly couple who said they had always wanted to fly on an airship before they died; a quiet, almost overawed younger couple; and a big, happily squabbling family. The riders' first impression, as the *Eureka* climbed to a thousand feet, was how quiet and comfortable the airship was—and how slow. For the circuit around Moffett Field and north toward Stanford University, the *Eureka* cruised at just thirty-five miles per hour. Cars sped past on the highways below. Birds passed without paying the *Eureka* any mind.

It might seem implausible that cargo operators and the military would be interested in something so slow. But in logistics, speed *isn't* everything. Airships boast certain advantages over other modes of transport. Airships are safe with proper planning, comparatively inexpensive to buy and maintain, highly fuel-efficient in certain modes, and can be scaled upward to a truly massive size. That last point is what has got the military interested. If and when the Pentagon takes the airship plunge, commercial operators can't be far behind.

To be clear, the *Eureka* is not a military aircraft. It's mostly for what Brian Hall calls "flight-seeing"—that is, aerial sightseeing—plus some advertising. But as Hall sees it, that's just the beginning. "At Airship Ventures, we are building a solid foundation via the proven application of airships in tourism—but we also have an eye toward the future with regards to security and military applications of airships. Our team has experience operating nearly every airship that has flown commercially—as well as some that were flown experimentally—since the 1980s and has military backgrounds and the requisite security clearances."

It might not be obvious to the several thousand tourists who have mo-tored tranquilly over lush Northern California in the *Eureka*'s cushy gon-dola, but the American zeppelin is a sort of unofficial test model for the coming renaissance in military lighter-than-air operations. Airships are primed to profoundly change the way we move stuff from A to B.

At Airship Ventures, one man lies at the three-way nexus of flight-seeing, military airship experimentation, and the coming lighter-than-air renaissance. That would be Jim Dexter, Airship Venture's senior crewman and one of the most experienced of the roughly forty airship pilots in America.

Dexter, fifty-three, has dark features and an unflappable calm accentu-ated by the stylish sunglasses he wears with his leather jacket and under-stated, hatless pilot's uniform. Sitting in the lefthand seat of the *Eureka*'s two-person cockpit, he listens to air-traffic control through a lightweight headset and steers the airship using a traditional yoke like you might see in any passenger jet. For the post-fog flight in late February, Dexter says noth-ing to his passengers for the entire ninety minutes of their flight-seeing tour. Instead, a nonrated Airship Ventures employee—essentially, a flight atten-dant—makes the safety announcements and chitchats with nervous fliers.

Dexter got his start in 1981 flying the world-famous Goodyear blimps. Since 1925, Goodyear, a $3 billion tire and rubber company, has used airships

The *Eureka*'s pilot, Jim Dexter, pilots the airship over Northern California in February 2010.
DAVID AXE

to advertise its products. Today Goodyear has three blimps—one each based in Ohio, Florida, and California—that together travel some 100,000 miles a year to hover over sporting events.[11]

Goodyear used to mass-produce airships for sale. The company collaborated with Zeppelin to produce the *Akron* and the *Macon* plus hundreds of small, manned blimps, all for the navy. But Goodyear shuttered its airship lines in the 1960s and today builds only the blimps it needs for its own advertising purposes. The three Goodyear blimps in active service in 2010 were built between 2000 and 2006 to a basic design dating from 1969. The end of Goodyear's commercial airship manufacturing left the American Blimp Corporation in Oregon as America's major airship-maker.[12]

Dexter had a commercial pilot's license when he joined Goodyear. The rest of his training was on the job. From Goodyear, he moved on to Germany—the world's other hub for airship design and production—to work for Zeppelin. After that, back to the United States to fly for American Blimp. In 2007, he joined a U.S. Navy project to test an American Blimp A-170 model for potential military applications. By the time he joined Airship Ventures, Dexter had around nine thousand hours of flight time in airships. He even held the airship world speed record—57.7 miles per hour in a British-made model—from 2000 until 2004, when adventurer Steve Fossett flew a Zeppelin NT to 69.4 miles per hour.[13]

As part of the navy airship team, Dexter witnessed firsthand the military's growing interest in airships. It was not without its hiccups.

■ ■ ■ ■

It had been forty-four years since a navy blimp had operated from Lakehurst Naval Air Station, the traditional home of the navy's East Coast airships. In May 2006, a 180-foot, $3.5 million A-170 built by American Blimp Corporation began flying from Lakehurst's Hangar 6, a thousand-foot-long building constructed to house patrol blimps in World War II. The A-170, re-designated "MZ-3A" by the navy, had four pilots assigned: two from navy test squadron VX-20 and two, including Dexter, hired from the tiny pool of American commercial airship pilots.

With the pilots taking turns, MZ-3A began flying low-altitude missions to test new sensors. The army had been using tethered, unpiloted balloons to carry cameras high over Iraq and Afghanistan; the navy wanted to see if it could do the same thing over the sea. The answer, apparently, was yes. But VX-20 was never happy with the airship. The then–thirty-one-year-old squadron had spent most of its career flying such high-performance aircraft as the sub-hunting P-3 Orion and the E-2 radar plane. By comparison, the MZ-3 was slow, light-lifting, and probably plain boring to navy aviators. VX-20 gave the airship "mixed reviews," Dexter says, and in 2007 the blimp test program was allowed to lapse.

Regardless of VX-20's attitude, the navy was still interested in blimps. In 2008, the sea service rented a British-made Skyship 600 and flew it over the Gulf of Mexico for two months in a series of tests that continued Dexter's work on the MZ-3. The MZ-3 itself was quietly picked up by the Navy Research Laboratory for possible future experiments. While all this was happening, Steve Huett, a member of the navy's Advanced Development Program Office, was thinking several steps ahead. In September 2009, he proposed that the navy develop an eight-hundred-foot-long airship capable of lifting five hundred tons of cargo in one sortie. It would be like the *Akron*, the *Macon* or even the *Hindenburg*, but much safer and more powerful by far.[14] As a bonus, Huett wrote, a large military-style airship could be used as a humanitarian Angel Ship, delivering massive amounts of aid directly to needy communities without the difficult sea-land interfaces required by ships.[15]

Huett's proposal was actually the latest in a series of think pieces by military officials dating back to at least 2005. That year, as army truckers were fighting for their lives on Iraq's highways, DARPA awarded funds to Lockheed Martin and Aeros Aeronautical Systems Corporation for initial work on what might become an airship cargo craft capable of hauling a thousand tons over global range. The so-called Walrus airship would lift battalions of five hundred or more soldiers and all their equipment in a single flight. Despite the concept's promise, DARPA pulled funding just a year later, as the Pentagon had decided to refocus the research agency on saving truckers in Iraq and other near-term problems.[16]

Huett essentially resurrected the Walrus idea. The navy version would "embark a ready-to-fight combat force—troops, armor, helicopters, supplies—at its base of origin" and transport them up to four thousand miles at a top speed of around a hundred miles per hour "without loss of unit cohesion or physical [or] mental 'readiness to fight,'" Huett wrote. Such an airship could land large numbers of forces in areas without airports or seaports. Its theoretical operating costs would be 60 percent less, per ton-mile, than an airplane, Huett claimed.[17]

Some navy traditionalists surely rolled their eyes, but what Huett was proposing wasn't mad science. Boeing was even developing a civilian version of an ultra-large airship for commercial applications. The Boeing JHL-40, if it proves viable following its planned first flight around 2012, could eventually join the military to fulfill Huett's vision—this despite DARPA earlier abandoning large airships. You just can't keep airships down.[18]

■ ■ ■ ■

Back aboard the *Eureka*, Dexter and his passengers are halfway through their languid tour. Dexter demonstrates the airship's controls. Propellers mounted on the airship's rigid, internal skeleton vector backward or downward for directional control, but trim and altitude are adjusted by shifting fuel across different tanks and tweaking the pressure in a series of bladders, each holding helium or air and contained within the zeppelin's outside envelope. Controlling the *Eureka* requires only gentle movements. "There's almost no pilot fatigue," Dexter explains. Flying an airship is pure Zen.

Nor does the airship itself suffer much fatigue. The outside envelope can wear out and should be replaced every seven or eight years, but the main structure and dynamic components work very gently. Dexter says he knows of some advertising blimps with basic frames that are more than forty years old and still work just fine. Fixed-wing aircraft, by contrast, require frequent, deep maintenance to counteract flight stress. Helicopters last only twenty years or so, on average, before the constant vibration tears them apart. In the coming era of declining defense resources, airships could make great economic sense.

The way ahead for airships depends on the navy's experiments, the performance of Boeing's forthcoming heavy-lifting model, the findings of any ongoing Pentagon studies, and the continuing safe operations of civilian airships such as the *Eureka*. "What's the prospect?" Dexter asks rhetorically. "If there is a market and a need to get heavy equipment from point A to point B, an airship could easily be designed to do the job. With today's weather technology and GPS, you could easily avoid the weather."

Huett seems to have banked on those conditions when he proposed the battalion-hauling navy airship in September 2009. All the technology for a vessel of that type would be ready by 2011, Huett wrote.

"I've been in the industry a long time and seen a lot of changes," Dexter says, inscrutable behind his sunglasses. "It's encouraging to see this renewed interest."

Future air logistics may very well boast fleets of huge airships. In the meantime, the U.S. military is finding new ways to use its existing, heavier-than-air craft to sustain one of history's greatest aerial supply efforts.

11

Air Donkeys

The train of tan-painted, dirt-encrusted vehicles comes to a halt in a cloud of thin, rising dust. Their rear ramps drop slowly, heavily, and men clad in grayish uniforms and helmets clamor out, fanning out across the dry, loose ground. They are American soldiers, and they have a job to do. An unglamorous one.

A boy stands watching. Beside him, a donkey stares straight at the ground mere inches from its face. The boy holds the donkey's reins, but that's clearly unnecessary. The five-foot-tall animal has no interest in going anywhere.

She will soon change her mind.

It's October 16, 2009, in Baraki Barak, an agricultural district in Logar Province, south of Kabul in mountainous central Afghanistan. The vehicles are variants of the MRAP trucks designed by the Pentagon to protect U.S. Army logistical troops in Iraq. In Afghanistan, the MRAPs function essentially as battle taxis, hauling four or five soldiers apiece across districts where improvised explosive devices sprouted like massive, fiery flowers.

The IEDs that took root in the Iraq War as the insurgents' weapon of choice for attacking U.S. military convoys, soon spread to Afghanistan via globetrotting Islamic extremists and secretive websites. In the early years of the Afghanistan war, gunfire and accidents were the biggest killers. By 2009 IEDs assumed that awful mantle.

With their angled hulls and high-tech, layered armor, MRAPs are good at deflecting the explosive force of roadside bombs. But Afghanistan is very difficult terrain for the lumbering vehicles. An MRAP amounts to a commercial truck chassis—basically a big rig minus the trailer—wrapped in armor. They aren't what anyone would describe as "off-road."

In Iraq that doesn't much matter, as the highways are modern and fairly well-maintained, and the terrain is basically flat from the southern border with Kuwait, all the way to the Kurdish-controlled north, where mountains belatedly sprout near the border with Turkey. An MRAP, all twenty-to-thirty tons of it, can roll along smoothly, albeit heavily. "The MRAPs were bought for Iraq," said marine brigadier general Michael Brogan, program manager for the blast-resistant vehicles. "They weren't bought with any vision of needing to handle the rough terrain that's common in Afghanistan."[1]

Afghanistan is bigger than Iraq to begin with, and the population centers are more widely spread. More than half the country is mountains. In Afghanistan, the sparse cities and towns accumulate in the valleys like litter in a ditch. Traveling between two towns means passing over the mountains, sometimes thousands of feet tall, that ring them like the jagged rims of monstrously tall bowls—then crossing between mountain ranges on roads that barely qualify as such.

The terrain makes good roads especially vital to any kind of reliable ground transport. The same terrain, and its accompanying harsh weather, means roads are very, very hard to build and maintain. Factor in decades of warfare and pervasive government corruption, and it should come as no surprise that Afghanistan's logistical infrastructure is all but nonexistent.

All that added up to big problems for the MRAPs. The first of them arrived in Afghanistan in late 2007, just a few months after their debut in Iraq. The troubles started almost immediately. "The axles began failing at an alarming rate," said Kim Yarboro, a civilian working under Brogan. Suspensions lasted just weeks before a once-smooth ride became bone-jarring, joint-smashing torture for an MRAP's passengers.[2]

On steep slopes, the heavily laden, diesel-powered trucks guzzled fuel. In 2009, accounting firm Deloitte estimated that the Pentagon burned twenty-two gallons of fuel per soldier per day in Afghanistan—the highest per-capita fuel consumption in the history of mechanized warfare.[3]

Better MRAPs was a very partial solution to a very big problem—but it was better than doing nothing. The marines designed a better axle and suspension, and the marines and army teamed up to buy a totally new model of the truck called the MRAP-All-Terrain Vehicle, or M-ATV. Oshkosh designed a lighter, higher-riding vehicle with a beefed-up, fully independent suspension and snagged the initial billion-dollar contract in June 2009. The air force flew the first M-ATVs into Afghanistan in September to rave reviews from the ground troops. "I love the M-ATV," said Pfc. Nicholas Marshall.[4]

But the soldiers in Baraki Barak are still using the old-style MRAPs, and it shows in the relief on their faces when they leap out of their idling vehicles. Moving from point A to point B in Afghanistan can be a terribly unpleasant activity, even when the Taliban isn't detonating bombs in your path.

The troops from Able Troop, Third Squadron, Seventy-first Cavalry Regiment, part of the aptly named Tenth Mountain Division, have been tasked with resupplying a mountaintop observation post. A thousand feet directly above them, a handful of their comrades sit surrounded by sandbags, armed to the gills, peering through sophisticated scopes at the town in the valley below. "Observation Post Spur," as it is known, is decked out with sensors and weapons. But they all require a constant flow of electricity, and one of OP Spur's generators has just quit. The soldiers at the base of the mountain have brought a replacement.

Problem is, the MRAPs can't climb the mountain's steep slope. The air force has the ability to drop in equipment using GPS-guided parachutes, but even the best of these silk-and-hardware models are too imprecise to land a generator on OP Spur's narrow summit. Worst of all, no helicopters are immediately available. The waiting list for chopper service is now several days deep. Able Troop has to haul the generator up the slope some other way.

In what probably seemed like a moment of inspiration worthy of Lawrence of Arabia, someone had proposed doing things the Afghan way and renting a donkey from a local farmer. It's that donkey and his handler that await Able Troop's arrival on the October afternoon. If the boy or his animal realize the scale of Able Troop's miscalculation as the soldiers lift the heavy generator out of an MRAP, neither shows it. Able Troop doesn't know that a single donkey isn't enough to carry a three-hundred-pound load a thousand feet up a thirty-degree slope.

The soldiers place the generator on a sled and tether the sled to the donkey. The Afghan boy whips the donkey with a short leather strip, starting her forward. For the first hundred yards, it seems like this half-baked scheme might actually work. Then the donkey decides she has had enough. She halts, brays, and refuses to budge even when the soldiers join the boy in whipping her flanks.

S.Sgt. Donald Coleman, a talkative, sunburned man, looks around at his soldiers, down the slope at the idling MRAPs, and up to the waiting OP. He stared at the protesting donkey. "Looked good on paper," he muses, then tells his men to pick up the generator and carry it, by hand, the rest of the way up the mountain. Which they do—muscles straining, faces reddening, boots slipping. The donkey, relieved of her impossible burden, blissfully follows the grunting soldiers up the mountain.

Soldiers from the U.S. Army's Seventy-first Cavalry haul a generator to Observation Post Spur in Logar Province, Afghanistan, in October 2009. DAVID AXE

This day in Baraki Barak is the Afghan war in a nutshell. More than Iraq, more than any naval soft-power mission to Latin America, more than most American conflicts, the Afghan war hinges on logistics. Whether by hand, donkey, truck, chopper, or plane, moving people and stuff quickly and efficiently between two distant points over rough terrain, through harsh weather, against violent opposition, is the key to any sort of military victory. The winner is the party that can move freely.

The U.S.-led coalition benefits, and suffers, from history's most exquisite logistical systems and techniques. Never before has a military had so many transport options and so much logistical potential. But the same power tempts the Pentagon to place forces in even the most remote locations—because it *can*.

But residing at the farthest extremes of the supply routes means these forces are the first to go without when systems fail. Far-flung troops who routinely enjoy satellite-guided aerial food drops and incoming swarms of multi-million-dollar, night-flying cargo helicopters also find themselves reduced to renting donkeys from Afghan boys.

■ ■ ■ ■

When President George W. Bush ordered the U.S. military to invade Afghanistan to hunt down Osama bin Laden and his protectors in the Taliban Islamic group, planners realized they had few options for deploying large numbers of U.S. troops to the country. Afghanistan is landlocked and surrounded by nations wary of, or outright hostile to, any U.S. presence. The government of Pakistan—no friend of the Taliban—was eager to help, and equally eager not to be seen helping, in light of the extremist tendencies of many of its own citizens.

A direct land assault was out of the question. An assault strictly by sea was, of course, impossible. Coming in by air seemed the only choice, but the only nearby airbases even theoretically available to the Americans were in Pakistan. Islamabad would allow only supporting aircraft, not the invasion force itself.

The solution was a mixed air and sea assault requiring the special skills of the U.S. Marine Corps, a force that blended the qualities of an army, a navy, and an air force into one seamless whole. Marine brigadier general James Mattis, a stern, beady-eyed Washington State native who eighteen months later would lead the marines' attack on southern Iraq, oversaw weeks of delicate planning.

Two flat-deck amphibious ships, sisters of USS *Kearsarge*, gathered with their aircraft, escorts, and supply ships in the northern Indian Ocean. Extra helicopters shuttled to the vessels. A contingent of marine KC-130 aerial tankers and logistical troops quietly set up shop at Pakistani airbases. U.S. Special Operations Forces teams already on the ground in southern Afghanistan hastily built helicopter landing zones and stocked them with fuel.[5]

The marines would lead the attack in their CH-53E helicopters, the same model that seven years later would ferry Nicaraguan patients to the medical bays aboard the *Kearsarge*. The seventeen-ton CH-53s and their escorting

AH-1W gunships—slim, sleek aircraft armed with guns, missiles, and rockets—would launch from the amphibious ships and hook north over Pakistan and descend on a walled hunting lodge that navy SEALs had identified outside Kandahar, the Taliban's main stronghold in southern Afghanistan.[6]

The KC-130 tankers flying out of Pakistan would refuel the cargo choppers in mid-air. The AH-1s, lacking refueling equipment, would land at the ground fuel points when necessary, essentially leapfrogging across Afghanistan to keep up with the CH-53s.[7]

At just shy of four hundred miles, the flight would represent the longest helicopter-borne air assault in history. And the riskiest. Nobody had ever pushed helicopters that hard before. Nobody was sure the finicky machines would hold together for what would amount to a quarter-day of hard flying over water, mountains, and desert.

The CH-53s were particularly worrying. A navy variant of the aircraft was the sea service's most crash-prone aircraft, tumbling out of the air at twice the rate of other choppers. A CH-53 crash in Iraq in January 2005 would kill thirty-one people, contributing to the bloodiest single day of the Iraq War for U.S. forces. Maintenance problems with the helicopters or missed refuelings could derail Mattis's whole fragile operation. The logistics had to work perfectly to avoid disaster.[8]

As night fell on November 25, 2001, a company of marines, around 150 strong, climbed into six CH-53s organized in two waves. The birds lifted off the deck under a deafening blanket of noise from their three forty-four-hundred-horsepower General Electric engines, driving seven forty-foot-long rotor blades. The comparatively tiny gunships, seating two marine aviators back-to-front, were flies buzzing around the horses' heads of the blocky, lumbering CH-53s. The aircraft were invisible to the naked eye. Their crews wore night-vision goggles that cast everything in unearthly shades of green.[9]

Alison Thompson, a tall, severe woman, piloted one of the CH-53s. In 2001 she was still a fairly junior flier. Seven years later, she would outpace all of her female Naval Academy classmates to become the Marine Corps's most experienced woman pilot, with some fifteen hundred flight hours under her belt. She would mark her achievement by deploying to Nicaragua to ferry medical patients to the *Kearsarge*.

Thompson was lucky to make it to Nicaragua at all. Early in the Afghanistan mission, the complex CH-53s began giving their operators trouble. "The three helicopters in the second wave would have difficulty conducting aerial refueling," the marines' official history noted, reducing a nightmarish scenario to bloodless prose. For the aviators, "difficulty" meant the terror of hurtling through the air inside a vast machine that just might decide to stop working. To their great relief, the Super Stallion pilots finally managed to connect their fueling probes to hoses reeled out behind the droning KC-130 tankers.

Their travails weren't over. The CH-53 is a notoriously temperamental beast, with three thirsty, powerful engines connected to a maze of wires and pipes that steadily leak fluids. Experienced navy officers know not to wear their white dress uniforms while riding in a CH-53: it's impossible to escape the drip-drip of the yellowish lubricants from the aircraft's exposed guts.

The chopper's innate complexity was compounded by Central Asia's brutal conditions. The air itself was dirty with suspended sand. Maybe it was the sand, maybe something else was to blame. Either way, somewhere over the arid expanse of southern Afghanistan, Thompson's CH-53 suffered a compressor stall as the internal workings of one of the engines fell out of synch. The helicopter lost power—and fell.

Later Thompson would describe skimming over sand dunes in the dying CH-53, desperately trying to jump start the aircraft's power plant. She would describe the near crash, and her salvation from certain death, in the driest possible terms. The stalled engine roared back to life. The CH-53 regained power. Thompson climbed back to cruising altitude.

The assault force landed before midnight. There was no opposition. KC-130s bearing reinforcements flowed in. By morning, there were nearly five hundred Americans on the ground at what would be called "Camp Rhino." A thousand more would arrive in the next week. News reports from reporters embedded with the marines at Camp Rhino celebrated the stoic attitudes of young riflemen waging this new war of vengeance in a strange, alien land. "Welcome to the world of the grunts," crowed CBS News's Allen Pizzey in a spot highlighting Afghanistan's "vicious and unrelenting" wind and the makeshift gyms marines set up to keep in shape between long hours standing guard.[10]

But few would draw attention to the heroic work—by planners, ship handlers, aircraft mechanics, fuel specialists, and pilots—that had delivered those young marines four hundred miles inland through a ring of hostile or ambivalent countries to a chunk of desert with little infrastructure.

The establishment of Camp Rhino was a singular logistical feat. It was also a harbinger of coming challenges. From the marines' tiny toehold, the U.S.-led war effort expanded. Tens of thousands of American, British, and European troops joined legions of friendly Afghan militiamen. Major cities fell one by one.

By 2009 the now NATO-led Afghan campaign involves a hundred thousand foreign troops, around a hundred and fifty thousand Afghan security personnel, and tens of thousands of mercenaries. The war's emphasis has changed, from invasion and attack, to winning the hearts and minds of Afghans while helping build up the Afghan military and government.

What hasn't changed are Afghanistan's essential qualities and the logistical challenges they pose. Afghanistan remains distant, landlocked, and inhospitable to routine transport. In 2009 as in 2001, the only reliable way to get people and stuff into the country is by air. The logistical feat that landed a company of marines at Camp Rhino has bloomed into one of history's most complex aerial supply efforts.

■ ■ ■ ■

The Nevada Air National Guard–assigned C-130, radio call sign "Torque 41," lifts off from Bagram Airfield, a former Soviet base an hour's drive from Kabul, and turns south. The boxy, four-engine cargo plane with the odd, upturned nose climbs fast in order to clear the tall mountains that surround Bagram.

In the cockpit, aircraft commander Lt. Col. Billy Toney—a lean man with a bushy moustache and deep smile lines—threads the plane through streams of other aircraft coming and going around one of the world's busiest military airports.

In the thirty-year-old C-130's cargo hold on that cool October morning, loadmasters Chief M.Sgt. Gary Lanham and S.Sgt. Renaye Lavin check and recheck the eight pallets of food and water, each attached to a disposable parachute made of recycled plastic and latched into a roller system embedded in the cargo plane's metal floor.

Several hundred miles away in the vicinity of Kandahar, a battalion of U.S. Marines—successors of the original American invaders—await the badly needed supplies. Poor roads and the constant threat of Taliban attack mean that, eight years into the war, many U.S. and NATO combat forces have come to rely almost entirely on aircraft for resupply.

Lt. Col. Bill Toney, from the 774th Expeditionary Airlift Squadron, pilots his C-130 airlifter over southern Afghanistan in October 2009. DAVID AXE

Where possible, the airlifters land at a forward airstrip—often just a clear stretch of dirt—to offload supplies by forklift. Where there are no airstrips, the planes deliver the supplies by parachute. The latter is becoming increasingly common as coalition troops spread farther out across the Afghan countryside in search of their elusive enemy. In March 2009, the air force dropped more than 3 million pounds of supplies, a monthly record for the air service. Six months later, the air force shatters that record. Aircraft are dropping so much stuff that the cost of parachutes is becoming a real concern, hence the new recycled model Torque 41 is carrying.

Not only does the final delivery of matériel within Afghanistan usually fall to aircraft, much of NATO's supplies come *into* Afghanistan by air, as well. While some supplies—around one hundred standard shipping containers per day by 2008—travel by rail south from Russia through Turkmenistan or Kazakhstan, and an equal amount winds through mountain passes straddling the Pakistani border after reaching Karachi by sea, these represented sideshows to the far more impressive aerial supply campaign.

Traditionally, just 10 percent of supplies for a U.S.-led war travel by air. In Afghanistan in 2009, it's 30 percent and growing.

The proportion of matériel arriving by air has grown at an accelerating rate as the Taliban has begun targeting the convoys coming through Pakistan. In December 2008, Taliban fighters swarmed a truck depot just inside Pakistan, killing a guard and setting fire to 150 vehicles carrying NATO matériel. Dozens of such assaults over the years have destroyed hundreds of vehicles.[11]

"You probably couldn't ask [for] or find a tougher place, from a logistics challenge [perspective], of getting the stuff in," air force general Duncan McNabb, TRANSCOM boss, told the Senate Armed Services Committee in March 2009. "We will be there," he was quick to add. "We'll figure it out and make sure you never have to worry about this."[12]

But U.S. lawmakers did worry. Their mounting concern was the reason McNabb was spending so much time at committee meetings promising ever-greater logistical feats to keep the war effort fueled and fed.

If it came down to it, McNabb told the senators, "you would see a Berlin airlift"—a repeat of the international effort between 1948 and 1949 to feed, by air, the 2 million people living in West Berlin, deep inside Soviet-controlled East Germany.[13] The Soviets had blocked rail and road access in a bid to consolidate their control over the occupied city. To break their blockade, the U.S. Air Force and the Royal Air Force flew some two hundred thousand flights carrying around 2.3 million tons of food and fuel into the city.[14]

As it turned out, another Berlin airlift is much like what happened in Afghanistan. Over time, aircraft took up more and more of the war's logistical burden. "We just don't have the land lines to bring things in sufficiently," explained air force brigadier general Steve Kwast, commander of an air force wing based at Bagram. "Everything that comes in through Afghanistan comes in through here, if it has any short-term requirement." And in 2008 and 2009, as the Iraq War wound down, the War in Afghanistan escalated—and more and more military matériel came stamped "urgent."

That means airlifters, hundreds of them—everything from contracted civilian light planes, to the air force's agile C-130s and lumbering 250-foot-long, four-hundred-ton, four-engine C-5s and equally large Antonovs chartered from Russian and Ukrainian firms. For flights within the country, the planes were joined by hundreds of helicopters. The army's twin-rotor CH-47 cargo chopper has become such a ubiquitous sight in Afghanistan that some

Afghan artists include it in the background of the popular Photoshopped portraits that Afghan men order to commemorate their army or police service.

At Bagram a plane or helicopter takes off or lands on average every five minutes, twenty-four hours a day, every day. All that traffic amounts to history's biggest sustained airlift—bigger even than the Berlin Airlift by most measures.

Still, it isn't enough. On the front lines, a shortage of aircraft and other logistical shortfalls force units like Able Troop to improvise. Sometimes the improvisation works. Sometimes it results in stubborn donkeys refusing to take another step and soldiers resorting to man's original logistical system: his own muscles.

■ ■ ■ ■

Many of the airlifters for the vital Afghan supply effort are based at Bagram. Those that aren't permanently based there at least spend much of their time at the air base on stopovers between supply runs.

Approaching Bagram by road, visitors see the streams of aircraft overhead long before they see the base's earthen walls. With hundreds of aircraft, big and small, calling Bagram home—and hundreds more visiting—parking quickly becomes an issue. In 2009 air force engineers and Afghan workers labored day and night to add concrete aprons for the expanding airplane population.

As the biggest and most centrally located airfield in Afghanistan, Bagram quickly becomes the main logistical hub for the whole war effort. As Bagram grows too crowded, the military rushes to expand a smaller airfield outside Kandahar, as well as several even smaller satellite strips.

To support the airlift, the air force gathers all its people and planes into functional pools. Everybody flying a particular type of plane lives and works together in Afghanistan, regardless of their old, previously sacrosanct squadron affiliations. For C-130s like Toney's—"H" models—the air force formed a new "expeditionary" airlift squadron, the 774th, and populated it with people and planes from Air National Guard units all over the United States. That keeps down overhead and eliminates downtime between squadron deployments.

Once established, the expeditionary squadrons remain in Afghanistan permanently. Crews and airplanes periodically rotate home to their original squadrons for rest and repair, but the 774th keeps chugging right along. The air force sets up similar expeditionary units for the newer, faster, J-model C-130s and even the larger C-17 airlifters that were considered a "strategic" asset—in other words, especially vital to national defense. The "Afghan airlift" is of such urgency that it shatters old parochial attitudes and breaks down long-standing organizations.

Lt. Col. Dan Krall, a balding, low-talking man, is in charge of one of these new ad hoc units. The way he sees it, the air force hasn't gone far enough in reorganizing its logistical efforts.

In late 2009, Krall commands 120 airmen with the 455th Expeditionary Aerial Port Squadron, a unit that has been created from scratch at Bagram. It was the squadron's job to receive, hold, and prepare for onward delivery all four hundred tons of air cargo and one thousand passengers arriving at Bagram every day. "Massive and complex" is how Krall describes his job.

Krall says planners in the Pentagon and at Central Command, which oversees the wars in Iraq and Afghanistan, tend to have a fairly naive view of Afghan logistics. The planners' attitude toward the frontline logisticians, Krall complains, is to "send it to them 'til they scream—and then keep sending it."

"They tend to think in terms of mass volume, without considering the physical realities on the ground," Krall says. The result by late 2009 is too much stuff arriving at Bagram too fast for Krall to efficiently ship it off to its final destination. That means customers—the army or marines usually—waiting extra days for the supplies they ordered. It also means the army or marines occasionally taking matters into their own hands, as Able Troop does at OP Spur.

Things are improving, slowly. In October 2009 the air force is building a new, bigger passenger terminal and a new, bigger cargo yard at Bagram using some of the $1.3 billion the Pentagon set aside for Afghan construction in 2009. But the yard isn't Krall's only problem. Even with sufficient yard space for orderly, temporary storage, there's a shortage of military airlifters—helicopters and C-130s—that limits how fast Krall can ship things out to the combat units.

That's a problem that will not go away anytime soon. The dearth of military aircraft means Krall relies on contractors—such as KBR and countless Eastern European firms—for some deliveries. The problem there is the contractors' policies. KBR, for instance, requires several days' notice for any shipment. And some contractors refuse to deliver to Afghanistan's most dangerous districts.

Lt. Col. Dan Krall, commander of the 455th Expeditionary Aerial Port Squadron at Bagram Airfield, Afghanistan, in October 2009. DAVID AXE

Their concern is not unfounded. A Russian-made Mi-26 helicopter, operated on a NATO contract by the Moldovan firm Pecotox Air, was hovering with a load of supplies near the town of Sangin in southern Afghanistan on July 14, 2009, when Taliban fighters fired on it with a rocket-propelled grenade. The crew of an accompanying helicopter saw the rocket sheer off the Mi-26's tail boom. All six Ukrainian crew members on board—and an Afghan boy on the ground—died when the thirty-ton chopper spiraled to the ground.[15]

Less than a week later, on July 19, a civilian Mi-8 helicopter operated by a Russian company crashed at the NATO base in Kandahar, killing sixteen passengers and crewmen.[16] In November another contracted Mi-8 crashed in Logar, Able's Troop's province, killing the three crewmen.[17]

The escalating danger posed by Taliban fire and mountainous terrain limits which supply routes civilian contractors will work. Using only military aircraft for certain destinations shrinks the pool of aircraft available to many commanders. That contributes to the growing mountain of stuff accumulating in Krall's cargo yard. By late 2009 Krall's cargo handlers are stacking pallets two stories high at Bagram.

As with the C-130 squadron shuffle, Krall says he wants a new layer of organization to help mediate between the planners back in the States and the tactical logisticians like him. A so-called "theater distribution center" might help smooth the flow of cargo as more and more stuff arrives to supply more and more U.S. and NATO troops. What Krall is asking for, in essence, is to duplicate UPS's regional hub system. For America, military logisticians copy their civilian counterparts at least as often as the civilians take their cues from the military.

■ ■ ■ ■

The cargo streaming into Krall's yard includes a steady stream of MRAPs and M-ATVs to equip the growing NATO army and to replace trucks destroyed in ambushes. By the spring of 2010, Bagram is receiving around thirty blast-resistant vehicles every day. For the aerial porters working Bagram's flight line, this meant dirty, dangerous, and delicate work.

The chartered Atlas Cargo 747-200 freighter is still taxiing to one of the airfield's remote aprons when the aerial porters climb into their pickup trucks, bulldozers, fuel trucks, and thirty-ton-capacity loaders—a sort of massive, motorized, elevating ramp controlled by a single operator sitting in a cube-shaped cabin—and sortie to meet the plane. With military planes such as the C-17 and C-5, unloading MRAPs is easy: unchain them and drive them right off the rear ramp.

With a 747, which has no ramp, just a side door, what should be a simple, ten-minute operation can turn into a ninety-minute ordeal. A 747 fits five M-ATVs—barely—lined nose-to-tail inside the freighter's two-hundred-foot cargo hold. Removing them means angling them out the side door, a task akin to fitting a ten-foot sofa through the three-foot-wide front door of your apartment. Except in this case the sofa is a fifteen-ton armored vehicle worth a million dollars.

The Air National Guard's deadline for enlistment is thirty-four years. S.Sgt. Vinton Velez joined at thirty-four and a half, after losing his job at a shipyard in Guam. With smooth skin and an easy smile, the now-forty-one-year-old Velez looks too young to lead a team of highly skilled airmen performing a dangerous and vital job at one of the world's busiest air bases. But you can't argue with his results.

Velez's crew deployed to Bagram from Guam and joined other airmen from all over the world to form the 455th Expeditionary Aerial Port Squadron. On a typical day, Velez and his six airmen might unload two planeloads of M-ATVs. The 747s are the toughest. "Our record is thirty-four minutes," says Airman First Class Brandon Arleth, one of Velez's forklift drivers. Times depend on all the 747's systems working perfectly—especially the electrically powered rollers installed on the plane's floor. "If the rollers are okay, it's easy," Velez says.

Today, the rollers aren't okay. The Atlas plane's two loadmasters try to angle the M-ATV nearest the cargo door. One of them, a burly middle-aged man with an imposing moustache, twists the joystick mounted to the fuselage wall that under normal circumstances would control the rollers, rotating the vehicle about its vertical axis, angling it to slide out the door with just a couple inches' clearance.

But the M-ATV is too heavy. The rollers whine and strain but don't budge the massive vehicle. The man with the moustache rolls his eyes. "We're going to have problems." He calls to Velez, who is busy untying the green nylon tethers lashing the M-ATVs to the deck. "We need more people to manhandle the trucks!"

Velez and another airman join the two Atlas loadmasters. The rollers might not be able to rotate the truck, but they still afford a lower friction coefficient. That's the only way just four normal men can drag a fifteen-ton object several feet. They pull the MRAP backward to the very rear of the hold, tug on one corner to rotate it at the right angle to fit, and help it the first few inches out the door.

They try again with the joystick. This time the rollers, partially relieved of their burden, manage to creep the vehicle forward, out of the plane, and onto the sliding metal surface atop the raised platform of the first loader.

The loader, with its huge, scissors-style telescoping supports, lowers the M-ATV to a second loader, lined up with the first. The second loader is set at its lowest level, its platform resting on its chassis with its ten huge wheels. The loader's surface is designed to slide back and forth to transfer its load from one end to the other without the load having to move on its own. The first M-ATV eases across the loaders, away from the 747, finally clearing the airplane's left wingtip.

A forklift deposits a simple steel ramp at the end of the second loader. Another forklift pries loose heavy wooden chocks from beneath the MRAP. Now the truck can drive under its own power. One of Velez's crew members yanks open the thick armored door and climbs into the driver's seat.

Aerial porters from the 455th Expeditionary Aerial Port Squadron unload M-ATV blast-resistant vehicles from an Atlas Cargo 747 freighter at Bagram in March 2010. DAVID AXE

The M-ATV's interior is swathed in protective plastic. Connectors and cables terminate where radios and other gear are due to be installed by the receiving unit. The factory-fresh truck still has that new-car smell. The aerial porter presses the ignition button, shifts the truck into reverse, and backs it down the ramp. Shifting into drive, the porter maneuvers to the head of what will be eventually be a baby-duck row of lifesaving trucks.

By now Velez and crew are in a groove. The overburdened rollers have slowed them down, but their efficient teamwork helps make up some of the lost time. It takes ninety minutes to download all five M-ATVs. That's far short of their record but not bad considering the kludgy system they're dealing with: a brand-new vehicle that no one worked with before a couple months ago, crammed with inches to spare into a cargo plane that was never designed for such loads.

It's dark when the last M-ATV comes off the loaders, and the porters have to work by the forklifts' headlights. At last they park their loaders and forklifts, and climb into the M-ATVs to drive them across the runway, past rows of C-130s resting after a long day's work, to Krall's cargo yard. The receiving unit—from the army, most likely—can pick them up in the morning.

Behind the wheel of the last M-ATV in the line, Arleth shrugs. "It's only five M-ATVs," he says. It's nearly 9:00. He's been out on the ramp shifting cargo all day without a break. Moreover, he's worked all day, every day, since arriving at Bagram more than a month before. His first day off is coming up. "I'll come into work in my PT gear"—shorts and a T-shirt—"watch TV and watch everybody else work," he says.

■ ■ ■ ■

All day and all night, the C-17s, C-5s, 747s, and other large freighters keep coming. All day and all night, the aerial porters download their cargo and shift it to the yard. By day, the 774th and other airlift squadrons fly back-to-back missions, chipping away at the mountain-like backlog.

With around a dozen C-130s to fly up to several missions per day, the 774th's plywood huts, clustered along the middle section of the Bagram's parallel, ten-thousand-foot runways, buzz with activity around the clock. A couple hours before takeoff, Toney's five-person crew—the two loadmasters plus a copilot, a navigator, and a flight engineer—gather around cups of coffee for a briefing. They don their survival gear, including emergency radios and handguns, and ride a van out to the flight line, where maintainers have just finished fueling and performing systems checks on Torque 41.

For relatively easy airdrops, old-fashioned parachutes will do. In 2009 the air force is using a disposable chute made from recycled plastic—similar in texture to a tarp you might buy at a home-improvement store—to replace expensive fabric parachutes that for economy's sake had to be recovered, cleaned, repaired, and reused. For tougher drops where accuracy really matters, the air force has a GPS-guided model.

Torque 41's mission doesn't call for the pricey, GPS-steered Joint Precision Air Drop System, but it still demands a high degree of precision lest stray pallets strike an Afghan home or fall too far away from the marines to be recovered. Toney and the flight crew's focus hones to a razor's edge as they approach the drop zone, keeping an eye out for hand-launched unmanned aerial vehicles belonging to a nearby British Army unit. In the cargo hold, Lanham checks the load while Lavin opens the ramp. Torque 41 is mere seconds away now.

Like flying, mechanical versions of pack donkeys, C-130s in Afghanistan handle a wide array of missions. Besides the regular supply drops and the routine shuttle flights carrying people and supplies into the country by way of Bagram, Hercules also function as air ambulances and aerial tankers. Helicopters, especially the powerful CH-47s, are probably the most important aircraft for the Afghan war effort, but C-130s are close behind. This despite the high average age of the American C-130 fleet. Torque 41 is pushing forty years old.

The new-generation C-130J is a regular sight at Bagram and at the smaller, more austere southern hub of Kandahar, but many of the Hercules are E and H models that have already seen decades of hard service. Old airplanes add an extra element of risk.

At Bagram, Maj. Christopher Day commands the 455th Expeditionary Aeromedical Evacuation Squadron, tasked with transporting injured troops to hospitals in the United States and Europe. For all but the longest flights, Day's five-man teams and their patients ride in C-130s.

In the evacuation role, the transport plane can accept stretchers and medical equipment including a cardiac monitor and defibrillator plus oxygen and bags of medicine. While the medics' focus is on keeping their patients healthy and comfortable, they must also deal with all the risks associated with air travel—especially air travel in an ancient military transport.

Day recalls one evacuation mission on a C-130 bound for Kandahar. "We were twenty minutes out over the wire when the [auxiliary generator] on the C-130 caught on fire." As the smoking aircraft angled in for an emergency landing, Day's team braced the patients. "We did the emergency landing, did an emergency egress—meaning we took all patients possible off aircraft." The walking patients were the first off. Once they were at a safe distance, Day's people raced back into the aircraft to retrieve the two litter patients. "There wasn't any time to think," Day adds. "My crew actually did everything right."

That isn't always the case. As Torque 41 nears the marines' drop zone on the October morning, Toney tells his loadmasters to open the ramp and prepare to drop the supplies. Lavin, a reservist and the junior loadmaster on the flight, presses the button to open the ramp—but fails to open it all the way. Lanham has to get on the intercom and correct her as the Hercules drones inexorably toward the marines' location. Just in time, Lavin gets the ramp fully open.

Toney yanks back the stick. The C-130's nose rises, its tail drops, and eight pallets of food and water rattle along the metal rollers in the floor and slide out the open ramp. Parachutes blossom. The supplies swing side-to-side as they fall toward the hungry and thirsty marines down below. Lanham climbs through the hold to the still-open ramp to check on the rapidly shrinking chutes. He appears satisfied.

Pallets safely on their way, the loadmasters close the ramp. "Good recovery on that drop, loads," Toney tells Lanham and Lavin as he turns the aircraft back toward Bagram. "It's not an easy thing to do."

■ ■ ■ ■

Despite the heroic efforts of aircrews like Toney's and cargo handlers like Krall's, supplies pile up in ever-higher stacks in yards at bases like Bagram. C-130s and the occasional ground convoy can move a large proportion of the accumulated materials, but many deliveries—especially those to frontline units in populous, mountainous areas—require helicopters. The roads are too dangerous for trucks. And air drops demand huge swaths of empty ground to ensure the falling pallets don't accidentally kill civilians. Only helicopters can deposit people and supplies with precision and safety in even the most crowded, hostile environments.

It was a rotating shift of army helicopters that delivered the supplies that Able Troop used to build the mountaintop OP Spur. Most of Able Troop's supplies, and all of its visitors, arrive by helicopter at the unit's soccer-field-size landing zone. Forget the Taliban, Al Qaeda, the Al Haqqani extremist group, and assorted violent criminals infesting Logar Province. "My biggest headache," says Lt. Col. Thomas Gukeisen, commander of a combined U.S. and Czech battalion that includes the generator-hauling Able Troop, "is vertical lift." Meaning helicopters.

It's a warm day in October 2009 at Gukeisen's headquarters, built around an old compound that once belonged to a Turkish gravel company. The American base, just outside the town of Altimur, sprawls over an area the size of several football fields. Parking for the battalion's hundreds of trucks accounts for approximately half of the base. A large helicopter landing zone covers most of the rest. Several times a day, military and civilian helicopters chase the sounds of their rotors through the mountains to Altimur, running a regular shuttle between Gukeisen's unit and its parent command at a nearby base called Shank.

The constant, energetic groan of helicopters is a signature of the Americans' presence. Just a year earlier, there was mostly silence. At that time, there were just a hundred Americans in all of Logar, hunkered on a hilltop at the center of what would become Gukeisen's Forward Operating Base Altimur. With no one to resist them, the Taliban and other violent elements dominated the province. Then, in early 2009, the Pentagon began shifting troops from Iraq to Afghanistan. Around a thousand made their way to Logar, expanding the existing hilltop base and establishing numerous, smaller outposts across the province. Each was a wedge inserted forcibly into the solid block of Taliban control.

Each wedge required a forceful push by a small armada of helicopters. It's the helicopters, with their ability to quickly haul people and supplies over the heads of the bad guys with their roadside bombs, that are the key to any U.S. operation. The hundreds of helicopters in NATO's arsenal represent the alliance's greatest strength in Afghanistan. But they also are its greatest weakness. Helicopters enable the coalition to expand into areas that otherwise would remain out of its reach. But the troops, once inserted, are almost totally reliant on the helicopters to keep them fed and supplied and to evacuate the wounded. With its helicopters, NATO has become addicted to a lifesaving drug.

It took a year and literally thousands of helicopter flights, but by late 2009 Logar is mostly under NATO control. But coalition troops have yet to expand as widely in neighboring Wardak Province. It falls to twenty-five-year-old U.S. Army first lieutenant Colin Riker and around a hundred young infantrymen to do in Wardak what Gukeisen's troops have done in Logar. In August, Riker's Bravo Company, Second Battalion, Eighty-seventh Infantry Regiment, is ordered to build a new outpost in Wardak's Nerkh District.

The first troops go in by road, fighting the whole way to the location of their new base in the district's restive west. Spc. Justin Pellerin dies and several soldiers are hurt when a huge buried bomb splits an MRAP in half. Blackhawk medical choppers swoop in to retrieve the body and the injured. Despite their losses, the Americans reach their destination in Nerkh and throw up an earthen wall.

Outpost established. Now Bravo Company just has to hold it.

Riker decides the road that claimed Pellerin is too dangerous for regular ground convoys. All movements between Bravo's main outpost and the new outpost will have to be by helicopter. The distance amounts to barely four miles. The average flight time is just three minutes. Even so, a regular shuttle is too taxing for the stretched-thin aviators at Shank. Flight cancellations frequently strand Bravo's soldiers at the patrol base for days longer than planned.

Riker is at an impasse. "We can't do anything here until we own the roads," he says. "The helicopters are a stopgap solution." But it's a stopgap that risks becoming permanent in Nerkh and across Wardak and the rest of Afghanistan. Like Gukeisen and Able Troop, and like the whole Afghan war effort, Riker is at the helicopters' mercy.

12
UPS—in Space

The Pentagon was acutely aware of its helicopter problem in Afghanistan. After a flurry of studies, Secretary of Defense Gates concluded in April 2009 that the number of choppers wasn't the real problem. In all, the U.S. military owned some six thousand helicopters—by far the world's largest chopper fleet. In 2009 alone the army would spend $7 billion to buy nearly two hundred new helicopters—a single-year purchase that was larger than most nations' entire chopper fleets. Navy and Marine Corps purchases in the same year added scores more helicopters.[1]

"The primary limitation on helicopter capacity is not airframes but shortages of maintenance crews and pilots," Gates asserted at a Pentagon press conference. His investigators had found a 20 percent shortfall in army aircrew levels. The ground-combat branch said it needed around fifteen hundred new chopper pilots per year to meet demand but was getting only twelve hundred. So Gates promised an extra $500 million in 2009 for "recruiting and training more Army helicopter crews."[2]

Eight days later, Gates dropped by the army's main helicopter schoolhouse at Fort Rucker, Alabama, to underscore his plans. The extra money, Gates said, would "increase the throughput of pilots and maintenance crews for our helicopters" and "help train more instructors, help with the infrastructure and possibly get more airframes" for training.[3] "Welcome news," Bobby Bright, congressman for Rucker's district, said of Gates' plans.[4]

While the Pentagon poured money into the chopper force, military scientists were asking if there weren't a better way. One thing U.S. troops needed, they surmised, was a "just-in-time" delivery capability similar to UPS's—

something small, light, and fast for moving vital supplies on short notice, with minimal fuss.

A militarized UPS might not fully replace helicopters and C-130s—which, after all, are scaled for bulk deliveries—but it could help relieve some of the logistical burden, say by dropping off a generator at Able Troop's mountain-top observation post or by shuttling food, water, and ammunition between Riker's two outposts in Nerkh District.

In 2005, the Pentagon's fringe research wing had turned to robots to eventually replace army truck drivers on Iraq's bloody highways. Four years later, researchers proposed that robots begin supplanting some helicopters in Afghanistan, too.

There was precedent for cargo-hauling 'bots. In 2001, Canadian tech firm Mist Mobility flew the first example of its SnowGoose robot parafoil. Essentially a small-capacity cargo pod fitted with a tiny computer "brain," a propeller, and a parachute-like sail, the $250,000 SnowGoose took off from the back of a truck or launched out the back of a C-130.

Like a hang-glider, it motored along under its parafoil at just thirty-five miles per hour, guided by GPS, and dropped its cargo over a designated location before turning around and heading home. "It's not complicated," said Clark Butner, a navy robot specialist. "The most complicated thing may be repacking the parasail after a mission."[5]

But that simplicity came at a price. SnowGoose could carry just a couple hundred pounds for a couple hundred miles, under the best of conditions. It was a niche capability for hauling such things as propaganda leaflets, small batches of blood plasma, or a few hundred rounds of ammunition. SnowGoose was strictly for emergencies.[6]

For that reason, only U.S. Special Operations Command, or SOCOM, was interested. It bought its first three SnowGooses in 2003 and laid plans for another twenty-five or so. It would take six years of bloody conflict for the military to get serious about truly effective cargo robots.[7]

■ ■ ■ ■

The marines were the first to take the leap. In October 2009 the Corps approached Boeing and chopper-maker Kaman and asked them to build a cargo 'bot bigger and more powerful than SnowGoose. Both companies already had robots that could be modified to suit the marines' needs.

Boeing's A-160T unmanned helicopter—a spin-off of the Robinson R-22 light chopper design—was thirty-five feet long and cruised at twenty thousand feet for up to eighteen hours. It could make nearly 150 miles per hour in a dash or trade speed for a payload of more than one ton.

The A-160 had been designed eleven years prior for surveillance missions, but its large payload made it a potentially excellent cargo carrier. "We are confident in its ability to meet the requirements of this critical mission," crowed John Groenenboom, the Boeing program manager.[8]

The marines gave the Chicago-based company $500,000 for a series of tests. The plan was to "deploy" an A-160 to a simulated forward operating base somewhere in the United States and have it fly mock cargo runs between the base and another outpost for three days straight.[9]

Connecticut-based Kaman got $860,000 to run similar tests using the pilotless version of its K-MAX chopper, which features separate twin rotors that intermesh as they rotate. That, and an ultra-slim fuselage, give the K-MAX one of the most impressive payloads of any aircraft: up to thirty-five hundred pounds for a helicopter weighing just five thousand pounds.[10]

While the two chopper-makers prepped for their cargo trials, other armed services caught the robotic-logistics bug. The navy said it might assign its new Northrop Grumman-built MQ-8 unmanned spy helicopters to supply missions, flying between ships. And in October 2009, the air force announced that it, too, would develop an unmanned airlifter, with substantial funding beginning in 2011.[11]

It would be a racehorse compared to the navy's and marines' donkeys. The air force said its cargo 'bot should fly 250 miles per hour out to a range of five hundred miles, while hauling up to three thousand pounds. And it should be able to take off on a runway no longer than three hundred feet, as well as glide out the back of a larger cargo plane, much like the SnowGoose.[12]

"An interesting set of attributes," mused one aviation writer, for no normal helicopter was capable of such speed, and no normal airplane could glide out the back of another. The most likely candidate would be a ducted-fan design: essentially, a disk-shaped UFO with a downward-pointing propeller in its middle. Several companies had tested ducted-fan 'bots, but so far no army or air force had bought any. They were just too weird.[13]

For one Marine Corps scientist, weird was no obstacle. To Roosevelt Lafontant, a saucer-shaped robot was downright mundane. For all its UFO-like appearance, a ducted-fan flying robot represented fairly modest technology. When Lafontant imagined the future of just-in-time military logistics, he pictured something truly out of science fiction.

His idea—to boost people and supplies into space, and back down, aboard a two-stage, reuseable "space plane"—was born that fateful night in November 2001 when Thompson and her fellow marine aviators flew four hundred miles into Afghanistan aboard their ancient, leaky, stall-prone CH-53 helicopters.

■ ■ ■ ■

In the winter of 2001, Lafontant—a then-forty-four-year-old New Yorker—was working in the Pentagon as a satellite-reconnaissance specialist. He and his coworkers had paid close attention to the unfolding Afghanistan war. Reading about the marines' risky, long-range assault on Kandahar, Lafontant found himself feeling troubled. "There had to be a better way," he recalls thinking.

By the spring of 2002, U.S. forces in Afghanistan were locked in bloody cave fighting as they looked for Osama bin Laden. They would turn up nothing. Years later, intelligence reports would surface that indicated bin Laden had evaded capture by mere days.

In April, Lafontant lunched with his friend Franz Gayl in the Pentagon cafeteria. Gayl, a balding forty-nine-year-old former marine with a toothy grin, was a science adviser to a high-level Marine Corps office. The two men got to talking about ways the United States might have gotten troops into Afghanistan, faster and without all the hassle of negotiating with Pakistan.

To Lafontant, easy access meant space. A nation's airspace extends to an altitude of fifty miles. Above that, nobody owns anything, and nobody can stop you from flying right through. Problem is, fifty miles is very nearly orbital altitude. It would take a rocket ship to fly that high. So a rocket ship is what Lafontant pitched to Gayl.

Lafontant described his concept in broad strokes, leaving the details to future engineers. The rocket ship should take off from the U.S. carrying a squad of marines and their gear—that's thirteen people and around a ton of stuff—and deliver its cargo anywhere in the world within two hours. For ease of use, the ship should probably take off and land like an airplane. It should be reusable, in order to keep down costs. It would be, in essence, an airplane traveling in space—a space plane.

Rockets, even reusable rockets capable of lofting heavy payloads and landing like an airplane, are old hat for NASA. The space agency already possessed a system closely matching Lafontant's basic concept. That would be the Space Shuttle, a multiuse transport capable of entering orbit and returning, in just hours'time.

But NASA's Shuttle missions are actually few and far between, and quite risky. In thirty years of service ending in 2011, the five operational Space Shuttles flew just 135 missions, each at a cost of around $500 million. Two crashed, killing their whole crews. Every mission required months of advance planning. To be militarily useful, a Space Shuttle–like transport would have to be much cheaper, safer, much more responsive, and capable of far heavier use.[14]

Still, to Lafontant the idea seemed sound. Gayl agreed but pointed out that developing a military space plane from scratch would be expensive and time-consuming. Lafontant thought about it and guessed it might take thirty years. "We should start getting to work on this now," he said, if either men were to see a military space plane take flight in his lifetime.

First, Lafontant and Gayl gave Lafontant's idea a name. They called it Small Unit Space Transport and Insertion—SUSTAIN for short. The two men sketched out SUSTAIN's theoretical parameters—how much it should carry, how far, and how fast—and presented the proposal to Gayl's boss, Lt. Gen. Emil Bedard, the Marine Corps' deputy commandant for plans, policies, and operations.

Marine generals are not known for their flights of fancy, so it's testimony to the feasibility of Lafontant and Gayl's vision that Bedard endorsed SUSTAIN. Suddenly, a space transport was on the marines'official wish list.

But going from some "maybe someday" list to actual, funded development was a big leap—one that many far-out weapons systems ideas never made. To get any traction in the real world, SUSTAIN would need a sponsor organization within in the Pentagon bureaucracy.

Lafontant's space plane eventually found its patron in the form of the Marine Corps's tiny Space Integration Branch in Virginia. Here, a pugnacious colonel named Jack Wassink directed a team of a hundred space specialists whose job it was to keep marine commanders supplied with satellite intelligence. Wassink was a surprisingly quick convert to the gospel of SUSTAIN.

"All SUSTAIN is, is a requirement to move marines very rapidly from one place to another," Wassink says. "Space lends itself to that role because that's the environment to get the speed to move a force anywhere in the world inside two hours."

But there was a problem. The Marine Corps is a small force with just 170,000 active-duty personnel. The Corps is technically subordinate to the navy, and its needs usually place a distant second to the navy's—and to every other military branch's, for that matter.

Historically, the marines get just six percent of Defense Department funding, despite possessing more than 10 percent of the Department's active manpower. "It's certainly not something the Marine Corps would be able to acquire on its own," Wassink says of SUSTAIN.

Wassink's boss agreed. "For affordability, we must coordinate . . . our technology needs with other Department of Defense and nonmilitary users," Brig. Gen. Richard Zilmer told Congress in July 2003. Zilmer mentioned NASA as a potential partner. Lafontant added the air force and DARPA to that list.

In SUSTAIN's early years, advocates mobilized to win over other agencies, industry, and Congress. "We saw the entire gamut of reactions," Wassink muses. "Some people didn't get past the past the giggle factor."

In other words, however feasible it might be in reality, SUSTAIN just *sounded* outlandish. Lafontant says he understood the laughter. When congressmen and military planners imagined marines in space, their minds probably latched onto the only images they could recall, and those were all from science fiction, which few of them took seriously.

The heroes from Robert Heinlein's borderline-fascist young-adult novel *Starship Troopers*. The space infantry from the lesser James Bond flick *Moonraker*. The Colonial Marines from *Aliens*. To win over the people who held the purse strings, SUSTAIN would have to overcome decades of accumulated sci-fi clichés.

Then, in 2004, something happened at a remote airstrip in the Mojave Desert that stopped people giggling. In June a simple, egg-shaped vehicle called SpaceShipOne—designed, built, and paid for by private entrepreneurs—boosted to an altitude of more than fifty miles, then landed like an airplane, demonstrating in one dramatic flight how SUSTAIN might look, for real.

Over the next five years, privately funded space planes from the Mojave would parallel, and propel, Lafontant's vision of a military space plane, demonstrating once again the intimate link between military and civilian transport and logistics that underpins American power and prosperity.

■ ■ ■ ■

SpaceShipOne was the child of brilliant parents. In the late nineties, famed aerospace designer Burt Rutan began tinkering with concepts for simple, cheap spaceflight. At the time, NASA was trying to master the science and engineering behind "single-stage" access to space—in other words, getting into orbit using just one rocket, instead of the more expensive stacked, multiple-stage rockets that were then standard.

By contrast Rutan kept two stages but broke them into two separate vehicles: a high-flying airplane "mother ship" and a simple rocket-powered vehicle that would launch from the mother ship, benefiting from that craft's altitude boost, spend several minutes on the edge of space, and then land on its own like an airplane.

Rutan's faithfulness to the proven two-stage concept paid off as NASA's single-stage efforts all failed one by one, at the cost of billions of dollars. In 2001 Microsoft billionaire Paul Allen agreed to underwrite Rutan's mother-ship-and-rocket-plane combination, to the tune of $20 million.[15]

The goal was to develop a reliable space plane that could carry tourists into near-orbit for a tidy profit. Tickets for Rutan's space planes began selling years before any vehicles were actually ready for paying customers. A reservation cost up to $200,000. Reportedly hundreds of tickets had sold by 2009, even though the first commercial flight was still years away.[16]

Rutan and Allen weren't the only people interested in space tourism. They were just the most prominent members of a movement calling itself "New Space" that wanted to get back to basics in space travel. So many New Space startups were chasing space planes by the early 2000s that a nonprofit group made a formal competition out of it. The X Prize Foundation offered $10 million to the first team to loft the same manned spacecraft to an altitude of one hundred kilometers twice in two weeks.[17]

On June 21, 2004, Rutan's White Knight mother ship launched the SpaceShipOne rocket on its first test flight. The four-ton, six-foot-diameter SpaceShipOne, with a single pilot aboard, fired a rubber-and-laughing-gas motor and climbed at eighty-four degrees for just over a minutes, tracing a thin arc over the Mojave.[18]

When the ship touched down, it represented the first successful private spaceflight. Four months later, Rutan's space plane would complete the two back-to-back flights required to win the X Prize.

Air Force Brig. Gen. S. Pete Worden, Director for Development and Transformation at Air Force Space Command, was sitting in the stands at the Mojave airport that October day as White Knight and SpaceShipOne proved that cheap spaceflight was possible. Worden knew of SUSTAIN and favored the concept's development. "It's just a scaled-up version of that that would do this [SUSTAIN] mission," he commented later.

With SpaceShipOne's impressive feat in the backs of everyone's minds, Lafontant and the other SUSTAIN boosters continued making the rounds in Washington, trying to impress upon anyone who would listen the feasibility, and desirability, of a military space transport. "The giggle factor is gone now," Lafontant says.

But that didn't mean anyone in the federal government was ready to throw actual money at building SUSTAIN. Even if technically feasible, the space transport would stretch American aerospace engineering and military strategy—and potentially the federal government's wallet, as well. For that reason, SUSTAIN would remain a "fantasy," said military analyst John Pike.

Dwayne Day, a space analyst, was less harsh but still highly skeptical. "Keep in mind that SpaceShipOne's payload is limited. If you want to carry a lot of armed combat troops and their equipment, you need a much bigger ship."

And that would demand huge advancements in science and engineering, pointed out Preston Carter, a space researcher at Lawrence Livermore National Laboratory. SUSTAIN, Carter said, "is beyond normal propulsion and normal structures."

SUSTAIN advocates realized that in addition to SpaceShipOne's proof-of-concept, they would need two things: some serious research muscle to back the program and patience. Lafontant estimated it would be 2012 before all the technology was ready. And that was before the 2008–2009 global economic crisis took a big bite out of federal research budgets.

In their first conversation about SUSTAIN, Gayl had told Lafontant that it might take thirty years before the space plane flew an operational mission.

Gayl had tossed out that number just to mean "a long time." But it became increasingly clear that SUSTAIN might *literally* take thirty years.

■ ■ ■ ■

With a growing sense of realism toward the challenges it faced but propelled by the image of SpaceShipOne arcing into low orbit, Wassink's space office, SUSTAIN's first official sponsor, continued drumming up support.

Worden was key. In 2004, the bespectacled officer retired from the air force and, after a stint advising Congress, joined NASA as the director of the Ames Research Center, located at Moffett Field, the airship base outside San Francisco. Worden gave the SUSTAIN boosters access to the space agency's research.

The avuncular former general also helped sell the SUSTAIN concept to the Air Force Research Laboratories, which had a $100 million program called Falcon, aimed at developing an aircraft that had a lot in common with space planes like SpaceShipOne and SUSTAIN. Falcon would be "hypersonic"—that is, capable of speeds faster than Mach 5.

With the weight of NASA and the air force behind him, an empowered Worden personally solicited the final holdout, DARPA.

DARPA said no. It was a big blow to the SUSTAIN team. But Worden was philosophical. "If the air force pursues this and shows more feasibility, DARPA might be a future player," he says.

Even without DARPA, Wassink's office had forged sufficient ties to capture a great proportion of the technology needed to build SUSTAIN. "One of the critical aspects of SUSTAIN is ultimately the ability to access space with 'aircraft-like'operations," Wassink says. "It does us no good to have the ability to get anywhere on the globe within two hours if it takes us days, weeks, or months to get ready to do so."

In addition to quicker prelaunch procedures, that means durable heat shields in place of the fragile tiles used by older rocket craft such as the Space Shuttle. And while two stages are a given, which combination of stages is best depends on whom you ask. SpaceShipOne used the subsonic White Knight mother ship, powered by old-fashioned jet engines, as its first stage—and fired its own rubber-and-laughing-gas engine for its second stage.

A military version of SpaceShipOne might call for more powerful propulsion. That could mean a mother ship based on the air force's Falcon vehicle, flying at hypersonic speed, then launching a separate vehicle powered by its own rocket engine.

If SUSTAIN used a hypersonic mother ship, it would entail yet more choices. With hypersonic aircraft, "there are several different approaches" to propulsion, says Jim Pittman, a NASA scientist. "The use of rockets to boost the vehicle to hypersonic speed is one approach. [Or] you could look at an air-breathing solution from take-off to hypersonic speed to landing."

Or you could mix rockets, old-fashioned jet turbines, and so-called scramjets (basically brute-force jets for super-high speeds) in what Pittman calls a "combined cycle."

Regardless, a hypersonic mother ship would require big advancements, including new, super-tough construction materials capable of withstanding, over and over again, the intense heat generated by the vehicle's powerful motors. For those materials, SUSTAIN could draw upon a navy program called RAT-TLRS, short for Revolutionary Approach to Time-Critical Long-Range Strike.

RATTLRS, which was meant to produce a hypersonic cruise missile, compelled the navy to experiment with all sorts of "new alloys, composites, ceramics," according to Bob Duge, a manager from Rolls-Royce North America working on the program.

NASA proposed that new materials might not be necessary if you shaped a SUSTAIN-like vehicle the right way. "New materials are required for coatings that can take multiple [flights], but a lot of the thermal issues are creative design issues," says David Glass, a researcher for the space agency. "Creative design" means shaping a vehicle in ways that transfer heat away from sensitive components and people.

Laughing-gas motors, hypersonic mother ships, advanced ceramics, creative shaping—in the flurry of new ideas suddenly swirling around SUSTAIN just a few years after its inception, it was easy to lose sight of the concept's two biggest problems.

The lesser of the two was financial. How much would SUSTAIN cost to actually build and operate? No one seemed willing to even hazard a guess. But a single Space Shuttle flight cost $500 million, not counting the decades of research and development supporting the Shuttle program. Factor in the R&D, and each Shuttle flight cost more than $1 *billion*.

It wasn't hard to imagine a strictly military space plane winding up an even bigger financial drain. Rutan, the man behind SpaceShipOne, predicted that SUSTAIN would probably end up being "relatively expensive" for the capability it delivered.

Military analyst Thomas Barnett was less sanguine. "Here's the kicker: huge cost," Barnett wrote about SUSTAIN. "And what does this spaceship deliver?" he scoffed. "Thirteen combat troops and their weapons."[19]

But space expert Eric Sterner, from the Marshall Institute in Washington, D.C., recalled that FedEx founder Fred Smith had encountered the same resistance thirty years ago when he proposed overnight package delivery at what was then perceived as a high price. "The legend is that . . . people laughed at him, and lo and behold, now people are willing to pay ten bucks to get a letter from one place to another."

Worden had the last word on the cost issue, for the time being. "Can we afford it? That's the whole question," Worden says. Again, he pointed to SpaceShipOne and the estimated $20 million it cost to design, build, and fly the egg-shaped space plane on several flights in 2004. "If commercial folks with their own money are developing these things, yes [we can afford it]," Worden says. His implication is that SUSTAIN had to stick closely to SpaceShipOne's model and avoid the "gold-plating" that traditionally jacks up the complexity and price of military systems.

That said, in the early years cost wasn't really SUSTAIN's biggest problem. After all, SUSTAIN was still purely a concept, assigned as a side project to an obscure Pentagon space office. All the real tech development was being funded separately, for separate and officially unrelated initiatives like Falcon and RATTLRS. Up to 2008, SUSTAIN hadn't really cost anyone a penny.

No, five years after Lafontant dreamed up his space transport, the concept's biggest problem was *conceptual*. Once you've designed and built a militarized version of SpaceShipOne, piled in a bunch of marines, and landed them halfway around the world just two hours after taking off, how do you get them home when the mission's over?

SpaceShipOne required a mother ship, and that mother ship needed a runway and lots of support personnel on the ground to service it. If you had those things waiting at the marines' destination, the argument went, you wouldn't have needed to land the marines from space to begin with: you would've simply chartered a 747.

SUSTAIN was for delivering people to the middle of nowhere, through hostile airspace, practically instantly. "Probably the most difficult challenge,"

Wassink confesses, "would be extracting the personnel," after delivery. Without extraction, any SUSTAIN mission would be strictly one-way. Americans have never much embraced suicide missions.

■ ■ ■ ■

The extraction problem was an obvious one but one that Lafontant and the other SUSTAIN boosters had first ignored and later downplayed in their eagerness to promote their space transport. But as Falcon and RATTLRS and other programs began slowly proving the technology that would eventually make SUSTAIN possible, and the date approached when someone would have to ask Congress for real money to start bending metal, SUSTAIN's advocates had to face the music. Their original concept simply wouldn't work in the real world.

As that realization dawned, key figures left the fold. Lafontant retired and took a job with Schafer, a Massachusetts-based company that builds space equipment. He continued advising on SUSTAIN but only unofficially and informally. Bedard retired. Gayl got into some controversy arguing for faster purchases of MRAPs for marines in Iraq and wound up sequestered in a dead-end posting. Wassink left the Space Integration Branch for another position, and that organization gave up its space plane advocacy role. By 2008 it looked like SUSTAIN might wind up grounded by its own enormous ambition.

But SUSTAIN had always been a marine's idea, and marines aren't known for giving up easily. "I admire marines for their persistence," Worden says. True to Worden's assessment, marine colonel Paul Damphousse rode to SUSTAIN's rescue.

Damphousse, with the Pentagon's secretive National Security Space Office, assumed sponsorship of SUSTAIN in 2008. In just one year, he totally revamped the concept and sold the new, improved version to all the most important people in Washington and the aerospace industry.

One solution, Damphousse realized, was to skirt the people-recovery problem—by removing the people. Once again, robots saved the day. And in doing so, they helped transform SUSTAIN from a somewhat loopy, potentially very expensive assault ship, into a much more versatile, and potentially affordable, logistical vehicle. Instead of human pilots and passengers, SUSTAIN would at first have a robotic pilot and a strictly matériel payload.

Lafontant's manned, space people transport, became an unmanned space *cargo* transport.

Damphousse's changes represented a growing sense of reality inside the SUSTAIN team. The space plane would have to evolve slowly, from an initially modest, robotic capability into something taking full advantage of the near-orbital medium—with people at the controls. "To go to rapid-response, point-to-point manned capability is a giant leap," Damphousse says, "[but] after some sort of unmanned point-to-point—after that, a manned demonstrator would be valid."

The vehicle's payload would evolve, too, from material to human. "In certain scenarios, we would still like to put people on the ground," Damphousse says. But for the first few years of SUSTAIN operations, the space plane would probably only deliver cargo. The payload might be actual supplies, like those the air force's C-130 crews haul around Afghanistan every day. SUSTAIN could drop the supplies by parachute and use its remaining altitude to make for a nearby friendly country with long runways.

Or the mother ship-boosted SUSTAIN might itself turn into a mother ship once it reached the target area and deploy unmanned aerial vehicles in areas "where we don't have UAVs," Damphousse proposed. The UAVs, if they were of the cargo variety, could then fan out, simultaneously delivering critical supplies to small ground teams spread across hundreds and hundreds of miles of contested terrain. Configured like that, SUSTAIN would represent a sort of military super-FedEx.

Damphousse's proposals forced a whole new way of thinking about the space plane. Instead of using it for the initial assault into enemy territory, the Pentagon would send in troops by other means—and use SUSTAIN to feed and supply them, super-fast.

In that way, SUSTAIN joined SnowGoose, , K-MAX, and the air force's projected robotic airlifter—not to mention the Urban Challenge racers and CAST the robot truck-driver—as key parts of the Pentagon's plan for robotic logistics.

With the conceptual problem mostly solved, Damphousse worked fast to tweak the tech-development strategy for SUSTAIN. Where previous SUSTAIN cheerleaders had counted on big, separate military programs like Falcon and RATTLRS to produce the technology that would go into the space plane, Damphousse preferred an entrepreneurial approach. Two years prior, Worden had stressed that SUSTAIN would have to mimic SpaceShipOne in order to be truly affordable. Damphousse took Worden's words to heart.

In the fall of 2008, he convened a hush-hush panel of senior Pentagon officials to mull over SUSTAIN's "concept of operations"—CONOPS, in military-speak. Officials representing the various military branches plus SOCOM decided how their respective forces might actually use a space plane, provided the marines managed to build one.

They combined their conclusions into a CONOPS document. In February 2009, Damphousse invited representatives from across the space industry—including starving engineers from what amounted to garage-based New Space startups—to the very first SUSTAIN engineering conference.

He disseminated an unclassified version of the CONOPS to the assembled scientists, engineers, and managers. The idea was to get the industry folks thinking about ways they might be able to help build SUSTAIN and how they might benefit from the project.

In 2003 General Zilmer had told Congress that the marines would have to find partners inside *and* outside government in order to make SUSTAIN a reality. But for SUSTAIN's first five years, the marines mostly worked within the Pentagon and NASA to advance their space plane. This was at a time when the only new, viable space plane anywhere was Rutan's SpaceShipOne, a commercial design. It wasn't until Damphousse came along that the Marines really began selling SUSTAIN to the people who were in the best position to build it.

"We are interested in leveraging and catalyzing," Damphousse explains later. He says making SUSTAIN a strictly government program was the best way to kill it, as its cost would surely escalate just like the Space Shuttle's had. Not to mention Pentagon-only tech development is notoriously slow. "If you leave it in the traditional military procurement system, you've got long way to go," Sterner says.

Nobody wanted to repeat the shuttle's tragic history or spend decades building SUSTAIN. To keep things fast and cheap, the military would play the role of distant, benevolent deity to the crafty mortals toiling to build SUSTAIN. The Pentagon would continue to evolve the basic parameters of the SUSTAIN concept, while leaving the execution to hungry private entities.

If a company came up with a viable military space plane, the Pentagon would buy it directly or license the design. The originating firm could still build their own copies for space tourism, substituting the Pentagon's robotic pilots and payload for people and using it in far less demanding circumstances.

In the event that the space tourism industry encountered design problems, the military could provide targeted bursts of R&D funding or could offer up government test facilities and government engineers to help overcome any development problems, Damphousse says. And the Pentagon could sponsor competitions like the X-Prize, to sustain the technologies that might evolve into SUSTAIN. One possible contest Damphousse describes would award cash to a team demonstrating a "soft-landing" capability allowing a space plane to land on rough airstrips or open fields.

In late 2009 the NSSO hosted its second engineering confab for SUSTAIN. The purpose of this meeting was to craft what Lafontant calls a "technology-roadmap" document that "identifies the key technologies in systems, vehicles, and propulsion technologies, the best development path options, specification of methods for technology evaluations, and methods of risk mitigation and management which are required to finally accomplish these space-access goals," Lafontant says.

"The panel included the government, commercial stakeholders with the national aerospace industry, including, in full partnership, the New Space companies. The significance of this is that these guys participated on their own dime, no financial support from the government. This included the big guys, like Boeing and Northrop Grumman."

And, for the first time, DARPA got on board. It had taken seven years, but the Pentagon's most powerful research agency finally believed in SUSTAIN. It was a profound endorsement.

■ ■ ■ ■

In his many years as a space journalist, Taylor Dinerman has heard his share of silly ideas. Early on, SUSTAIN seemed like just another in a long tradition of space fantasy. "When I first heard about it, I was like, 'Who are they trying to kid?'" Dinerman says. But year after year, Lafontant's seemingly outlandish space transport kept gaining momentum and credibility, with big boosts from Rutan and New Space.

"It's an idea that refuses to die, I think, because it's a good idea," Lafontant says in 2009, by which time "no one was laughing." "Around

2012, 2013, we should be at a level where the technology should start to accelerate," Lafontant adds. "In a few years, what we think is impossible will really start coming together."

"In the time frame they're looking at, it made sense," Dinerman says. The key, he admits, is plugging away at the individual technologies that might eventually be combined into a usable space transport. "Having the marines supporting this means that the small tech work has some support. And it helps ensure that the small amounts of money available for research won't get cut every time [Congress] needs to plus up accounts for . . . Space Shuttle repairs."

SUSTAIN "is not a pipe dream," Lafontant stresses. "It just needs to gel." Once the individual technologies were ready, the next step would be integration. "All you have right now is individual programs. We hope somebody has the vision to bring all those things together."

It should have come as no surprise that that somebody was Burt Rutan, the SpaceShipOne creator. Retiring SpaceShipOne to the Smithsonian in 2005, Rutan and his engineers disappeared into their workshops, laboring in secrecy to develop a bigger, tougher version of their pioneering rocket ship.

The so-called SpaceShipTwo, launched by a bigger "White Knight Two" mother ship, was meant to carry eight people—two crew members and six passengers—versus SpaceShipOne's theoretical three-person capacity. From 2008, Marine Corps documents related to SUSTAIN cited SpaceShipTwo, rather than its predecessor, as the basis for a military space plane. White Knight Two took flight for the first time in December 2008. Rutan unveiled SpaceShipTwo at its Mojave factory in December 2009.

SpaceShipOne cost around $30 million to develop. Rutan didn't say how much SpaceShipTwo cost, but his business plan hinged on selling rides on the craft for $200,000 apiece.

By 2009 reportedly hundreds of customers had booked flights. A full flight would represent $1.2 million in revenues for Rutan and his partners. That revenue had to cover the cost of that flight, plus a portion of the development cost spread over potentially decades of service. In other words, SpaceShipTwo would probably cost significantly less than a million dollars per flight, compared to a billion dollars per flight for the Space Shuttle.

If SUSTAIN ends up looking like SpaceShipTwo, it could turn out to be surprisingly affordable. For comparison, just one of the air force's more than two hundred C-17 airlifters cost $200 million to buy and as much as $80,000 to operate for a typical long-range flight. Based on these figures alone, SUSTAIN might not seem prohibitively expensive. It might be cheaper to buy than one C-17, but more expensive, per flight, to operate.

That said, it's important to note that the C-17 carries much, much more than SUSTAIN ever could: one hundred and seventy thousand pounds for the C-17 versus a realistic goal of just five thousand pounds for SUSTAIN. The other factors are speed, range, and access. The air force describes the C-17's range as "global, with in-flight refueling." But at a top speed of five hundred miles per hour, a twelve-thousand-mile trip to the opposite side of the planet would take twenty-four hours on a C-17.[20]

SUSTAIN, in theory, could reach any spot on the earth in just two hours. Just as FedEx and UPS customers are willing to pay a premium for speed, so might the U.S. military. In 2009 Damphousse says the Pentagon was still studying what kinds of payloads might justify SUSTAIN's premium.

While space planners mulled over which cargoes were worth an amortized delivery cost of several million dollars, something happened on America's doorstep that forced military supply specialists to think hard about the opposite end of the logistical spectrum, where huge amounts of materials must be delivered steadily over a long period of time.

In January 2010 one of the greatest natural disasters to strike the Americas in modern times required the United States to mobilize the full range of its civil and military logistical capability. It was the test of the century for our ability to move people and stuff from point A to point B.

PART **FIVE**

A Bowling Ball through a Soda Straw

It's another night in teeming, torrid Haiti. With 10 million people and a GDP of just $7 billion, the country is the poorest and most underdeveloped in the Americas. On the evening of January 12, 2010, U.S. Army lieutenant general Ken Keen is just sitting down for a chat with U.S. ambassador Raymond Joseph in the ambassador's hilltop office in the capital of Port-au-Prince, when the ground seems to turn to liquid beneath them.

It's an earthquake, the biggest to strike the island nation in two centuries. Its epicenter is a mere ten miles southwest of Port-au-Prince and just nine miles below the surface. By quake standards, this one is a monster.[1]

Though unharmed themselves, Keen and Joseph immediately sense the scale of the disaster. "We were able to see from a high point over the city some of the devastation," Keen says. "And we could hear the screaming and the yelling of the people in the valleys below. So we immediately knew that what we had just experienced was a tremendous tragedy that was going to have unforeseen circumstances the next morning."

Keen, a Kentucky native with a prominent chin and ears, is second-in-command of U.S. Southern Command, the regional command responsible for all of Latin America. With nearly two decades' experience as a paratrooper, Keen is acutely aware of logistics. After all, when you're jumping from the belly of a transport plane straight into enemy territory, you can't rely on infrastructure on the ground for food, water, and spare parts. You must get by with what you carry on your back and what the planes can drop alongside you. For paratroopers, logistical constraints are a constant concern—even obsession.

Keen assesses the unfolding disaster through that filter. His mind imme-diately fixates on the country's two major ports of entry: the Port-au-Prince seaport and Toussaint Louverture International Airport.

The seaport, Keen learns just a few hours later, is damaged beyond safe use. "There's only one way to get supplies and equipment and people into Haiti right now to any degree," Keen says six days later, "and that's through their in-ternational airport. It's an international airport with one runway, one taxiway."

Quoting U.S. vice president Joe Biden, Keen compares sending cargo through the airport to "pushing a bowling ball through a soda straw."

In truth, it's very nearly like pushing a bowling ball through a brick wall. "We are fortunate," Keen says. "We have the best airmen in the world, who arrived here within twenty-four hours of the earthquake and set up the air-field for twenty-four-hour operation immediately thereafter."

The effort Keen refers to represents the heroic beginning of a logistical campaign like no other, one that tests the capability and capacity of all the most powerful supply and transport entities in America, both military and civilian. If recent years have been a reeducation in the importance of U.S. lo-gistics, Haiti is the final exam.

■ ■ ■ ■

The phone rings at Hurlburt air force base, in eastern Florida, just hours after the quake. Information is still spotty: indications are that Louverture airport is damaged but still useable. Someone needs to get in there, survey the damage, and get the airport running at full capacity as soon as possible.

Already government, nonprofit, and corporate aid groups have volunteered scores, even hundreds, of airplanes to haul relief workers and emergency sup-plies into Haiti. Planes are lined up at airports and air bases all over the world, waiting for someone to tell them Port-au-Prince is ready to receive them.

Other groups send their aircraft without waiting for a proper assessment. Dozens of aircraft have threaded into Haiti without air-traffic control and without anyone on the ground to receive and unload them. There are reports of relief supplies piling up on the airport tarmac where crews have simply shoved them out of their cargo holds. It's a logistical mess, and it isn't doing the people of Haiti any good.

"For the foreseeable future, you have this huge funnel at one end that is north of Haiti that is all the goodwill. . . . Everyone wants to pour something into Haiti," says Col. Steve Shea, from the Air Force Office of Logistics Readiness. "And then you have this very constricted pipeline of how to get it in there, which is the Port-Au-Prince airport. And you can clog that funnel so that nothing will get through. On the other end, south of the funnel is the needs of the Haitian people, which we also know is huge," Shea adds.

"If something happens to that airfield, we are in trouble to get supplies there until the seaports are open," says air force lieutenant colonel Brad Graff, commander of an air force unit in Florida that will eventually help manage Haiti traffic.

"From our experience in special tactics, we know that these first seventy-two hours are very critical," points out Maj. Jason Daniels, from the Air Force's 720th Operations Support Squadron, based at Hurlburt. It falls to Daniels' airmen and others from the colocated Twenty-Third Special Tactics Squadron and First Special Operations Wing, both part of Air Force Special Operations Command—or AFSOC—to salvage what remains of those critical first three days.

Trained to infiltrate commandos deep behind enemy lines aboard specially modified C-130 airlifters, AFSOC is probably the only organization in the world capable of opening Toussaint Louverture on short notice. To do so, they treat the airport like it's a defended enemy facility on the opening night of a war. In essence, the airmen assault and capture Port-au-Prince, for the sake of all Haitians.

The quake struck on January 12. The AFSOC C-130s leave Hurlburt on the afternoon of January 13 and arrive that evening around 8:00. There are no air-traffic controllers to guide the pilots, no local weather forecast to advise about wind and storms, no airport radars to warn of potential collisions with other aircraft, no airport personnel on the ground to direct the planes to safe parking spots on the tarmac.

The pilots use their own radars, their eyes, and, as night falls, their night-vision goggles to slip into Haitian airspace and find a safe vector to the airport. The quake offers the pilots just one consolation prize: despite extensive damage to the airport, the runway lights are still working. As soon as the transports touch down, the pilots slam the brakes, trying to use as little as possible of the potentially damaged runway.

The C-130s' ramps drop and air force security troops storm out. It's their job to secure a safe perimeter for the other airmen to work in. A chaotic sight greets the security troops. The runway and the runway lights might be operational, but the rest of the facility is in ruins.

Buildings are pancaked. The tower appears mostly intact, but its structural integrity is suspect. Radars and weather equipment are a tangled mess—and powerless. Vigilante relief planes pack the tarmac. Piles of supplies form dark mountains between the planes. No one is in charge. What the earthquake has spared, a lack of organization has rendered useless. The airport is on the brink of totally shutting down.

The first thing is to set up a makeshift control tower. Only there's no time to build an actual tower. The airmen haul radios from the C-130s and begin trying to reach the aid planes streaming toward the airport. "My men got on that airplane with radios on their backs and walked off that airplane ready to start talking to airplanes," Nelson says.

The controllers drag some tables out to a grassy strip alongside the tarmac and pile their equipment on top. From there, they can see the runway to one side and the tarmac to the other.

The idea is to keep the planes flowing at a steady rate—and a rate that's neither too slow nor too fast. Too fast will overwhelm the airport. Too slow, and planes might have to turn back, denying Haiti the food, water, and medicine in their holds. That would also deny foreigners stranded in Haiti the opportunity to get out of the country. Already, thousands of foreign nationals are streaming toward the airport in the hope of catching planes home.

While the controllers marshal the incoming and outgoing planes, other airmen begin corralling the aircraft already on the ground. "The men and women of the Twenty-Third Special Tactics Squadron really have their hands full," squadron commander Lt. Col. Brett Nelson says twenty-four hours after the airmen arrive. "It's a small number of people on the ground, and they're continuously marshaling airplanes and parking airplanes and trying to maximize the number of airplanes they can put on the ground at any one time but still ensure that aircraft can continue to take off and unload and offload cargo and equipment as necessary."

One of the biggest problems is a lack of ground support equipment, Nelson says. "There are only two fuel trucks and two tow bars available at Port-au-Prince airport, so when an aircraft lands and requires fuel or . . . has to be moved around on the airfield by towing, it significantly delays us processing that aircraft and getting it back out." At one point on January 14, there are forty-four airplanes on the Toussaint Louverture tarmac at the same time, dropping off cargo and loading evacuees. It's a circus.

"You can imagine if we just bring stuff into the airport and we have no way to get it off, no way to distribute it out in the country, then we're going to just clog our airport," Shea says.

"We're trying to make order out of chaos," observes Chief M.Sgt. Tyler Foster, one of the controllers. On January 18, fellow controller S.Sgt. Don Travo is guiding in a C-130 when he realizes he has no place for it to park. "I can't get him in," Travo tells a *Wall Street Journal* reporter. He radios the C-130 to break off its approach and orbit until a spot on the tarmac opens up.

With the air force's expert management, and with new equipment being flown in, the situation improves. By January 21 an average of 140 flights a day flow into and out of Toussaint Louverture—three times the number the airport handled before the quake.

"On a given day in Haiti, we are flying more stuff in . . . than we do right here at my home airport, Tucson International," says Col. John Romero, whose airmen at Davis-Monthan Air Force Base in Arizona begin overseeing the air supply lines for Haiti within days of the quake. "As a matter of fact, we do twice as much. So I think we're doing a good job."

■ ■ ■ ■

The C-17 cargo plane, radio call sign "Reach 240A," takes off from March Air Force Base outside Riverside, California, on January 27 and turns east. Over the next five days, the plane and its seven crewmen—aircraft commander Lt. Col. Jim Daronco plus his copilot and a backup pilot, two loadmasters, two aircraft mechanics, and two security guards—will fly three times between East Coast bases and Haiti, delivering relief workers and supplies on the inbound leg, and evacuating survivors while outbound.[2]

By the time the plane returns to March on February 1, it has hauled 171,400 pounds of cargo and twenty-five troops into Haiti, and brought 263 evacuees and aid workers out. The C-17's epic journey is all the more astounding for being so common. Scores of U.S. airlifters duplicate the C-17's feat in the weeks following the Haiti quake.[3]

First, Reach 240A flies empty to Louisville, Kentucky, and picks up a pallet of supplies and fifteen soldiers from Fort Knox plus their vehicles. Then it's straight on to Port-au-Prince, touching down at midnight. The controllers working from their foldout table direct the 275-ton plane to a quiet corner of the tarmac, where U.S. Air Force aerial porters wait to download the equipment.[4]

It's dawn by the time the C-17 is downloaded and cleared for takeoff. For the first return flight, the cavernous hold is all but empty. Just eight aid workers, their stints in Haiti completed, occupy the nylon seats lining the plane's fuselage. The C-17 lands in Orlando on the morning of January 28. Her crew has been at work for forty-two hours straight.[5]

After fourteen hours of rest in Orlando, they're back in the air in the middle of the night, heading north to Pope Air Force Base in North Carolina. At Pope, the loadmasters tie down sixteen pallets containing insect nets, tents, office supplies, and ten mobile showers. Two soldiers trained to operate the showers are the only passengers, squeezed into the slim spaces on either side of the bulky cargo.[6]

It's daytime and rush hour when the airlifter reaches Toussaint Louverture for the second time. Congestion in the circuit and on the ground keeps the C-17 orbiting for twenty minutes. Aerial porters, sweating in the sun, their forklifts and loaders hot to the touch, drag the pallets out of the hold, making space for 176 evacuees—aid workers and U.S. passport–holders—lining up on the tarmac. "Many of them were exhausted and dehydrated from the heat," writes Capt. Ashley Norris, an air force reporter.[7]

The C-17 has just fifty-four nylon seats. Those go to the elderly and injured. The rest sit eight across in rows on the cargo-hold floor. The loadmasters tie them down like pallets using a heavy woven strap that doubled as a seatbelt. "None of us had ever floor-loaded anybody before," Daronco muses.[8]

An hour and a half in the air, then the C-17 touches down at Orlando. The passengers cheer.[9]

Daronco and his crew are on the razor's edge of exhaustion. After Orlando, they fly onward to South Carolina's Charleston Air Force Base, home to a huge C-17 force, for a day and a half of rest. On January 31, the crew—fresh and well fed—hop one state over to Robins Air Force Base, Georgia, to pick up a squad of eight air force communications specialists plus thirty tons of cargo and several vehicles.[10]

"The third flight to Port-au-Prince went smoothly," Norris writes. Seventy-nine evacuees climbed aboard as the sun set in the west. The plane landed in Orlando before midnight and immediately takes off for the flight home. The C-17's fourteen tires, each nearly half as tall as a man, touch Californian concrete at 2:00 in the morning, local time.[11]

■ ■ ■ ■

With the airport open and working at full capacity, emphasis shifts to optimizing the mix of airplanes. With so many governments, aid groups, and even publicity-hungry celebrities such as John Travolta trying to shoehorn their planes into Port-au-Prince, the airspace over Haiti gets rather tangled. And on the ground, there's no rhyme or reason to the mix of supplies flowing in.

The air force controllers on the ground can guide planes in to a safe landing, but they aren't up to the much more complicated task of sorting the traffic to prioritize, say, a plane full of medicine over Travolta's personal 707 carrying Scientologists aiming to practice "touch therapy" on injured Haitians. Which planes arrive, and when, comes down to chance and the audacity of particular pilots.[12]

It's a problem, Romero says. He thinks about what would happen if pilots had the same attitude flying into New York. "Imagine at JFK International you have twice as many people coming in there that weren't supposed to. Everyone thought they had a priority; however, they never called and got a landing time for JFK or in this case a slot time to go into Haiti. But it didn't deter them. They showed up anyway."

The Haitian government, itself nearly disabled by the earthquake, can only issue broad directives—send more water, for instance, or ease up on emergency rations. Beyond that, someone has to prioritize individual aircraft, like UPS's industrial engineers do all day.

That job falls to two U.S. Air Force air-movement planning cells: Romero's in Arizona and another under Graff at Tyndall Air Force Base in Florida. Between the two cells, just under a hundred airmen work phones, radios, and computer networks to schedule arrivals for nearly a thousand incoming flights per week.

"We are trying to properly apportion between all of the interested parties," Graff says. "You can imagine how many different parties there are involved now in this international effort, which is a somewhat different experience for us. We've never operated in this broad of a scope."

"Trying to balance all of those wants and needs—there's some political implications," Graff says. He's not wrong. By week two, aid groups are accusing the air force of prioritizing American planes over non-U.S. ones, and military planes over civilian ones. The governments of France and Brazil lodge official protests. Paris says Toussaint Louverture has become an American "annex."[13]

But no other country could have handled the job of instantly building the logistical networks required to feed, clothe, and provide medical care and shelter to 3 million Haitians displaced by the quake. To underscore that reality, in the days following the disaster U.S. naval forces follow the air force controllers into Haitian territory.

The seaborne relief force, codenamed Task Force 41, is led by the nuclear-powered carrier USS *Carl Vinson*, escorted by the destroyer USS *Higgins*. Other ships are en route. At its peak, Task Force 41 numbers no fewer than a dozen large vessels carrying thousands of sailors and scores of aircraft. The relief ships' aggregate tonnage makes them roughly the fifth biggest navy in the world, around the same size as the entire Chinese navy.

Off the Haitian coast, these ships take the concepts pioneered by the *Kearsarge*, the *Comfort*, and other soft-power vessels and expand it exponentially. And rather than relying solely on unreliable helicopters, boats, and landing craft to act as ship-to-shore connectors, as the *Kearsarge* and the *Comfort* did, the Haitian sea base diversifies, reviving an old but sturdy bit of hardware. The eventual addition of a floating causeway transforms what might have been a loose flotilla of vessels into a fully engaged humanitarian sea base capable of powerfully shaping events on shore.

"The *Carl Vinson*, with its speed and flexibility, along with the *Higgins* and other units that were in the area, are the perfect first responders," says Rear Adm. Victor Guillory, commander of the navy's Latin American Fourth Fleet. "They're providing critical help when it's needed most. Very soon, we'll have our sea base in place—the right ships with the right capabilities for sustained relief operations from the sea."[14]

"Sea basing's really unique capability lies in the movement of traditionally land-based logistics functions to the sea: arrival and assembly, supply, sustainment, reconstitution, etc.," analyst Greg Parker writes for the Brookings Institution, a Washington, D.C. think tank. "It is, at its core, a port and airfield at sea—with associated billeting, medical and command-and-control facilities.

. . . And it is when the port and airfield on land are unavailable or disabled—
as has been the case in Haiti—that sea basing shows its strength."[15]

The *Vinson* arrives off Haiti on January 15. She anchors a few miles offshore of the wrecked Port-au-Prince seaport. Her thousand-foot flight deck
essentially doubles the number of active runways in Haiti. While above deck
flight operations got under way, the ship's fifty-strong medical department
prepared their wards to receive injured Haitians.

Theirs is indeed a first-responders' role. The carrier's sole surgical bay represents the very first additional trauma facility to arrive in Haiti in the
quake's aftermath. Other navy ships are steaming in to add to the carrier's
medical capacity The assault ship USS *Bataan*, a sister ship of the *Kearsarge*,
will arrive on January 18. The *Comfort* is on her way from Baltimore, but
her seventeen-knot top speed means she won't reach Haiti until January 20.

On January 15 nineteen navy helicopters begin flying short hops from the
Vinson's deck to landing zones in and around Port-au-Prince. Hovering over
fields thronging with Haitian survivors, the chopper crews shove water, food,
and other supplies out their side doors.

The choppers evacuate their first medical patient that day. An air force
rescue specialist who flew in with the airport team has freed a man from the
ruins of the famed Hotel Montana. The man has lost both legs below the
knees. A navy SH-60B from Helicopter Sea Combat Squadron 9 aboard the
Vinson answers the rescuer's radio call and spirits the survivor to the carrier
for surgery. The next day, the navy lists the man as stable.[16]

Behind the *Vinson* sailed the cruiser USS *Normandy*. Her job is unique.
On January 16 the *Normandy* takes up station between Florida and Haiti
and turns her air-search radars to full power. Damage and power outages
have rendered Toussaint Louverture a "non-radar environment," air force officer Romero says. So the *Normandy* provides her radar coverage to help the
air force sort the incoming aircraft. The ten-thousand-ton, $1 billion cruiser
with the arsenal of 130 missiles, plus guns and torpedoes, finds herself filling in as makeshift airport tower.

"We're an air-defense ship," explains Capt. Geoffrey Griffin, the
Normandy's skipper. "Our specialty is the ability to track and potentially
engage hostile aircraft." It isn't a huge step for the crew to apply their skills
and technology to guiding airplanes, rather than shooting them down.
"We're keeping a good air picture," Griffin says.

The *Normandy* has the best radar in and around Haiti but not the best communications systems. Those belong to the *Vinson*. So the *Normandy* relays her radar data via a radio data-link to the aircraft carrier, where highly trained military air-traffic controllers pass the information to the air force.

In the same way that the *Vinson* helps the *Normandy* with her air-control job, the *Normandy* assists the *Vinson* and the other ships in their roles as floating hospitals and humanitarian assault ships. The *Normandy*'s two SH-60 helicopters shuttle patients from Port-au-Prince to the various medical ships.

"We've only got room for two stretchers, so we're kind of limited as to space," says Lt. Michael Hanson from the cruiser's helicopter detachment. But with the toll of injured rising by the hour during those early days following the quake, every little bit helps.

Sailors from the *Normandy* also help their comrades from the *Bataan* and other ships scout coastal sites around Port-au-Prince that might be suitable for beachheads. In World War II, American soldiers and marines, supported by the navy, stormed enemy-held beaches to secure these vital entry points for invading forces. Nearly seventy years later, beachheads would facilitate a "humanitarian invasion" of Haiti.

■ ■ ■ ■

The air force pulled off a minor miracle in reopening Toussaint Louverture and quickly tripling its throughput. But there's a natural limit to the amount of incoming material any airport can handle. It's sheer physics. Within days of the quake, U.S. military planners realize they've maxed out the Port-au-Prince airport.

They turn their attention to the sea. "Clearly the ability to use a seaport enables both international community and the Department of Defense to move large tonnage of supplies that will be needed there at a capacity that exceeds what we can do by airlift," Shea says.

But the Port-au-Prince seaport is heavily damaged. How damaged, no one knows for sure, but probably more so than the airport. For the first few weeks, at least, the U.S. Navy might have to make its own seaport, using amphibious ships and equipment to land supplies directly on Haitian beaches.

The assault ship *Bataan* is in Norfolk, Virginia, when the earthquake hits. She has just returned from a seven-month deployment to the Indian Ocean and is in the process of offloading her sailors and marines and their equipment when the call comes to reverse the process and get down to Haiti ASAP.

Two smaller amphibious ships, USS *Fort McHenry* and USS *Carter Hall*, will join her. "A lot of effort has gone into getting organized and getting the gear prepared and onto the ships," says marine captain Clark Carpenter, the *Bataan*'s spokesman. Thirty-six hours after getting the call, the forty-thousand-ton vessel is under way.

While sailing the more than a thousand miles to Haiti, intelligence analysts on the *Bataan* work overtime trying to "get a clear picture of what we're getting into," Carpenter says. They plug into the military's usual channels for information: TV news, satellite imagery, and photos and video from overflying aircraft. What emerges is a tragic portrait of death, destruction, and desperation that moves the *Bataan*'s sailors and marines. "The world knows us as warriors," Carpenter says, "but we are equally compassionate."

The scale of Haiti's need is clear. What isn't clear is exactly how Keen might ask the *Bataan* to help. "As to what we'll specifically be doing, we don't exactly know," Carpenter admits. "We're very capable of providing more than just relief effort. We've got lot of bodies that can support whatever we're asked of." That might include forming the core of a sea base. "We have great capability to sea-base," Carpenter says.

With sea-basing, sailors and marines will live on the *Bataan*. "It reduces strain on the infrastructure" ashore, Carpenter explains. That's no small consideration. At the moment, Haiti can't even feed its own millions, much less the tens of thousands of aid workers surging into the country.

Indeed, how to feed and house relief crews has been one of Keen's early concerns. "We want to balance that—make sure have enough but not put too big a footprint on Haiti," he says.

To keep their impact small, the *Bataan*'s crew can use landing craft and helicopters to shuttle the ship's sailors and marines into Haiti every day then bring them back at night to eat, sleep, and prepare for the next day's work. By the same token, the landing craft and choppers can bring Haitians to the ship for medical care before transferring them back home or onward for follow-up care. But these methods are limited by the same reliability problems that vexed sister ship *Kearsarge* in Nicaragua. The Haiti sea base demands better methods.

What role the *Bataan* plays depends greatly on the condition of the Port-au-Prince seaport and the air force's progress in maintaining or expanding the air bridge. At the moment, there are more questions than answers.

The *Bataan*'s group reaches Haiti on January 18, by which time the situation on the ground is clearer. Conditions are worse than many expected. Before the *Bataan* even weighs anchor, her helicopters join choppers from the *Vinson* and the *Normandy*, ferrying relief supplies ashore.

Inside the ship's steel belly, amid a buzz of activity, the medical department gets ready to receive patients. They make beds, set aside drugs and bandages, and sketch out a basic division of labor between the *Bataan* and the *Vinson* and—once she arrives from Baltimore—the *Comfort*.

For several weeks, the *Comfort* will represent the biggest and most sophisticated hospital in Haitian territory. Her capabilities are impressive. "They're bringing about six hundred medical personnel and about a thousand-bed hospital facility," says Cdr. William Wallace, a navy surgeon attached to the *Bataan*. "They also have other heavy equipment like CT scans, MRIs, a lot more X-rays than we do. They're also bringing other supplies such as blood—lots of blood, about five thousand units——and they can serve as many as about one thousand patients."

It's up to the *Bataan*'s medical department to help prepare for the *Comfort*'s arrival. "In the whole area, there's just about fifteen hundred medical providers that are here," Wallace adds. "We're all working together as ships arrive to basically build that up, but it's one of those things that's kind of changing. Obviously, the hospital ship isn't here yet. She will arrive later on today or tomorrow morning, and when she brings in, she'll play a larger role."

"Right now she's in the distance," Wallace continues, "but basically as the ships arrive, we bring everybody in, see what capabilities we have, and then we kind of do a little bit of adjustment in the organization to make sure that any patients that are brought out to the ship are put into place where they can receive the best care—so that no one ship is going to be overwhelmed by everybody going there. Obviously, everybody won't go to *Comfort*."

Medical care is just part of the equation for *Bataan*. "This is a multipurpose amphibious ship," says Cdr. Melanie Merrick, *Bataan*'s senior doctor. In addition to adding fourteen intensive care unit beds and thirty-eight ward beds to the *Vinson*'s fifty-one beds and, eventually, the *Comfort*'s thousand, the *Bataan*'s marines and her navy beach party sport bulldozers and trucks for debris removal; in addition to her helicopters, the *Bataan* carries landing craft that can shuttle people and equipment ashore. The ship represents a full-service disaster-relief shop that, in a pinch, can support all her own people at sea.

It soon becomes clear that this was exactly what the *Bataan* must do. The MSC salvage ship USNS *Grasp* reaches Haiti the same day the *Bataan* does. A joint team of army and navy divers immediately begins assessing the condition of Port-au-Prince's seaport. Aid groups are already using the port's piers to unload ships full of supplies when the military begins its assessment.

"From above, the pier doesn't show significant damage other than the approach," says Brian Crowder, a navy engineer. "But with the divers conducting underwater inspections on the pier, we were able to identify significant damage to the foundation of the pier."[17]

The U.S. Coast Guard gives one Haitian shipper permission to use the pier "gingerly" to unload 123 containers of aid. But the structure simply isn't safe for the scale and intensity of operations the navy has planned. Besides the airport, the U.S. military needs another way into Haiti. The *Bataan* will anchor a sea base for sailors and marines working to establish a brand new port of entry into Haiti.[18]

That's where the *Bataan*'s traditional military use comes in handy. She's designed to land marines and their equipment on any beach, against any opposition. Now her crew puts this capability to good use in a noncombat situation, landing people and supplies on a Haitian beach—in essence, creating a "humanitarian beachhead" to supplant the damaged seaport.

The *Bataan*'s landing craft are vital to this operation—her hovercraft, especially. "The Landing Craft Air Cushion that will be on the USS *Bataan*, they can seek additional entry points other than the airport in Haiti, so we can find a beach and we can set up a place where we can bring supplies ashore at that beach," Carpenter says.

The first members of the beach party wade ashore from their landing craft just hours after *Bataan*'s crew sights land. "The primary goal right now is establishing a forward presence—basically getting people on the beach, getting a site secured so they can get humanitarian aid into position so we can start dispersing it," Wallace says.

In following days, additional ships and equipment arrive to expand Bataan's beachhead. MSC mobilizes the transport USNS *1st Lt. Jack Lummus*. The 675-foot, forty-thousand-ton container ship loads 120 pallets of supplies from the U.S. Agency for International Development, another 90 pallets from the Federal Emergency Management Agency, twenty-four thousand gallons of gasoline, twenty-four thousand gallons of diesel fuel, three army port-repair kits, and a slew of Marine Corps trucks and construction vehicles. In a single trip between Florida and Haiti, the ship carries more cargo than four hundred heavy-lift airplanes—and unloads it far faster, thanks to one specialized set of equipment.[19] That equipment, a floating causeway called "lighterage," is the key to the Haiti sea base's success.

The *Lummus* carries components of the lighterage system with her from Florida. It amounts to a set of interlocking, motorized, floating platforms designed to link up and quickly move vast amounts of cargo from anchored ships to a beachhead. The basic design of the lighterage dates to World War II but has been updated over the decades to better handle high winds and choppy seas.[20]

The *Lummus* arrives off Haiti on January 21. She cranes the lighterage barges into the water. Some linger while at least one other—a sort of pontoon—races to shore and jams through the surf and up onto the beach. While sailors secure this pontoon pier, crane operators aboard the *Lummus* ease containers over the side and onto the waiting lighterage barges.[21]

The ship also drops a ramp installed on her tall, blocky stern, opening a wide passageway into her vehicle deck. The lighterage crews carefully align their ungainly craft with the ramp and hold them there while vehicles roll from the ship to the barges. The lighterage chugs toward the beachhead and sidles up to the pontoon. A wheeled container handler picks up the containers and moves them ashore while vehicles roll right off the lighterage, down the pontoon, and into action.

It has taken more than a week to put all the pieces in place, but finally the U.S.-led, full-scale humanitarian invasion of Haiti is under way. Aircraft guided by the air force and navy's ad hoc air-traffic control sustain a trickle of urgent materials into Toussaint Louverture, while the bulk of supplies flow from the offshore sea base directly into Port-au-Prince, and the sick and injured stream in the opposite direction to the medical bays of the assembled ships.

Decades of logistical development have culminated in the most sophisticated relief effort ever, to help one of the world's poorest nations recover from one of recent history's most devastating natural disasters.

■ ■ ■ ■

As always, the frontline logisticians have their own logistical needs. The *Vinson*, the *Bataan*, the *Comfort*, the *Lummus*, and the other ships require fueling within a couple days of arriving on station. Several days later, they need fresh batches of other consumables, plus extra humanitarian supplies for onward distribution to Haitians.

MSC anticipates the demand. The day after the quake, the command orders crews for more than twenty of its ships to mobilize, just in case Southern Command asks for them. "We offered everything we had available," says Capt. Michael Graham, from MSC's East Coast division. "It was all push and no pull."[22]

Sure enough, that day SOUTHCOM asks for a tanker. MSC tapped USNS *Big Horn*, 680 feet long and displacing forty thousand tons—most of that off-loadable fuel. By sheer coincidence, the vessel's master is Thomas Finger, the same man who took the *Comfort* south to Haiti and other countries on her last routine humanitarian cruise.

"I received a call at 3 a.m. the morning of the 13th telling me that they were considering *Big Horn* for tasking to Haiti," Finger says. "An hour later, another phone call confirmed it." Finger places his own calls. Between him and the command, they get seventy-seven crew members—all but four of them civilians—out of bed and out to the pier to prep the ship.[23]

"We left the pier at Naval Station Norfolk for refueling at Craney Island Fuel Terminal as soon as we could, and we got underway for Haiti by five that afternoon," Finger says. The *Big Horn* reaches Port-au-Prince on the 17th and finds "customers" figuratively lined up, desperate for the tanker's ministrations. With her hoses she offloads 2.6 millions gallons of fuel. She also cranes over 618 pallets of supplies. And then she's empty. The *Big Horn* turns around and heads north to Florida to get more fuel and stuff.[24]

And so it goes, Finger's ship sailing back and forth between Haiti and Florida to keep the humanitarian sea base fueled and fed. After a month of nonstop work, a fresh tanker, USNS *Leroy Grumman*, relieves the *Big Horn*. The ship and her exhausted crew head north to Norfolk for a much-deserved break.

By then the scale of relief work in Haiti has ballooned beyond anything anyone predicted. The humanitarians are burning through supplies as fast as they come in. To meet rising demand, on January 19 MSC mobilizes a second Norfolk-based ship, USNS *Sacagawea*, the second T-AKE built by NASSCO in San Diego. She arrives off Port-au-Prince three days later.

The barely three-year-old ship carries nearly half a million packaged meals, plus an extra 235,000 pounds of food, seven truckloads of bottled water, and ten water-purification systems. The supplies filled seventeen thousand standard pallets. The ship's 135 crew members worked around the clock for several days to load the forty-thousand-ton vessel, finishing just an hour before she was due to sail.[25]

"We had a sense we would be called to duty as soon as we heard about the earthquake," says George McCarthy, *Sacagawea*'s skipper. "MSC's motto is, 'We Deliver.' Now *Sacagawea* has added the line, 'We care, and we are coming.'"[26]

As the most modern ship in the MSC inventory, the *Sacagawea* can do things her cousin vessels can't. For one, she carries helicopters, where many MSC ships don't. For the several weeks that both the *Sacagawea* and the *Big Horn* are on station together, the *Sacagawea*'s choppers work for both ships. "Its helicopters made it possible to rapidly get our disaster relief cargo to the amphibious ships and then on to the beach," Finger says. "We couldn't have done it without the helicopters."[27]

The flight ops take place simultaneously with UNREPs and "skin-to-skin" supply transfers, where other ships tie up right alongside *Sacagawea*, their hulls separated only by bumpers while their crews crane pallets across. "In a very dynamic environment, all 1,700 pallets of provisions and cargo were transferred to 13 ships in six days," says Cdr. Mark Pimpo, assigned to *Sacagawea*.

"We transferred critical medical supplies to *Comfort* upon arrival in Port-au-Prince harbor. We also transferred more than 40,000 gallons of water to amphibious assault ship USS *Bataan* when both of the ship's evaporators stopped functioning."[28]

As with the *Big Horn*, *Sacagawea*, once empty, hurries back to Florida for a top-up. The ships form a sort of shuttle service that expands as MSC progressively mobilizes additional vessels. USNS *Lewis and Clark*, the first T-AKE built, arrives in early February. Before her departure from Florida, navy admiral Vic Guillory visits the *Lewis and Clark* to remind the crew of their importance. "The Navy is uniquely equipped to respond to disasters like this earthquake in Haiti." Guillory says. "The supplies you are carrying will save lives."[29]

■ ■ ■ ■

With the airport open, the sea base well established, and the beachhead growing, the military can breathe a little easier. The first and biggest problem—

access—has been solved for the time being. Now planners can begin thinking ahead to Haiti's long-term needs. With 3 million homeless and the
Haitian government in ruins, it's likely the U.S. military will provide some
level of support for months to come. "We understand it's a long-term mission," Shea says.

When it became clear that the Iraq conflict would take years to resolve and
that insurgents could disrupt long-term plans by attacking supply lines, the
Pentagon was forced to "harden" the logistical system. Those measures included the blast-resistant MRAP trucks and increasingly autonomous robots
that might eventually transform U.S. ground forces.

In Afghanistan, the conflict proved even more protracted—and even more
logistically demanding. To keep the U.S. military in Afghanistan fed, fueled,
and fully armed, the Pentagon has constructed history's most sophisticated
aerial supply system.

By the same token, long-term Haiti relief demands big-time innovation.

The dust is still hovering over Port-au-Prince, and aftershocks still rattle
the rubble and the teeming masses of survivors, when the air force lays out
a plan for a semi-permanent Haiti airlift. It would look a lot like the Afghan
airlift, only somewhat smaller. It takes root at a mostly dormant air force
base in southern Florida.

Homestead Air Force Base was once a thriving facility. A round of budget-
driven base closures in the 1990s stripped away Homestead's resident F-16
fighter jets and all but shuttered the facility. By 2010 the base permanently
supports just a handful of fighters that rotate in from other bases and fly air
patrols over the southeastern United States. But the base's runways and tarmacs
are intact. Half as far from Haiti as many of the military's East Coast air hubs,
it's the perfect staging point for a sustained airlift into the ruined country.

With the active-duty air force preoccupied flying supplies into Afghanistan,
much of the responsibility for the Haiti airlift falls to the Air Force Reserve.
Even before it's official, Reserve commander Lt. Gen. Charles Stenner begins making preparations for the lift. "When that kind of news comes out on
the TV and radio, the phone starts ringing, because people know there's
going to be a requirement," Stenner says.

He promptly orders every available plane, plus the required ground crews,
to the Florida base. "Everything we have has been delivered to Homestead,"
Stenner says. On January 20 the crews are just waiting for Romero and

Graff's controllers to assign them slots into Toussaint Louverture. "We put things on the ramp waiting for the airport in Haiti to accept airplanes," Stenner says.

In the meantime, Stenner lays plans to call up more of his reservists, requiring them to put their civilian jobs on hold and switch to full-time military work. "We're prepared to bring folks down to Homestead on a rotational basis to keep up the effort," he says. "We're prepared for the long haul."

■ ■ ■ ■

A month after the quake, Keen begins cutting the U.S. military force in Haiti. His goal, he says, is to slowly transition the relief effort to civilian control. "As we see this transition occurring, we see our civilian partners increase their capabilities—both the government here in Haiti as well as the non-government organizations—we see the need for our military assistance dwindling," Keen says.[30]

But not so fast! "At the present time, there is still great need across the board," Keen stresses. To fully replace the military, civilian agencies will need to continue reinforcing their logistical systems. For some agencies, that means UPS.[31]

"One of big problems when disaster strikes is logistics," says Ed Martinez, director of philanthropy for UPS. "Infrastructure is damaged, people have needs, you have a world that wants to respond but doesn't know how." Aid groups know what kinds of things disaster victims need, "but may not be equipped to get goods from the dock to the people who need it"—especially in large quantities over a long period of time.

In an emergency the scale of the Haiti earthquake, aid groups rely on the same companies that everyone else does to haul cargo: FedEx, DHL, UPS. For these companies, aid work isn't strictly charity. In UPS's case, the company views disaster relief as a long-term investment in its markets. "If you have a strong community, you have a strong UPS," Martinez says.

UPS traditionally partners up with UNICEF, the American Red Cross, the Salvation Army, CARE International, and the UN World Food Program. "As soon as the earthquake struck on January 12, we began mobilizing with our partners," Martinez says. The first step was assessment. "UNICEF was on the ground. CARE was on the ground. We began communicating over the weekend about what the conditions were on the ground."

As information trickled in, UPS began working with its aid clients to craft a distribution plan. At the company's disposal was its fleet of air freighters plus its trucks and its ship-charter operation. Airplanes were fastest and would be the focus of initial efforts. "We identified Miami International Airport—the home base for our operations into Latin America—as the tip of the spear for us," Martinez says.

But UPS's planners faced the same problem that military planners did in the early days following the quake—that is, "getting into Port-au-Prince," Martinez said. There was no shortage of aircraft, volunteers, or aid supplies. The problem was where to deliver these things. In the first week after the air force opened Toussaint Louverture, the damaged airport handled just a fraction of the aircraft made available by governments and private charities. Though the Pentagon denied it, it seemed that military aircraft were getting priority.

So UPS tapped Santa Domingo in the Dominican Republic as its initial entry point, while continuing to work the Toussaint Louverture problem. For starters, UPS planners would form road convoys to haul supplies from Santa Domingo to the NGOs' distribution centers inside Haiti. "From that point on, it became a question of mobilizing our internal people," Martinez says. More than enough UPS employees had volunteered to help. The company picked a handful to accompany the aid groups into the field. UPS also dispatched two of its senior logisticians from to Santa Domingo to begin organizing the convoys.

The trucks would be a mix of brown UPS trucks plus others hired from Dominican fleet operators. It turned out that gathering trucks was the easy part. Far more difficult was finding navigable roads free of bandits. The fear of hijacking and ruined roads delayed the departure of the first UPS convoy by several days, till the third week of January.

There would be no single, easy solution to Haiti's transportation problem. UPS planners decided to simultaneously pursue all three modes of transport—air, land, and sea—in hopes of eventually finding the right mix for a sustainable relief effort. "We're moving on parallel tracks," Martinez said.

Ground convoys are cheap and mean the fewest bottlenecks but are slow and vulnerable to minor delays resulting from poor roads and security. Airplanes are fastest but more expensive and most susceptible to total bottlenecking owing to Toussaint Louverture's capacity problem. The cheapest

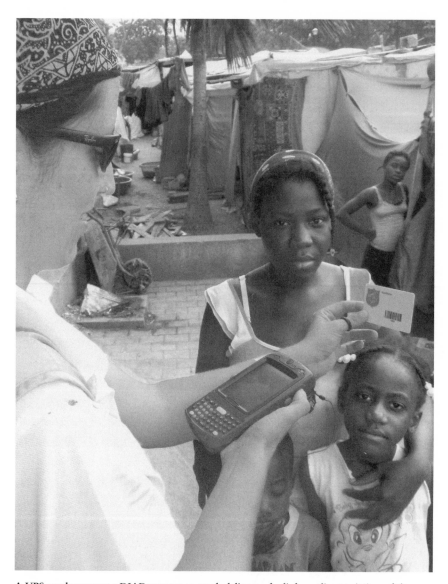

A UPS employee uses a DIAD scanner to track delivery of relief supplies to victims of the January 2010 Haiti earthquake. SALVATION ARMY

method of all is for UPS to charter a ship, but ships need a seaport, and Port-au-Prince's was still in shambles.

A big factor in the mix of modes was the time-sensitivity of the cargo. For truly urgent supplies, UPS pushed hard for a landing slot at the airport and sent in a plane. Less vital materials could go by road or, in time, by sea. "We don't drive that," Martinez says. "We look to the NGOs to make that determination."

The sheer complexity of the situation prevented UPS from doing what it did best: massaging a distribution process in order to eke the best time-cost balance for itself and its customers. Stateside UPS operations balance on the fine point of perfect cost-effectiveness and timeliness. The company even monitors how hard and how often its drivers apply their brakes, in order to pinpoint where individual drivers might trim a few minutes from their delivery times. In Haiti, that kind of fine-tuning was impossible at first.

"At this point, we have not been able to establish a natural flow," Martinez laments. "We would assume, as relief efforts shift into recovery efforts, that will come."

■ ■ ■ ■

And so one of the greatest human tragedies in decades became part of the vast, complex, and, for most people, largely ignored overhead of America's power and prosperity. Just as our logistical systems maintain our high standard of living and sustain our disproportionate influence abroad, they now provide for a devastated nation of 10 million struggling for survival just a few hours' flight time from our southernmost states.

At the time of writing in the spring of 2010, U.S.-led Haiti relief operations are ongoing but rarely make the news. The Haiti humanitarian campaign remains one of the most astounding examples of logistical brilliance in memory. It's testimony to how frequently Americans pull off such transportation miracles that we hardly notice them anymore.

Overseas in Iraq and Afghanistan, and at home on our highways and on the Great Lakes, American logisticians battle insurgent enemies, the elements, and sometimes the laws of physics—to move more and more stuff, cheaper and faster, from point A to point B. In most cases, the logisticians win.

That, more than anything else, will ensure another century of American power and prosperity, despite the recent and continuing economic downturn. But we must not take for granted that our logisticians will do what they must all on their own. World-beating logistics requires investment on a national scale. That kind of investment requires political will.

We can change the world by moving it, one truck-, ship-, and planeload at a time. But only if we want to—and pay for it.

Notes

PART ONE

Chapter 1: "They're the Lifeline"

1   Coalition Provisional Authority Briefing with Brigadier General Mark
    Kimmitt, April 16, 2004: http://govinfo.library.unt.edu/cpa-iraq/transcripts
    /20040416_Apr16_KimmittSenor.html.

2   Medill Washington, "Lightening Soldiers' Loads Harder than Ever," UPI, June 18,
    2009: http://www.upiu.com/articles/lightening-soldiers-loads-harder-than-ever.

3   United States Transportation Command 2003 Annual Command Report:
    http://www.dtic.mil/cgi-bin/GetTRDoc?AD=ADA427443&Location=
    U2&doc=GetTRDoc.pdf.

4   Naval Historical Center, "U.S. Navy in Desert Shield/Desert Storm":
    http://www.history.navy.mil/wars/dstorm/ds4.htm.

5   Frederick Godfrey, "The Logistics of Invasions," *Army Logistician*, Nov.-Dec.
    2003: http://findarticles.com/p/articles/mi_m0PAI/is_6_35/ai_110459247/.

6   United States Transportation Command 2008 Annual Command Report:
    http://www.dtic.mil/cgibin/GetTRDoc?AD=ADA505158&Location=U2&doc=
    GetTRDoc.pdf.

7   Stephen Cohen, "Boom Boxes: Shipping Containers and Terrorists," Berkeley
    Roundtable on the International Economy, October 13, 2005:
    http://brie.berkeley.edu/publications/RP7.pdf.

8   U.S. Department of Transportation:
    http://www.dot.gov/perfacc2003/ataglance.htm.

9   Bureau of International Information Programs, "A U.S. Economy Linked to
    the World," September 15, 2009: http://www.america.gov/st/business-english
    /2009/September/20090916131014ebyessedo0.9084371.html.

10 U.S. Department of Transportation:
    http://www.dot.gov/perfacc2003/ataglance.htm.

11 "The Transportation Challenge: Moving the U.S. Economy" (2008), U.S.
    Chamber of Commerce, 53. http://www.nssga.org/government
    /Reauthorization/08_Section_3.pdf.

12 George Day, "Logistics: Bridge to Global Prosperity," Wharton Global Forum,
    Istanbul, June 8–9, 2007: http://www.wharton.universia.net/index.cfm?fa=
    viewArticle&id=1202&language=english.

13 Thomas Donohue, National Freight Forum, Washington, D.C., March 12,
    2002: http://www.uschamber.com/press/speeches/2002/020314tjd_freight.htm.

14 American Recovery and Reinvestment Act of 2009:
    http://publicservice.evendon.com/RecoveryBill1M.htm.

15 "Minnesota Collapsed Bridge Death Toll Rises to 5, 8 Still Missing," Fox
    News, August 3, 2007:
    http://www.foxnews.com/story/0,2933,291933,00.html.

16 Committee on the Marine Transportation System, "National Strategy for the
    Marine Transportation System: A Framework for Action," July 2008:
    http://www.cmts.gov/nationalstrategy.htm.

17 American Association of State Highway and Transportation Officials:
    http://www.transportation1.org/tif3report/intro.html.

18 Barack Obama and Joe Biden, "Strengthening America's Transportation
    Infrastructure": http://www.barackobama.com/pdf/issues/FactSheet
    Transportation.pdf.

19 American Society of Civil Engineers, 2008 Infrastructure Report Card:
    http://apps.asce.org/reportcard/2005/index.cfm.

20   Michael Cooper, "House Plan for Infrastructure Disappoints Advocates for
      Major Projects," *New York Times*, January 19, 2009:
      http://www.nytimes.com/2009/01/20/us/politics/20publicworks.html.

21   Scott Horsley, "Can Infrastructure Spending Rev Up the Economy?" NPR,
      December 8, 2008: http://www.npr.org/templates/story/story.php?storyId=
      97973470.

Chapter 2: Secret Sauce

1   Eric Schmitt, Edmund L. Andrews, "Cargo Flights Added to Cut Risky Land
      Trips," *New York Times*, December 15, 2004:
      http://query.nytimes.com/gst/fullpage.html?res=9B02E7DD1730F936A25751C
      1A9629C8B63&sec=&spon=&pagewanted=all.

2   Otto Kreisher, "Air Force May Need More C-17 Planes," Copley News
      Service, March 2, 2006: http://www.redorbit.com/news/technology/412759
      /air_force_may_need_more_c17_planes/index.html.

3   Noah Shachtman, "Military Security Threat: Bogus Bomb-Zapper's Bogus
      Countermeasure," *Danger Room*, July 16, 2007:
      http://www.wired.com/dangerroom/2007/07/nobody-wants-re/.

4   Tim Oren, "Urban Challenge 2007: Reflections," *Tim Oren's Due Diligence*,
      November 5, 2007: http://due-diligence.typepad.com/blog/2007/11/urban
      -challen-2.html.

5   Warren Brown, "A Vehicle That Would Drive Itself," *Washington Post*,
      October 28, 2007: http://www.washingtonpost.com/wp-dyn/content/article
      /2007/10/25/AR2007102502212.html.

6   University of Texas at Austin, "Self-Driving SUV Advances to DARPA Urban
      Challenge Semifinals," August 9, 2007: http://www.utexas.edu/news/2007
      /08/09/comp_sci/.

7   Dylan Tweney, "How Stanford's Robotic Car Passed Its Driving Test," *Gadget
      Lab*, June 15, 2007: http://www.wired.com/gadgetlab/2007/06/how
      _stanfords_r/#ixzz0mceQczZ7.

8   General Motors Collaborative Research Lab, "Tartan Racing Wins $2M
      DARPA Urban Challenge": http://gm.web.cmu.edu/news/boss.php.

9   Matthew Wald, "Sleepy Truckers Linked to Many Deaths," *New York Times*, January 19, 1995: http://www.nytimes.com/1995/01/19/us/sleepy-truckers -linked-to-many-deaths.html?pagewanted=1.

10   "Dead Tired: Desperate Drivers Defy Limits as Safety Net Falters," *Kansas City Star*, December 16, 2001: http://www.patt.org/Dead_Tired.php.

11   "No Hands Across America": http://www.cs.cmu.edu/afs/cs/usr/tjochem /www/nhaa/general_info.html/.

12   Stefanie Olsen, "Robot Car Competitors: Don't Call It a Race!" CNET, April 1, 2008: http://news.cnet.com/8301-10784_3-9908396-7.html.

13   Stefanie Olsen, "Robot Race Has Serious Consequences," CNET, October 19, 2007: http://www.zdnet.com.au/robot-race-has-serious-consequences -339283078.htm.

Chapter 3: Backseat Driver

1   Human Factors and Ergonomics Society: http://www.hfes.org/Web/Educational Resources/HFEdefinitionsmain.html.

2   Patrick Jordan, "A Vision for the Future of Human Factors": http://www.hfes -europe.org/books/firstpage1996/17.pdf.

3   http://www.intellidriveusa.org/whoweare/program.php.

PART TWO

Chapter 4: Frankenstein's Automonster

1   National Atlas of the United States: http://www.nationalatlas.gov/transportation.html.

2   Calum MacLeod, "China's Highways Go the Distance," *USA Today*, January 29, 2006: http://www.usatoday.com/news/world/2006-01-29-china -roads_x.htm.

3   Ibid.

4   William Pentland, "The World's Top Car-Owning Countries," *Forbes*, July 30, 2008: http://www.forbes.com/2008/07/30/energy-europe-automobiles-biz -energy-cx_wp_0730cars.html.

5   Gavin Wright, "Historical Foundations of American Technology," *Innovation. and U.S. Competitiveness,* (New York: The Conference Board, December 2007): http://www.conference-board.org/economics/workingpapers.cfm?pdf=E-0037-08-WP.

6   University of Michigan Ross School of Business, "Video: A Conversation with Dean Robert Dolan and The New York Times' Micheline Maynard," January 12, 2010: http://www.bus.umich.edu/NewsRoom/ArticleDisplay.asp?news_id=18351.

7   "America on the Move," The Smithsonian Institution: http://americanhistory.si.edu/ONTHEMOVE/collection/object_615.html.

8   P. J. O'Rourke, "The End of the Affair," *Wall Street Journal*, May 30, 2009: http://online.wsj.com/article/SB10001424052970203771904574173401767415892.html.

9   Ibid.

10 Ibid.

11 Thomas J. Sugrue, "Automobile in American Life and Society": http://www.autolife.umd.umich.edu/Race/R_Overview/R_Overview.htm.

12 Ibid.

13 Ibid.

14 O'Rourke, "End of the Affair."

15 Michael Moore, "Goodbye, GM," Michaelmoore.com, June 1, 2009: http://www.michaelmoore.com/words/mikes-letter/goodbye-gm-by-michael-moore.

16 Environmental Protection Agency: http://epa.gov/otaq/invntory/overview/pollutants/index.htm.

17 Ibid.

18 Sugrue, "Automobile."

19 Ibid.

20 Earth Policy Institute: http://www.earth-policy.org/index.php?/plan_b_updates/2010/update87.

21   Nate Silver, "The End of Car Culture," *Esquire*, May 6, 2009: http://www.esquire.com/features/data/nate-silver-car-culture-stats -0609#ixzz0mebxY9KJ.

22   Peter Bregman, "For 2010, Think of Self-Reliance as Progress," CNN, December 31, 2009: http://peterbregman.com/2009/12/31/for-2010-think-of -self-reliance-as-progress/.

23   Silver, "End of Car Culture."

24   Ibid.

25   Ibid.

26   Rosanne Skirble, "Falling New Auto Sales in US Could Signal End of Era," Voice of America, January 12, 2010: http://www1.voanews.com/english/news/usa /Falling-New-Auto-Sales-in-US-Could-Signal-End-of-Era—81240217.html.

27   Ibid.

28   Ibid.

29   Ibid.

30   Harvey Wasserman, "Is This the End of the Age of the Automobile?" *Counterpunch*, March 10, 2010: http://www.counterpunch.org/wasserman03102009.html.

31   Moore, "Goodbye, GM."

32   Break the Gridlock!: http://breakthegridlock.org/story/2009/11/57.

33   Ibid.

34   Wasserman, "Is This the End?"

35   Earth Policy Institute.

36   Ibid.

37   Ibid.

38   Wasserman, "Is This the End?"

39   Edward Glaeser, "What Would High-Speed Rail Do to Suburban Sprawl?" *New York Times*, August 18, 2009: http://economix.blogs.nytimes.com/tag /high-speed-rail-do-to-suburban-sprawl/.

40 Ibid.

41 Ibid.

42 American Bus Association: http://www.buses.org/files/ComparativeEnergy.pdf.

43 Environmental Protection Agency: http://www.epa.gov/oms/fetrends.htm.

44 Ibid.

45 Bruce Mulliken, "Safe and Efficient, Trains Won't Replace Dangerous Cars," *Green Energy News*, December 18, 2009: http://www.green-energy-news.com /arch/nrgs2009/20090095.html.

46 U.S. Department of Transportation: http://www.fhwa.dot.gov/interstate/faq.htm#question4.

47 Texas Transportation Institute, 2009 Annual Urban Mobility Report: http://mobility.tamu.edu/ums/.

Chapter 5: Mixed Breed

1 The White House: http://www.whitehouse.gov/issues/energy-and-environment.

2 Serbia Sanctions Case Study, American University: http://www1.american.edu/ted/serbsanc.htm/.

3 Dana: http://dana.mediaroom.com/index.php/press_releases/1575.

4 James Klatell, "Dana Corp. Files for Bankruptcy," CBS News, March 3, 2006: http://www.cbsnews.com/stories/2006/03/03/business/main1367076.shtml.

5 Bosch-Rexroth: http://www.marketwire.com/press-release/Testing-Begins-of-Rexroth-Hydraulic-Hybrid-Technology-in-NYC-Refuse-Trucks-996368.htm.

6 Ibid.

7 Michael Conrad, "Hydraulic Hybrid Vehicle Technologies," Clean Technologies Forum, Sacramento, CA, September 09, 2008: http://www.airquality.org/mobile /ctf/Events/20080909NearTerm-BoschRexroth-ConradM.pdf.

8 Ibid.

9   Arthur St. Antoine, "Asphalt Jungle: The Temple of Doom," *Motor Trend*, May 2008: http://www.motortrend.com/features/editorial/112_0805_asphalt_jungle/index.html.

Chapter 6: Parsing Parcels

1   "Competition Takes FedEx and UPS to the Forefront of Technological Innovation," *Rethink IT*, July 2004: http://findarticles.com/p/articles/mi_m0PAT/is_2004_July/ai_n6148566/.

2   United Parcel Service: http://www.ups.com/aircargo/using/services/services/domestic/svc-aircraft.html.

3   Daniel Terdiman, "UPS Turns Data Analysis into Big Savings," *CNET*, April 2, 2010: http://news.cnet.com/8301-13772_3-20001576-52.html.

4   Ibid.

PART THREE

Chapter 7: The Greatest Lakes

1   Jerome Idaszak, "Manufacturing's Share of GDP Will Recover and Hold Steady," *Kiplinger*, July 13, 2009: http://www.kiplinger.com/businessresource/forecast/archive/manufacturing_share_of_gdp_090710.html.

2   U.S. Merchant Marine Academy: http://www.usmma.edu/about/history.htm.

3   Ibid.

4   Ibid.

5   Ibid.

6   Lake Carriers Association letter to James F. Collins, president, Steel Manufacturers Association, July 1, 1997: http://www.lcaships.com/sma.html.

7   Henry Ford Museum: http://www.hfmgv.org/rouge/historyofrouge.aspx.

8   Bureau of Labor Statistics: http://www.bls.gov/oco/ocos247.htm.

9   Kimberly Quillen, "Stakes Are High for Louisiana Maritime Industry in Debate over Decades-Old Law," *Times-Picayune*, January 31, 2010: http://www.nola.com/business/index.ssf/2010/01/stakes_are_high_for_louisiana.html.

10 Ibid.

11 Ibid.

Chapter 8: Medical Care, Anywhere

1   Erik Barker, "Kearsarge, Continuing Promise Begin Surgeries Aboard," August 19, 2008: http://www.navy.mil/search/display.asp?story_id=39184.

2   U.S. Navy: http://www.southcom.mil/AppsSC/factfiles.php?id=53.

3   Ibid.

4   "Focus on 'Terror War' Downs U.S. Image to All-Time Low: Report," AFP, November 08, 2007: http://www.dailytimes.com.pk/default.asp?page=2007\11\08\story_8-11-2007_pg7_63.

5   Joseph Nye, "The U.S. Can Reclaim 'Smart Power,'" *Los Angeles Times*, January 21, 2009: http://www.latimes.com/news/opinion/commentary/la-oe-nye21-2009jan21,0,3381521.story.

6   Gordon Lubold, "A U.S. Military Leader Stresses Ideas over Firepower," *Christian Science Monitor*, July 3, 2007: http://www.csmonitor.com/2007/0703/p01s03-usmi.html.

7   U.S. Naval Heritage and History Command: http://www.history.navy.mil/wars/spanam.htm.

8   Federation of American Scientists: http://www.fas.org/man/dod-101/sys/ship/unrep.htm.

9   Eric Wertheim, *Combat Fleets of the World* (Annapolis, MD: U.S. Naval Institute Press, 2008).

10 Bob Work, "The U.S. Navy: Charting a Course for Tomorrow's Fleet," Center for Strategic and Budgetary Assessment, February 17, 2009: http://www.csbaonline.org/4Publications/PubLibrary/R.20090217.The_US_Navy_Charti/R.20090217.The_US_Navy_Charti.pdf.

11 Ibid.

Chapter 9: The $3 Billion Maritime Operating Company, with Guns

1   Michael Gannon, *Operation Drumbeat: Germany's U-Boat Attacks Along the American Coast in World War II* (New York: Harper Perennial, 1991).

2   Globalsecurity.org: http://www.globalsecurity.org/military/systems/ship/liberty-ships.htm.

3   Florida International University: http://www2.fiu.edu/~thompsop/liberty/photos/liberty_summary.html.

4   Globalsecurity.org.

5   "NASSCO Begins Construction of Product Carriers," *Mariner*, August 28, 2007: http://professionalmariner.com/Me2/dirmod.asp?sid=6D92E69F00EA4DF1919 EF5F48265F858&nm=News+and+Events&type=news&mod=News&mid=9A 02E3B96F2A415ABC72CB5F516B4C10&tier=3&nid=D61A0A4B313D4154 BBFE161147106647.

6   Ibid.

7   Naval History and Heritage Command: http://www.history.navy.mil/faqs/faq52-1.htm.

8   Ibid.

9   Stefano Ambrogi, "U.S. Navy Tanker under Apparent Pirate Attack off Somalia," Reuters, September 24, 2008: http://www.reuters.com/article/idUSTRE48N67320080924.

10 "U.S. Navy Admits Ship in Suez Canal Killed an Egyptian," *New York Times*, March 26, 2008: http://www.nytimes.com/2008/03/26/world/africa/26iht -canal.4.11445365.html.

11 U.S. Navy: http://www.navy.mil/Search/display.asp?story_id=45081.

12 Kagan, Frederick, "The Art of War," *New Criterion*, November 2003.

13 "War Shipping Administration Report, January 15, 1946," *American Merchant Marine at War*: http://www.usmm.org/wedeliver.html.

14 Salvatore R. Mercogliano, "One Hundred Years in the Making: The Birth of Military Sea Transportation Service (MSTS)," *American Merchant Marine at War*: http://www.usmm.org/msts.html.

15 Ibid.

16 Military Sealift Command: http://www.msc.navy.mil/N00P/overview.asp.

17 Ted Kim and Gary Mears, "Logistics: The Way Ahead," *Joint Forces Quarterly*, Spring 1994: http://www.dtic.mil/doctrine/jel/jfq_pubs/jfq0804.pdf.

18 Ibid.

PART FOUR

Chapter 10: Big Blimpin'

1 Martin Kelly, "The Hindenburg Disaster," *About.com Guide*: http://americanhistory.about.com/od/hindenburg/a/hindenburg.htm.

2 U.S. Centennial of Flight: http://www.centennialofflight.gov/essay/Dictionary/blanchard/DI10.htm.

3 Naval Historical Center: http://www.history.navy.mil/Branches/lta-m.html.

4 Ibid.

5 Ibid.

6 Ibid.

7 Airship Ventures: http://www.airshipventures.com/ourstory.php.

8 Ibid.

9 Ibid.

10 Ibid.

11 Goodyear: http://www.goodyearblimp.com/faqs/faqs_business.html.

12 Ibid.

13 Christian Michel, "Steve Fossett Breaks Airship Speed Record with Zeppelin NT," *Modern Airships*: http://www.modern-airships.info/en/zeppelin/fossett_record_2004.html.

14 Steve Huett, "Hybrid Aircraft: Envisioned Military Relevance," U.S. Navy Advanced Development Program Office, Airship Concepts, September 2, 2009: http://www.flightglobal.com/blogs/the-dewline/2009/12/how-serious-is-dod -about-airsh.html.

15 Ibid.

16 Ibid.

17 Ibid.

18 Ibid.

11: Air Donkeys

1   "Military Altering MRAP Suspension for Afghan Terrain," *Stars and Stripes*, June 10, 2009: http://www.stripes.com/article.asp?section=104&article=63187.

2   Yochi J. Dreazen, "Focus Shifts to Afghanistan, with Fleet Designed for Iraq," *Wall Street Journal*, June 9, 2009: http://online.wsj.com/article/SB124450375989595981.html.

3   Deloitte, "Energy Security, America's Best Defense," November 6, 2009: http://www.deloitte.com/assets/Dcom-UnitedStates/Local%20Assets/Documents /us_ad_energy%20security.pdf.

4   Elisebet Freeburg, "Driver Course Prepares Troops for New M-ATV," U.S. Army Public Affairs, December 1, 2009: http://www.army.mil/-news/2009/12/01 /31169-driver-course-prepares-troops-for-new-m-atv/.

5   "Unclassified Documents from Marine Task Force 58's Operations in Afghanistan," Strategy Page: http://www.strategypage.com/articles/tf58/.

6   Ibid.

7   Ibid.

8   David Ensor, Tomas Etzler, Octavia Nasr Cal Perry, Auday Sadik, and Mohammad Tawfeeq, "Deadliest Day for U.S. in Iraq War," CNN, January 27, 2005: http://www.cnn.com/2005/WORLD/meast/01/26/iraq.main/index.html.

9   "Unclassified Documents from Marine Task Force."

10   Allen Pizzey, "On the Scene: Camp Rhino," CBS News, Dec. 11, 2001:
     http://www.cbsnews.com/stories/2001/12/11/terror/main320967.shtml.

11   Laura King, "Attackers Burn 150 Supply Trucks in Pakistan," *Los Angeles
     Times*, December 8, 2008: http://articles.sfgate.com/2008-12-08/news/17129756
     _1_khyber-region-india-and-pakistan-tribal-areas.

12   Walter Pincus, "General Urges Confidence in Ability to Supply Troops in
     Afghanistan," *Washington Post*, March 22, 2009:
     http://www.washingtonpost.com/wp-dyn/content/article/2009/03
     /21/AR2009032101967.html.

13   Ibid.

14   Globalsecurity.org:
     http://www.globalsecurity.org/military/ops/berlin_airlift.htm.

15   Richard A Oppel Jr. and Taimoor Shah, "Helicopter Crash Kills 6 in
     Afghanistan," *New York Times*, July 14, 2009:
     http://www.nytimes.com/2009/07/15/world/asia/15afghan.html.

16   "Afghan Helicopter Crash Kills 16," BBC, July 19, 2009:
     http://news.bbc.co.uk/2/hi/8157939.stm.

17   "NATO Forces Find Crash Site of Helicopter in Afghanistan," Associated
     Press, November 27, 2009: http://www.foxnews.com/world/2009/11/27/nato
     -forces-crash-site-helicopter-afghanistan/.

Chapter 12: UPS—in Space

1   Frank A. DiStasio, Jr., "The Army Budget, Fiscal Year 2010: An Analysis,"
     Association of the U.S. Army, September 28, 2009: http://www.ausa.org/
     publications/ilw/ilw_pubs/SpecialReports/Documents/BudgetBookFY10LOWR
     ES_021009.pdf.

2   Secretary of Defense Bob Gates, May 13, 2009: http://www.defense.gov
     /Speeches/Speech.aspx?SpeechID=1351.

3   Representative Bobby Bright press release: http://bright.house.gov/index.php?
     option=com_content&task=view&id=135&Itemid=94.

4   Ibid.

5   Jim Garamone, "SnowGoose: UAVs Enter the Airlift Business," American Forces Press Service, July 16, 2003: http://www.defense.gov/news/newsarticle.aspx?id=28717.

6   "UAV Directory," *Flight*: http://www.flightglobal.com/directory/uav/mmist -21985/cq-10a-snowgoose-3530.html.

7   Ibid.

8   Boeing press release, June 2, 2009: http://boeing.mediaroom.com/index.php?s= 43&item=683.

9   Boeing press release, August 10, 2009: http://boeing.mediaroom.com/index.php ?s=43&item=785.

10 Kaman press release, February 8, 2010: http://www.kamanaero.com/images /PDFs/02-08-10%20KMAX-Unmanned%20Demo-Dugway-UT.pdf.

11 Stephen Trimble, "US Air Force and Army Seek Unmanned Cargo Aircraft Concepts," *Flight*, February 10, 2009: http://www.flightglobal.com/articles/2009/10/02/332965/us-air-force-and -army-seek-unmanned-cargo-aircraft-concepts.html.

12 Ibid.

13 Graham Warwick, "USAF Gets Interested in Unmanned Cargo," *Ares*, September 29, 2009: http://www.aviationweek.com/aw/blogs/defense/index.jsp ?plckController=Blog&plckScript=blogScript&plckElementId=blogDest&plck BlogPage=BlogViewPost&plckPostId=Blog%3A27ec4a53-dcc8-42d0-bd3a -01329aef79a7Post%3A775a40b1-2900-4c01-81e5-d65e4ac17796.

14 National Aeronautics and Space Administration: http://www.nasa.gov/centers /kennedy/about/information/shuttle_faq.html#10.

15 Alan Boyle, "Private Rocket Ship Breaks Space Barrier," MSNBC, June 21, 2004: http://www.msnbc.msn.com/id/5261571/.

16 Jason Paur, "SpaceShipTwo Christened VSS *Enterprise*," *Autopia*, December 7, 2009: http://www.wired.com/autopia/2009/12/spaceshiptwo-christened-as -vss-enterprise/#ixzz0mtC7aBgj.

17 Scaled Composites: http://scaled.com/projects/tierone/.

18 Ibid.

19 Thomas P. M. Barnett, "The Pentagon Feels the Need . . . the Need for
    Astronomic Speed!" *Thomas P. M. Barnett's Globlogization*, November 7,
    2008:
    http://www.thomaspmbarnett.com/weblog/2008/11/the_pentagon_feels_the
    _need_th.html.

20 U.S. Air Force fact sheet: http://www.af.mil/information/factsheets/factsheet
    _print.asp?fsID=86&page=1.

PART FIVE

Chapter 13: A Bowling Ball through a Soda Straw

1   Ned Potter, "Haiti Earthquake: Why So Much Damage?" ABC News, January
    14, 2010: http://abcnews.go.com/Technology/HaitiEarthquake/haiti-shallow
    -earthquake-magnified-damage-californias-san-andreas/story?id=9562379.

2   Ashley Norris, "March C-17 Crew Completes Mission to Haiti," Air Force
    Public Affairs, February 2, 2010:
    http://www.afrc.af.mil/news/story.asp?id=123188743.

3   Ibid.

4   Ibid.

5   Ibid.

6   Ibid.

7   Ibid.

8   Ibid.

9   Ibid.

10 Ibid.

11 Ibid.

12 Robert Mackey, "Travolta Flies More Scientologists to Haiti," *New York
    Times*, January 26, 2010: http://thelede.blogs.nytimes.com/2010/01/26
    /travolta-flies-more-scientologists-to-haiti/.

13   John Ibbitson, "Canada to Hold Haiti Summit amid Historic Relief Effort,"
     Globe and Mail, January 18, 2010: http://www.theglobeandmail.com/news
     /world/haiti/canada-to-hold-haiti-summit-amid-historic-relief-effort
     /article1434568/.

14   "*Vinson* Helicopters Perform Medical Evacuations; 'Sea Base' on the Way,"
     Navy Public Affairs, January 16, 2010: http://www.navy.mil/search/display.asp
     ?story_id=50582.

15   Greg Parker, "Sea Basing in Haiti: A Transformation Phoenix Rising from the
     Ashes?" The Brookings Institute: January 21, 2010:
     http://www.brookings.edu/opinions/2010/0121_haiti_dod_parker.aspx.

16   "*Vinson* Helicopters Perform Medical Evacuations."

17   Chris Lussier, "USNS *Grasp*, Task Force Conduct Port Assessment in Port-au-
     Prince," Navy Public Affairs, January 21, 2010: http://www.southcom.mil
     /AppsSC/news.php?storyId=2083.

18   Peter Slevin, "Quake-Damaged Main Port in Port-au-Prince, Haiti, Worse Off
     than Realized," *Washington Post*, January 28, 2010:
     http://www.washingtonpost.com/wp-dyn/content/article/2010/01/27
     /AR2010012705250.html.

19   "Navy Prepositioning Ship to Deliver Humanitarian Assistance and Disaster
     Relief Supplies to Haiti," Navy Public Affairs, January 19, 2010:
     http://www.msc.navy.mil/N00p/pressrel/press10/press01.htm.

20   Ibid.

21   Trish Larson and Mike Neuhardt, "*Lummus* & JLOTS Lift Hearts in Haiti,"
     Navy Public Afairs, March 2010:
     http://www.msc.navy.mil/sealift/2010/March/lummus.htm.

22   Bill Cook, "Unrep Ships Critical Platforms for Haitian Disaster Relief," Navy
     Public Affairs, March 2010:
     http://www.msc.navy.mil/sealift/2010/March/unrep.htm.

23   Ibid.

24   Ibid.

25   Ibid.

26 Ibid.

27 Ibid.

28 Ibid.

29 Holly Boynton, "4th Fleet Commander Visits USNS *Lewis and Clark* before
    Deployment to Haiti," Navy Public Affairs, February 5, 2010:
    http://www.navy.mil/search/display.asp?story_id=51125.

30 John J. Kruzel, "Demand Dwindles for U.S. Forces in Haiti, Official Says,"
    American Forces Press Service, February 17, 2010:
    http://www.defense.gov/news/newsarticle.aspx?id=57990.

31 Ibid.

Selected Bibliography

Ambrose, Stephen E. *Nothing Like It in the World: The Men Who Built the Transcontinental Railroad, 1863–1869*. New York: Simon & Schuster, 2001.

Ascher, Kate. *The Works: Anatomy of a City*. New York: Penguin, 2005.

Brooks, Rodney. *Flesh and Machines: How Robots Will Change Us*. New York: Vintage, 2003.

Carson, Iain, and Vijay Vaitheeswaran. *Zoom: The Global Race to Fuel the Car of the Future*. New York: Twelve, 2008.

Gannon, Michael. *Operation Drumbeat: Germany's U-Boat Attacks Along the American Coast in World War II*. New York: Harper, 2001.

Haydamacker, Nelson, and Alan D. Millar. *Deckhand: Life on Freighters of the Great Lakes*. Ann Arbor: University of Michigan Press, 2009.

O'Toole, Randal. *Gridlock: Why We're Stuck in Traffic and What to Do About It*. Washington: Cato Institute, 2010.

Reeves, Richard. *Daring Young Men: The Heroism and Triumph of the Berlin Airlift, June 1948–May 1949*. New York: Simon & Schuster, 2010.

Singer, P.W. *Wired for War: The Robotics Revolution and Conflict in the 21st Century.* New York: Penguin, 2009.

Wertheim, Eric. *The Naval Institute Guide to Combat Fleets of the World.* Annapolis, MD: U.S. Naval Institute Press, 2007.

Index

455th Expeditionary Aerial Port Squadron, 160, 161, 162, 164

455th Expeditionary Aeromedical Evacuation Squadron, 166

720th Operations Support Squadron, 193

774th Expeditionary Airlift Squadron, 157, 159

1052nd Transportation Company, 3, 5, 8, 72

A-170 airship, 145, 146

Aberdeen Proving Ground, 75

Adams, Douglas, 60

Aeros Aeronautical Systems Corporation, 147

Afghanistan, 6, 7, 11, 17, 18, 21, 34, 72, 73, 108, 122, 125, 135, 146, 149–61, 165, 168–69, 171, 172, 174, 183, 207, 211

AH-1W, 153–54

Air Force Office of Logistics Readiness, 192–93

Air Force Reserve, 207

Air Force Special Operations Command, 193

Airbus, 80

Airship Ventures, 141–45

Al Haqqani, 167

Al Qaeda, 167

Aldrich, Mike, 16, 17

Alexander, Brian, 107

Aliens, 176

Allen, Paul, 177

Altimur, Afghanistan, 167–68

AM General, 68; AM General Humvee, 4, 5, 9, 14, 15, 66, 68, 73, 85

American Blimp, 145, 146

American Bus Association, 57

American Legion Bridge, 61

American Red Cross, 208

Amtrak, 56

Anaconda, Logistics Support Area, 3, 5, 7–9, 14, 15, 19

Anacostia River, 120, 125

Angel Ship, 134, 146–47

Animashaun, Asisat, 29

Antonov, 18, 158

Arizona, 195, 197

Arleth, Brandon, 163, 165

Atlantic Ocean, 110, 122, 127, 130, 139

Atlas Cargo, 162–64

Austin, Texas, 86

Automotive Research Center, 39, 70–71

BAE Systems, 17

Bagram, Afghanistan, 72, 156, 158, 159–62, 164–67

Balad, Iraq, 5

Baraki Barak district, Afghanistan, 149, 151, 152

Barber, Brian, 107

Barnett, Thomas, 181

Battelle, 39

Battle of the Bulge, 71–72

Battlefield Extract Assist Robot, 35

Bedard, Emil, 175, 182

Bedford, England, 142

Berlin Airlift, 158–59

Biden, Joe, 192

Blanchard, Jean-Pierre, 139

Boeing 747, 18, 162–65, 181

Boeing 767, 80–81

Boeing A-160T, 173

Boeing AV-8B, 111

Boeing C-17, 17, 20, 159–60, 162, 165, 186–87, 195–97

Boeing CH-47, 20, 143, 158, 166

Boeing JHL-40, 147

Boeing V-22, 66

Bond, James, 176

Bosch-Rexroth, 70–76, 77, 85

Bradley, Omar, 10

Brazil, 198

Break the Gridlock!, 54

Bregman, Peter, 52

Bridges, Rashida, 82

Bright, Bobby, 171

Brogan, Mike, 17, 150

Brookings Institution, the, 198

Brooks, Rodney, 33–35, 38, 40

Brown, Lester, 53–55

Buffalo vehicle, 15–17

Burns, Larry, 22

Butner, Clark, 172

Camp Buehring, 19

Camp Rhino, 155, 156

Canada, 11, 91, 94

carbon dioxide, 57

carbon monoxide, 50

Carnegie Mellon University, 22, 23, 25, 27–28

Carpenter, Clark, 201, 203

Cartwright, Charles, 29

Cato Institute, the, 51

CH-53E, 117, 118, 153, 155

Chabot Space & Science Center, 142

Charleston Air Force Base, 196

Charleston, SC, 17

Chevy Tahoe, 22, 23, 26, 27, 65

China, vii, 47, 94, 114, 115

Chrysler, 31, 53, 63

Civil War, 114

Cleveland, OH, 86, 102

CNET, 83

Cohen, Greg, 58–61

Coleman, Donald, 152

Cologne, Germany, 142

Colonial Marines, 176

Columbia, SC, 79–83

Conrad, Michael, 76–77

Convoy Active Safety Technology (CAST), 28–30, 36, 37, 39, 41, 183

Conway Freight, 40

Cornell University, 26–27

Craney Island Fuel Terminal, 205

Cross-Bronx Expressway, 60

Crowder, Brian, 203

Cuba, 114

Cumbee, Jeremiah, 8

Dallas, TX, 55

Damphousse, Paul, 182–85, 187

Dana Corporation, 75–76

Daniels, Jason, 193

Daronco, Jim, 195, 196

Davis-Monthan Air Force Base, 195

Day, Christopher, 166

Day, George, 11

Defense Advanced Research Projects Agency (DARPA), 21, 22, 24, 26, 30, 36, 84, 147, 176, 179, 185

Delivery Information Acquisitions Device (DIAD), 83, 84, 129, 210

Detroit, MI, viii, 28, 31, 48–50, 63, 65, 71, 72, 77, 91, 92, 96, 97

Dexter, Jim, 142, 144–45, 146–48

DHL, 79–80, 126, 208

Dinerman, Taylor, 185–86

DiRico, Rocco, 76

Dominican Republic, 132, 209

Donohue, Thomas, 11

DRS, 20

Duge, Bob, 180

Earth Policy Institute, 53

Eaton, 77, 85, 86

Eighty-seventh Infantry Regiment, 168

English Channel, 139

Environmental Protection Agency, 50, 57, 73, 86, 87

Esquire, 52

Eureka, 141, 143–45, 147, 148

Falcon, 179–80, 181, 182, 183

Federal Emergency Management Agency, 203

Fedex, 59, 76–77, 79–80, 126, 129, 181, 183, 187, 208

Filipi, Zoran, 70–77, 85

Finger, Thomas, 131–34, 205–6

First Special Operations Wing, 193

Flint, MI, 50

Florida, 110, 145, 192, 193, 197, 199, 204–7

FMC M-113, 66

Forbes, 47

Force Protection, 16–18

Ford, 22, 31, 53, 63, 65, 93, 96, 97, 98

Ford, Henry, 51, 97

Forrestal, James, 128

Fort Rucker, AL, 171

Fossett, Steve, 146

Foster, Tyler, 195

France, 6, 198

Gayl, Franz, 174, 175, 178–79, 182

General Dynamics, 17, 68

General Dynamics M-2, 66

General Motors, 22, 23, 31, 50, 53, 54, 63, 65

Germany, 11, 122, 142, 143, 145, 158

Glaeser, Edward, 55

Global Positioning System, 38, 39, 83, 141, 148, 151, 165, 172

Goodyear, 141, 144–45

Graff, Brad, 193, 197, 198, 207–8

Graham, Quentin, 14

Great Lakes, 12, 87, 92, 93, 95, 97–102, 104, 105, 124, 211

Green Energy News, 58–59

Greenpeace, 53

Griffin, Geoffrey, 199

Groenenboom, John, 173

Gross Domestic Product, U.S., 11, 12, 91–92, 191

Guam, 162

Guillory, Victor, 198, 206

Gukeisen, Thomas, 167–69

Habitat for Humanity, 110

Haiti, 132, 133, 191–211

Hall, Alex, 142, 143

Hall, Brian, 142–44

Hall, Chris, 28, 29

Hall, Robert, 85–87

Harris, Frederick, 124

Harvard University, 55, 108

Heinlein, Robert, 176

Helicopter Sea Combat Squadron 9, 199

Highway Users Alliance, 58

hillbilly armor, 19–20

Hindenberg, 139, 140, 146

Hitchhiker's Guide to the Galaxy, The, 60

Homestead Air Force Base, 207–8

Honda, 39, 63; Accord, 39–40

Houston, TX, 55, 86

hovercraft, 203

Huett, Steve, 146–48

human factors, 35

Humvee. *See* AM General Humvee

Huntsville, AL, 85

Hurlburt Air Force Base, 192, 193

hybrid vehicle, 12, 57, 63–70, 72–78, 85–87, 103, 126

I-35W Mississippi River Bridge, 11–12

I-270, 61

I-495, 61

I-696, 42

I-710, 61

improvised explosive device (IED), 20, 21, 149, 168

Integrated Vehicle-Based Safety System (IVBSS), 39–41, 43

Intellidrive, 41

Ionatron, 21

iRobot, 33

Japan, 11, 35, 53, 121–22, 127

Jarvis, Peter, 29

Jochem, Todd, 25

John F. Kennedy International Airport, 197

Johnson, J. J., 3, 4, 5, 9, 10, 14–16, 30

Johnson, Karl, 124

Joint Precision Air Drop System, 165

Jordan, Patrick, 35

Joseph, Raymond, 191

Jumper, John, 20

Kabul, Afghanistan, 149, 156

Kaman, 172, 173

Kaman K-MAX, 173, 183

Kandahar, Afghanistan, 154, 156, 159, 161, 166, 174

Kansas State University, 108

Karachi, Pakistan, 72, 157

Keen, Ken, 191–92, 201, 208

Kellogg Brown & Root, 3, 4, 9, 14, 30, 160

Kernan, Joseph, 118

Khalil, Gus, 66–70, 85

Kim, Ted, 129

Kimmitt, Mark, 4

Krall, Dan, 160–62, 164, 167

Kuwait, 7, 8–9, 19, 129, 150

Kwast, Steve, 158

Lacollo, Ches, 107, 108, 119

Lafontant, Roosevelt, 173–78, 181–83, 185–86

Laisure, Mike, 75

Lakehurst Naval Air Station, 139, 146

Land Rover, 22, 26

landing craft, 110, 111, 117, 119, 134, 198, 201–3

Landing Craft Air Cushion, 203

Lanham, Clarence, 79–82

Lanham, Gary, 156, 165–67

Las Vegas, Nevada, 7, 86

Latin America, 96, 108–11, 114, 119, 130–32, 134, 152, 191, 198, 209

Lavin, Renaye, 156, 165–67

Lawrence of Arabia, 151

Lemon, Jerome, 4, 8, 30

Levis, Jack, 83

Liberty Ship, 122

Light Detection and Ranging, 37, 39

lighterage, 204

Lockheed Martin, 22, 29, 147; C-5, 17, 158, 162, 165; C-130, 20, 69, 143, 153–60, 162, 164–67, 172, 183, 193–95; KC-130, 153–55

Logar Province, Afghanistan, 149, 152, 161, 167, 168

Los Angeles, CA, 21, 61, 86

Louisville, KY, 195

M-14 rifle, 112

Mahan, Alfred Thayer, 114

March Air Force Base, 195

Marine Corps Space Integration Branch, 175, 182

Marshall Institute, 181

Marshall, Nicholas, 151

Martinez, Ed, 208–9, 211

Massachusetts Institute of Technology, 26–27, 33, 34, 36–38

Mattis, James, 153, 154

McCarthy, George, 206

McClary, Robert, 4, 9, 14–15, 19–20

McKinley, Landon, 131–32

McNabb, Craig, 68

McNabb, Duncan, 158

Mears, Gary, 129

Meerkat vehicle, 15

Mexico, 11, 94

Miami International Airport, 209

Microsoft, 177

Mil Mi-8, 161

Mil Mi-26, 161

Military Sea Transportation Service, 128. See also Military Sealift Command

Military Sealift Command, 7, 95, 96, 112, 120–28, 129–31, 133, 203, 205, 206

Mine-Resistant Ambush-Protected vehicle, 16–21, 30, 74, 86, 125, 126, 149–52, 162, 163, 168, 182, 207

Minneapolis, MN, 11, 77, 86

Mist Mobility, 172

Moffett Field, 141, 143, 179

Mojave Desert, 176–77, 178

Monahan, Kevin, 54

Moonraker, 176

Moore, Michael, 50, 53, 54

Mori, Masahiro, 35

Moseley, Michael, 20

Motor Trend, 78

Mulliken, Bruce, 58–59

M/V Henry Ford II, 97

Myrick, Julie, 82–84

MZ-3A, 146

NASA Ames Research Center, 179

National Aeronautics and Space Administration, 143, 175–77, 179, 180, 184

National Security Space Office, 182

National Space Center, 142

National Steel and Shipbuilding Company, 121, 123, 124, 130, 205

National Transportation Safety Board, 12

Navistar International, 16, 17, 39, 40, 74, 86

Navlab 5, 25

Navy Advanced Development Program Office, 146

Navy League, 127

navy SEALs, 154

Navy Yard, 125

Nekvasil, Glen, 98, 99, 101–5

Nelson, Brett, 194

Nerkh District, Afghanistan, 168, 169, 172

Nevada, 29–30

Nevada National Guard, 30, 156

New Space, 177, 184, 185

New York, 94, 142

New York City, NY, 11, 13, 76, 77, 94, 197

New York Times, 25

Nicaragua, 107, 112, 116–18, 134, 154, 201

Nokia, 37

Norfolk, VA, 110, 200, 205

Norris, Ashley, 196

North Atlantic Treaty Organization, 156–58, 161, 162, 168

North Carolina, 79, 196

Northrop Grumman, 20–21, 173, 185

Northrop Grumman MQ-8, 173

Nye, Joseph, 108, 109

Obama, Barack, 12–13, 63

Observation Post Spur, 151, 152, 160, 167

Ohio, 77, 93, 94, 98, 140, 145

Old Rhinebeck Aerodrome, 142

Omni-Directional Inspection System, 33

OnStar, 42

Operation Desert Storm, 6, 129

Oregon, 145

Oren, Tim, 22

Orlando, FL, 82, 196–97

O'Rourke, P. J., 48–50

Oshkosh, 23, 26, 68–70, 150; Heavy Expanded Mobility Tactical Truck, 68–70; M-ATV, 150–151, 162–65; Terramax, 26, 28

O'Toole, Randal, 51, 56

Pacific Ocean, 108, 124, 130, 143

Pakistan, 72, 153, 154, 157, 158, 174

Parker, Greg, 198

Pecotox Air, 161

PEI Electronics, 85

Pellerin, Justin, 168

Perceptek, 28–30, 36, 37, 84

Permo-Drive, 75

Persian Gulf, 131

Pimpo, Mark, 206

Pizzey, Allen, 155

Pomerleau, Dean, 25

Ponds, Frank, 108, 109, 118, 119

Pope Air Force Base, 196

Port-au-Prince, 191–97, 199, 200, 203–5, 207, 209

Portugal, 47

Puerto Cabezas, 107, 110, 119–20

Rajkumar, Raj, 23

Reach 240A, 195

recession, viii, 52, 54, 76, 99, 100, 102

Reconnaissance, Surveillance, Targeting Vehicle, 66

Reilly, Robert, 7, 125–28, 133–34

Revolutionary Approach to Time-Critical Long-Range Strike (RATTLRS), 180–83

Riker, Colin, 168, 169, 172

Robinson R-22, 173

Rolls-Royce North America, 180

Romero, John, 195, 197, 199, 207–8

Roosevelt, Theodore, 98, 115

Royal Air Force, 158

Russia, 157, 158, 161

Rutan, Burt, 177, 178, 180–81, 184–86

Ryan, Tom, 64

San Diego, CA, 25, 121, 130, 140, 205

San Francisco, CA, 33, 86, 141, 143, 179,

Sangin, Afghanistan, 161

Santa Domingo International Airport, 209

Saudi Arabia, 129

Sayer, Jim, 38–43, 71, 83, 84

Schmiedel, Gary, 69

Schoenherr, Ed, 28

Serbia, 71

Servello, Chris, 109

Seventy-first Cavalry Regiment, 151, 152

Shea, Steve, 193, 195, 200, 207

Shenandoah, 140

Sikorsky SH-60, 199, 200

Sikorsky UH-60, 168

Silver, Nate, 52

sky lantern, 139

Skyship 600, 146

Small Unit Space Transport and Insertion(SUSTAIN), 175, 176, 178–87

Smith, Fred, 181

Smuda, Bill, 34

SnowGoose parafoil, 172, 173, 183

Society of Automotive Engineers, 64

soft power, 108–10, 116–20, 122, 130, 135, 152, 198

Space Shuttle, 175, 179, 180, 184, 186

SpaceShipOne, 176–81, 184, 186

Spain, 114, 126

sport utility vehicle, 22, 56, 57, 65

St. Antoine, Arthur, 78

Stanford University, 23, 26, 27, 48, 143

Starship Troopers, 176

Stavridis, James, 108–9, 118

Stenner, Charles, 207–8

Sterner, Eric, 181, 184

Strohband, Sven, 23

Suez Canal, 126

Sugrue, Thomas, 49, 51

T-AKE, 121–26, 205, 206

Taliban, 72, 151, 153, 154, 156, 158, 161, 167–68

Tank and Automotive Research and Development Command (TARDEC), 28, 33, 34, 66–68, 72–73

Task Force 41, 198

telematics, 42, 83–84, 86

Teller, Seth, 36–41

Tenth Mountain Division, 151

Tether, Tony, 21, 23–24, 27, 28, 31

Texas Transportation Institute, 61

Theisen, Bernard, 29

Thompson, Alison, 154, 155, 174

Thrun, Sebastian, 23, 27

Tierney, Terry, 33

Tikrit, Iraq, 3, 9

Toney, Bill, 156, 157, 159, 165–67

Torque 41, 156, 157, 165–66

Toussaint Louverture International Airport, 192, 193, 195, 196, 198–200, 204, 208, 209

Toyota, 56, 63, 65; Prius, 56, 65

Travo, Don, 195

Travolta, John, 197

Tuttle, Dave, 22

Twenty-Third Special Tactics Squadron, 193, 194

Tyndall Air Force Base, 197

Ulrich, Harry, 109

UN World Food Program, 208

underway replenishment, 113–16, 122, 123, 206

UNICEF, 208

unmanned aerial vehicle, 165, 183

United Parcel Service, 6, 7, 59, 77, 79–87, 128, 129, 162, 171, 187, 197, 208–11

University of Michigan, 39, 71

University of Michigan Transportation Research Institute, 39, 40, 70–71, 83

University of South Carolina, 82

University of Texas, 22

University of Utah, 33

Urban Challenge, 22–28, 30–31, 36, 37, 41, 42, 183

U.S. Air Force, 17, 20, 22, 81, 94, 129, 139, 151, 153, 157–60, 165, 173, 176, 178, 179, 183, 186, 187, 192, 193, 195–201, 207, 209

U.S. Army, 3–5, 8, 9, 16, 19, 20, 25, 28–30, 33, 35, 36, 38, 66–68, 70–73, 75, 83, 94, 104, 117, 125, 127–29, 134, 146, 147, 149, 150, 152, 153, 158, 160, 162, 164, 167, 168, 171–73, 191, 203, 204, 208

U.S. Central Command, 160

U.S. Coast Guard, 95, 97, 105, 127, 203

U.S. Department of Defense, 68, 109, 125, 176, 200

U.S. Department of Transportation, 71

U.S. Fourth Fleet, 198

U.S. Marine Corps, 6, 17, 23, 24, 66, 67, 107, 109, 111, 117, 129, 130, 133, 150, 153–56, 160, 165–67, 171–76, 181, 182, 184, 186, 200–204

U.S. Navy, 95, 97, 107–11, 114–17, 119, 120, 122, 123–30, 133, 134, 139–41, 143, 145–48, 153–55, 171–73, 176, 180, 198–200, 202–4, 206

U.S. Postal Service, 59, 77, 80

U.S. Sixth Fleet, 109

U.S. Southern Command, 108–9, 191, 205

U.S. Special Operations Command (SOCOM), 172, 184

U.S. Transportation Command (TRANSCOM), 6–8, 10, 158

USNS *1st Lt. Jack Lummus*, 203, 204

USNS *Alan Shepard*, 122

USNS *Amelia Earhart*, 122

USNS *Big Horn*, 205, 206

USNS *Comfort*, 108, 130–34, 198, 199, 202, 204–6

USNS *Global Patriot*, 126

USNS *Grasp*, 129, 203

USNS *John Lenthall*, 126

USNS *Laramie*, 110–16, 120

USNS *Leroy Grumman*, 205

USNS *Lewis and Clark*, 121, 126–27, 206

USNS *Mercy*, 130

USNS *Robert E. Peary*, 122

USNS *Sacagawea*, 205, 206

USS *Akron*, 140, 145, 146

USS *Boxer*, 108

USS *Carl Vinson*, 198–200, 202, 204

USS *Carter Hall*, 201

USS *Cole*, 126

USS *Emory S. Land*, 109

USS *Fort McHenry*, 201

USS *Higgins*, 198

USS *Kearsage*, 107–13, 116–20, 130, 133, 134, 153, 154, 198, 199, 201

USS *Macon*, 140, 145, 146

USS *Marcellus*, 115

USS *Massachusetts*, 115

USS *Normandy*, 199–200, 202

Vecna, 35

Velez, Vinton, 162–64

Verhoff, Don, 70

Vickerman, John, 12

Virginia, 28–29, 37, 107, 110, 125, 175, 200

Virginia Tech, 27

Voice of America, 53

Volkswagen, 23; Passat, 23, 26

VX-20, 146

Wall Street Journal, The, 195

Wallace, William, 202, 203

Wardak Province, Afghanistan, 168, 169

Ware, James, 130, 133

Warren, Michigan, 66, 68

Washington, D.C., 7, 19, 21, 51, 61, 63, 64, 95, 120, 122, 125, 153, 178, 181, 182, 198

Wasserman, Harvey, 53–55

Wassink, Jack, 175–76, 179, 181–82

West Africa, 109

Whitaker, Norman, 24, 27

White Knight, 177–78, 179

Wilkinson, Catherine, 8

Worden, S. Pete, 178, 179, 181–84

Work, Bob, 109, 116, 123

World War II, 6, 47–49, 55, 93, 94, 111, 115, 116, 119, 121, 128, 129, 140, 146, 200, 204

Wright, Gavin, 48–49

X-Prize, 185

Yarboro, Kim, 150

Yaro, Robert, 13

Yemen, 126

Young, John, 21

Yugo, 71

Zeppelin Company, 139

Zeppelin NT, 141–47

Zilmer, Richard, 176, 184

About the Author

David Axe is a freelance war correspondent based in Columbia, South Carolina. Since 2005 he has reported from Iraq, Afghanistan, Lebanon, East Timor, Somalia, and Chad, among other conflict zones. His work has appeared in hundreds of magazines and newspapers, including the *Washington Times*, the *Village Voice*, *Popular Mechanics*, *Wired*, *Popular Science*, *Salon*, and *Columbia Journalism Review*, as well as on BBC Radio, C-SPAN, and PBS. He is the author of the graphic novel *War Fix* (2006), the nonfiction book *Army 101* (2007), and the graphic novel *War Is Boring* (2010).